"*China, A Macro History* was published before the student uprising in Beijing, an event in any case too recent to be documented well enough for a seriously useful history. But Huang's book, written with charm and an often engaging humor, will quickly place that event into the perspective of history, rendering it understandable to any sinophile, whether he or she be of video or academic suasion. It's one of the best "short" histories of any country I've read."

East West

"Only 277 pages for this sparkling survey of Chinese history over the last several thousand years. Huang is the author of the much-admired, *1587, A Year of No Significance.* In this latest book, he argues that much of what is happening in China today is due to a centuries-old restructuring, a modernization that will bring China further into the mainstream of Western civilization. Impressive anecdotes inform a lively synthesis by a respected scholar. An unusual book that is for both the scholar and the general reader. "An undeniable fact about contemporary China is that although until the 1920s the country was mathematically unmanageable, now it is on its way to becoming mathematically manageable." Most convincing, lucid, a brilliant view of Chinese history."

The Book Reader

"Huang's macro-history is most welcome. It builds a structure of novel interpretation and vivid anecdote on a solid base of original research and covers the whole sweep of Chinese history, making comparative references to Western history. Huang seeks to explain the present Chinese reforms as the culmination of a commercialization trend that has broken down the old peasant society and brought China into the mainstream of world history. It is debatable whether Imperial China was as stagnant as Huang says, and his theory of the breakup of traditional China bears a resemblance to old-fashioned modernization theory. Still, his book is a boldly opinionated, freshly written synthesis that will be read with pleasure and profit by all."

Library Journal

"An impressive book. A serious work by a mature scholar."
Derk Bodde, Professor Emeritus, University of Pennsylvania

"What I admire perhaps most is that this book appeals alike to the scholar (to whom it gives much food for thought) and, because it reads so easily, to the interested layman."
Herbert Franke, Professor Emeritus of Far Eastern Studies, University of München

"Professor Ray Huang's purpose was to reexamine and present the whole history of China in a broad perspective and in an entirely new light, keeping in mind that China's history, at least till the twentieth century, is incompatible with the history of Western civilization. At the same time, he wanted to produce a recounting of China's history that made a valid connection between the tradition of the past and the programs of the present. He has beautifully succeeded, and his book—whose content is well balanced between the facts, their explanations and their consequences, and which is very clearly written and accessible to the general reader as well as to the specialist—deserves to become a classic in the field of sinology."

Jacques Guillermaz, formerly Professor and Director,
Research and Documentation Center,
Ecole des Hautes Etudes en Sciences Social, Paris

"I have never enjoyed a read more than Ray Huang's history of China. We (as historians of science) have always been vitally concerned with the differences between the civilizations which made the Scientific Revolution possible in Europe and nowhere else. We have been accustomed to pointing to the differences between the types of feudalism in China and Europe—'bureaucratic feudalism' *versus* 'military-aristocratic feudalism.' Anyone who wishes to understand better what this means would read Ray Huang's book."

Joseph Needham, Director,
Science and Civilization in China Project, Cambridge University

"The author plunges into the depth of Chinese history, tireless in his effort to examine a multitude of material, and comes up with a crisp outline. Professor Huang is a keen observer; his words carry weight."

Wang Yuquan, Member,
Chinese Academy of Social Sciences, Beijing

"Ray Huang's *China: A Macrohistory* is a most clear, judicious and concise account of Chinese history from antiquity to the present. . . . This work is unique in that the author fruitfully combines his own rich lived experiences in an age of rapid change with scholarly researches into various aspects of the Chinese tradition. As a result, this study breathes new life into Chinese history, and the past and the present illuminate each other. This work is truly trail-blazing not merely as a textbook but as an introduction to China for the general reader."

Ying-shih Yü, Michael Henry Strater University Professor,
Princeton University; Member, Academia Sinica, Taipei

CHINA
A MACRO
HISTORY

RAY HUANG

An East Gate Book

M. E. SHARPE, INC.
Armonk, New York
London, England

An East Gate Book

Revised edition, April 1990

Epilogue Copyright © 1990 by M. E. Sharpe, Inc.
Copyright © 1988 by M. E. Sharpe, Inc.
80 Business Park Drive, Armonk, New York 10504

Available in the United Kingdom and Europe from M. E. Sharpe,
Publishers, 3 Henrietta Street, London WC2E 8LU.

Illustrations by the author.

Library of Congress Cataloging-in-Publication Data

Huang, Ray.
    China, a macro history.

    Includes index.
    1. China—History.   I. Title

DS735.H785   1988   951   87-28898
ISBN 0-87332-452-8 (Cloth)
ISBN 0-87332-728-4 (Paper)

Printed in the United States of America

This edition includes

**Epilogue:
Reflections on Tiananmen**

Contents

Maps and Chronological Tables *viii*

Preface *ix*

1 / Xi'an and the Loess Land *3*

2 / The Second Sage and the First Emperor *10*

3 / Soil, Wind, and Water *20*

4 / Behind the Terracotta Army *27*

5 / The First Empire: Establishing the Standard *36*

6 / Literati Turned Warlords *49*

7 / Prolonged Disunity *62*

8 / When Historical Components Sprawled
Far and Wide *70*

9 / On the Road to Reunification *78*

10 / The Second Empire: A Breakthrough That Failed
to Materialize *88*

11 / The Northern Song: A Daring Experiment *107*

12 / West Lake and the Southern Song *122*

13 / The Mongolian Interlude *137*

14 / The Ming: An Introverted and
Noncompetitive State *149*

15 / The Late Ming *164*

16 / The Role of the Manchus *180*

17 / 1800: A Point for Reflection *192*

18 / From the Opium War to the
Self-Strengthening Movement *200*

19 / The "Hundred Days," the Republic,
and May Fourth *213*

20 / Contemporary China and Its Place in the World *232*

21 / Taiwan, Hong Kong, and Macao *260*

Epilogue: Reflections on Tiananmen *267*

Index *271*

Maps and Chronological Charts

Map Sketches

China During the Warring States Period 11
Loess Land 21
Patterns of Air Flow 22
Fifteen-inch Isohyet Line 23
The Han Empire 44
Jin Invasions 64
The Tang Empire 91
Tripartite Relations During the Northern Song 113
Tripartite Relations During the Southern Song 126
The Mongol Conquest 140
The Ming in the Fifteenth Century 155
The Voyages of Zheng He 156
The Qing Empire at Its Zenith 190

Chronological Charts

China Prior to the Qin Unification 13
The First Empire 39
China Toward a Long Period of Disunity 66
China on the Way to Reunification 86
The Second Empire 89
The Third Empire 147

Preface

This is a book of current interest.

I have just returned from a short visit to China, my country of origin, after an absence of thirty-eight years. The last time that I was in Manchuria was in the spring of 1946. Then a junior staff officer in Generalissimo Chiang Kai-shek's Nationalist Army, I was with the troops pushing toward Harbin, recently evacuated by the Soviets. On the way we were blocked by Marshal Lin Biao's forces and learned firsthand and with horror what a "human sea attack" was like. Forty-one years later, I finally made it to the city, this time as a guest speaker addressing a historians' convention.

In Beijing I was treated to a duck dinner by General Cheng Zihua, a hero of the Long March whose hands had both been, rather freakishly, deformed by a single rifle bullet. In Harbin I was entertained by Professor Xu Lanxu, president of Heilongjiang University. During the banquet I had the good fortune to be seated close to Mr. Zhang Xianglin, commissioner of Cultural Affairs of Heilongjiang. When I revealed to him my Kuomintang (Nationalist) background he told me that that was also the party affiliation of his elder brother. But in 1946 he himself was mobilizing the local population for the Northeast Union Democratic Army, later a part of the People's Liberation Army. Our comparing of notes about the old days went on so well that he promised to call on me during his forthcoming trip to the United States, so that we could continue. The lieutenant-governor of Heilongjiang in charge of education, Mr. Jing Baiwen, took me for a ride across town. When I said that I was a graduate of the Kuomintang's Central Military Academy, generally known as Whampoa, he lost no time in telling me that so were both his parents. Mrs. Jing in particular holds the rare distinction of having been with the Women's Detachment in Wuhan. It must be noted that throughout the history of the academy it issued no more than 200 diplomas to female cadets, all from the Class of 1927. I then added that my father, Huang Zhenbai, was a member of the Allied Association, the revolutionary group organized by Dr. Sun Yat-sen in the pre-Republican era that was the forerunner of the Kuomintang. Mr. Jing responded that so was his grandfather.

With our revolutionary genealogy spelled out and laid down, reminiscence inevitably led to nostalgia. It seemed that we, like our forefathers before us, had grossly underestimated the length and breadth and complexity of a business called revolution. But looking back, how enchanting it was. With a full head of thick hair shining under the morning sun and regardless of what political indoctrination was in one's head, one could indulge in thinking that world affairs could be reshaped to his liking with just a little exertion on his part. A little more effort is all it takes! Decades later, the effort and exertion have given way to misery and nightmare, and our simple naïveté has been transformed into a labyrinth of confusion. Few of us, even the most undaunted, could have come out of it unperturbed, if still unscathed.

Yet 1987 is not another year of disillusionment. All indications are that the longest revolution in the world has come to a fruitful conclusion. China is now experiencing a genuine reign of peace, for the first time in her modern history. Time has assuaged the agony that came with war and upheaval. Foes of the past can now regard one another with not only sympathy but also admiration because they begin to see the long-term rationality of history, which has superseded revolutionary rhetoric of all kinds, and is by itself larger than the worlds of Mao and Chiang combined. It is in the same spirit that I, a non-Marxist historian and a naturalized citizen of the United States, can feel comfortable speaking before an assembly of scholars coming from all parts of China.

For me there is no better assurance of a settlement than a rendezvous I had with former friends of my youthful years. In 1938 I worked for a tabloid in Changsha called the *War of Resistance*. Its editor-in-chief was playwright Tian Han, whose "Volunteers' March" is now the national anthem of the People's Republic. But during the months I was with the paper Uncle Tian, participating in the general mobilization in Wuhan, had left the editorial responsibility to Liao Mosha, who was also my roommate. In those days we shared the business with scissors and paste along with bits of street-side reporting in addition to proofreading in the composing room without bothering to clarify who was responsible for what. Another worker in the office, still in his early teens, was Tian Hainan, Tian Han's son. As war with Japan engulfed the inland provinces, *War of Resistance* ceased publication and we parted ways. But Hainan and I went together to enroll in the military academy, then in exile in Chengdu.

About thirty years later, I learned to my dismay that Uncle Tian had died in prison, succumbing as one of the early victims of the Cultural Revolution. Mosha had achieved the prominence of being one of the three satirical writers whose joint column in a journal enraged Chairman Mao and had touched off the Great Proletarian Cultural Revolution in the first place. But for years to come, no one knew of Liao's whereabouts. Until his release from farm labor in 1979 few were even aware that he was still alive. (He is the only survivor of the three.) Upon graduation from the military academy, Hainan and I served as platoon leaders in the same 14th Nationalist Division, and later we were transferred together to the Chinese Army in India. But after V-J Day he voluntarily went over to Kalgan and subsequently made substantial contributions to the People's Liberation Army by designing training programs for its artillery and armored forces. Unfortunately, as his father was under criticism he too fell into disgrace and found himself imprisoned. Although rehabilitated a dozen years later, his early discharge from the service has hardly rectified an act of injustice which caused him and his family to suffer so much.

During our reunion in Beijing all the barriers of the past vanished. We could talk about the old days as well as recent days without any urge to evade an issue or dodge an answer. Amazingly, we managed to recapture a great deal of the "lost decades" in a matter of hours. The differences between and among ourselves were neutralized by the common understanding that after all, life is far more complicated than any of us had anticipated. I congratulated Mosha for having become such a celebrity, now that his name appears around the world in all the textbooks on the history of contemporary China. He replied nonchalantly: "Jiang Qing made it so." Hainan told me that he is determined to brush up on his English. He must be thinking that there are pursuits other than the armed forces.

Both of them looked younger than their age. How could they be so serene, to be able to shake off with scorn the ill-treatment that they had so wrongly received, instead of sinking themselves in self-pity and rancor? Then I remembered that revolution is a mass movement, and as such it provides little room for individual justice. Once one becomes reconciled with the historical act, one need not be contentious with the agents of history.

In any case, the release of a volume called the *Chronology of the Major Events Concerning the Chinese Communist Party*, also occurring during my stay in Beijing, should soothe somewhat those whose bitter memories of the troublesome past decades have not yet subsided. This book never spares praise of Mao Zedong wherever it is due; but it also lays the blame for the Cultural Revolution at the feet of the chairman himself. He planned the sequence of events and set traps for his comrades-at-arms. Those whose loved ones died or suffered for the Nationalist cause may feel equally comforted. In the past, partisan Communist propaganda created the impression that the Kuomintang forces, achieving nothing but evil deeds and aiming at preserving their own strength only, dealt with the Japanese halfheartedly. This volume puts the total Chinese casualties as a result of the war with Japan at twenty-one million. Of that number, 600,000 came from the Communist armed forces, while six million were civilians in the territories under their control. What is not stated bears silent testimony to the role played by the Nationalist Army; it could not have been inactive or minor. Turning back to Mao, the *Chronology* points out that his tomb was constructed against his expressed wish, thus arguing that his memorial in front of the Tiananmen Square should never have been built.

In my memory, no Chinese regime, imperial or republican, ancient or modern, has ever spoken of its leader with such candor and shown so much willingness to rectify itself. Incidentally, because the *Chronology* was prepared by the Party's history section, it should exert some influence on Chinese politics in the foreseeable future.

The openness is not universal, however. I cannot say that I never ran into strained situations during my weeks in China. The hardline ideology was still there. Back in New York and still under the spell of jet lag, I was wakened every morning by my wife Gayle; she wanted me to watch with her NBC's "Today" show, which had sent the Pauley-Gumbel-Scott team to China for a whole week. After saying many good things about China and the Chinese, at the conclusion of the program the host and hostess wondered why so many people were still afraid to speak up, and along the same line, why so many middle-echelon bureaucrats had to block the path of free communication, knowing that the eyes of the world were on them.

Indeed, why? This book does not endeavor to answer all the questions. Instead, it provides background information that may lead to a variety of answers. If it does not come specifically to a point on the contemporary scene, it should enable the reader to form his or her own opinions on general areas.

When we say that the Chinese revolution has come to a conclusion, we mean only that the period of trying to solve problems with bloodshed and violence has ended. In no sense do we suggest that China is entering into a problem-free era. On the contrary, at this moment China is facing an immense number of problems, many of them of an unprecedented scope.

An inspiring scene that any tourist in China cannot possibly overlook these days is the construction boom. In the cities, buildings were at first erected in blocks, then on whole acres, and lately they are even beginning to fill up entire square miles. A medieval town can change its skyline rapidly and dramatically, often in just a few years. Most of the high rises are not commercial buildings, but public housing for government workers. The apartments are leased to the tenants at nominal fees. My friend Liao Mosha's family, for instance, occupies an apartment situated only two blocks from Tiananmen Square. It has two bedrooms, a sitting-room/study, a dining room, a kitchen that is only large enough for one person to freely turn around in, and a washroom that is equipped with a wash basin and a toilet bowl but no bathtub. There is a separate entrance. The monthly rent, including heating and other utilities, is sixty yuan *renminbi*, or at the current exchange rate something close to US$16.

One may wonder how the land is requisitioned, what happens if the tenant is delinquent in the monthly payment or should lose his job, whether the right to occupancy is inheritable or not, what liabilities the contractors have in case of building hazards. Frankly, not all these questions can be answered. In most cases they have not even been raised. The fact is that behind every issue there is the government; and the bureaucrats are having a hard time making decisions. The latest I heard in Beijing is that the housing authorities are contemplating raising rents to a level adequate to provide building maintenance, and that alone may hike some payments to six or seven times the current level—a line of action that is likely to run into resistance if not technical difficulties.

This dilemma is only one of the obstacles to the "going private" movement, which alone can alleviate the bureaucratic burden.

When construction is undertaken on such an unprecedented scale, inevitably there is congestion and imbalance. We have heard complaints about broken windows and dirty corridors in high-rise buildings, of coal piled up in the yard, depriving children of their only playground, of hotels three or four years old already beginning to show signs of wear and tear, and of everywhere public utilities and services being taxed to the breaking point. No wonder. Shanghai alone has three million bicycles. Every day its bus service handles fifteen million riders. More and more waste, in millions of tons, has to be discharged through the city's sewage system. Modernization has come to China en masse. (That is why tourists, paying their way with foreign exchange, have to be treated as a privileged group.)

Decades ago when I traveled on the Beijing-Tianjin Railway, I saw mountains of rubbish piled up, unmarked graves crowding the patches of vegetable gardens, and shanties whose tarpaulin tops had to be weighted down with rocks in order to withstand the dust storms of North China. This time I could see that most of the eyesores are gone. Some of the shanties are still there, but only rarely. Stretching into Manchuria, the clusters of red brick houses with chimneys and Western-style roof tiles, some with TV antennas, warm the visitor's heart. The fields are large and integrated. One can imagine the great human cost that the population has paid for all this—the end product of collectivity and discipline. Still, deviation has not been entirely rooted out. Not too far from the railroad tracks signs are posted which give warning: Taking topsoil from this spot is strictly forbidden.

In some cases the sprucing up of the cities is only superficial. The unbroken line of trees arrayed along both sides of the highway leading from Harbin to its airport, mile after mile with equal height and spacing, is an impressive sight indeed. I cannot recall ever seeing anything like it anywhere else in the world. But behind the main thoroughfare of the city, the back alleys remain unpaved and contain water puddles even during the dry season. Orderliness as a social discipline also lessens when the stage is less public. The trams and buses in the national capital are always crowded. Passengers along the thoroughfares nevertheless queue up at the stops. But on Wangfujing Dajie, a mere two blocks away from the Beijing Hotel, it is everyone for himself; one has to fight his way aboard, the chaos providing an excellent hunting ground for pickpockets. Even though I had been forewarned of the situation, one that was not unfamiliar to me decades ago, I found reliving the experience difficult; I had thought that such things had been wiped clean by the revolution.

Yet, as discomfiting as the minor unpleasantness and inconveniences are, they are nothing compared to the red tape thrown around every transaction by the bureaucrats who, finding the changing world no less perplexing than we do, have to stick to their unchanging organizational logic in order to survive. It is not difficult to imagine the extent of irregularities in practice.

In sum, the China that we are dealing with is more a phenomenon and a movement than a settled entity. Robust with energy and never averted from experiment, it is by no means devoid of self-contradictions. We know that the mass has been stirred up, but we are not so sure where it is heading. Under the circumstances, it is most difficult to wrap up what one sees and hears with an opinionated theme. One is likely to be carried away by his first impression and sentiments.

The Institute for Development of the Research Center for Rural Development in Beijing is a very curious organization. It was started in 1979 by a group of young intellectuals who had been sent to the countryside during the Cultural Revolution. Convinced that rural China is the prime mover of the country's progress, they undertook to study and research the subject. In time they received financial aid from the Ford Foundation. The work expanded and several members traveled overseas to gain experience. Finally, four years ago, their publications attracted the attention of the State Council, which invited them to become a part of that governmental organization. They accepted, and with a work force of fifty persons, they continue to conduct field studies and publish research bulletins. Their office is rented from, of all the possible landlords, the People's Liberation Army.

Some members of the institute had read my historical interpretation of the current developments in *Chinese Intellectual* and expressed interest in my work. I, in turn, became convinced that their approach to problems could widen my vision as a historian. A mutual friend in New York wrote to introduce us. On a September day four senior members from the institute, all in their thirties, came to my hotel for lunch.

No doubt about it, their chief concern about contemporary China is with the primary accumulation of capital, which has to be developed from the agrarian sector. They describe the policy of the Chinese government in the past as "a pair of scissors." On the one side it collected foodstuff from the peasantry at low prices; on the other it sold the same to city dwellers at abnormally low prices. In this way it managed to keep both farm wages and industrial wages at a very low level, thus achieving forced savings. What remains unsaid is that the plant and equipment currently in use are also the product of this national sacrifice, which, indirectly, has fueled the present construction boom. But, according to one author, the potential of this belt-tightening has already been used up. Another author goes so far as to say that the policy to deny the peasants freedom of movement, if it had not been discontinued, would have caused general uprisings.

They are unanimous in holding that the subsequent policy of contracting individual farmers for production is a move in the right direction. After the initial benefits, the well-to-do peasants can also move on to take up auxiliary trades and start rural industries, creating further opportunities. Within the short span of the six years between 1979 and 1985, the institute's publication points out, one out of every five Chinese peasants has "relocated himself, taken a new vocation, or changed his social status." Of course, numerous new problems arise in the course of these changes. Within the same time span, China's urban population registered a net increase of 127 million. The current trend to develop rural industries at a high debt ratio, while accelerating growth, tends also to subject the macro-economy to recessional influences. Mr. Wang Qishan, head of the institute, showed some concern over the reemergence of the disparity between the rich and the poor; but there is more concern about the unsettled property rights and the lack of coordination among the various projects amid the flurry of economic activities.

Our discussion confirmed a basic belief of mine: From the historian's point of view a breakthrough has been achieved by China. The nation is shifting from the outdated agrarian-bureaucratic management to a mode of management by commercial principles, imperfect as it is at this point. Its whole domain is moving toward being mathematically managed, although just what the math is has yet to be determined. In such a milieu, the polemics over whether the Chinese are still within the fold of Communism or are on the threshold of capitalism become virtually meaningless. Those verbal archetypes of yesterday bear little semblance to current developments; their proponents' claims to exclusivity are even more absurd. We cannot see how the public sector of the national economy, so profound and so substantial, will or can fade into the background. On the other hand, private and semiprivate capital, just now being vigorously promoted and widely fostered to fill a vacuum, to form a secondary line and to provide services, are not being created in order to be taken over either. Above all, the current program, so massive and stupendous, will soon demonstrate its own characteristics. Future readjustments, therefore, are likely to be dictated more by technical instinct than ideological direction.

But, how can an issue of such paramount importance manage to escape wider discussion? How can thousands and millions of workers be engaged in this epoch-making task without being specifically told about it? I believe that the responsibility to speak up falls on historians of China, especially those of us who reside overseas unencumbered by any doctrinal line. In fact, a dispute over ideology is unnecessary. A recounting of Chinese history that makes a valid connection between the traditions of the past and the programs of the present is enough.

This book intends to accomplish just that.

Chinese history differs from the history of other peoples and other parts of the world because of an important factor: its vast multitudes. Its cross-section is denser. Owing to China's great mass, inner movement takes more time to be transmitted from one end to another. Its peasantry can only be maneuvered in blocks. Presiding over the land mass of the East Asian continent, the center of gravity of this enormous entity seems always to have been wrapped in some form of mysticism. In the imperial period as well as in the very recent past, practical problems had to be translated into abstract notions in order to be disseminated. In turn, at the local level the message had once again to be rendered into everyday language. Sometimes form counted more than substance. For the bureaucracy operating under such a system, truth resided with authority; both had to move from the top downward.

In military affairs, too, geographical imperatives dictated that quantity outweigh quality. Sieges of walled cities often featured an endurance contest of some kind. Thus for general organization the Chinese tended to look to homogeneity and uniformity, and things unusual were rarely regarded with favor. The impracticality of reaching a ramified division of labor inhibited technical analysis and the development of civil law. The national economy followed the lead of tax administration. The state had reason to hold the entire country as a conglomeration of village communities wherein the ideal citizen was the small self-cultivator. The demand for simplicity precluded any sustained drive to promote local interests of a specific kind. For governance the bureaucrats relied on the penal code, whose essence changed little over two thousand years. When that was not enough, social discipline under the guidance of patriarchal authorities did the rest. Yet, as the ideal situation could rarely be maintained, the worst features of the system often precipitated in the village cells, with usurious exploitation and peasant indebtedness running rampant.

What can the historian do?

In view of the latest developments, I intend to reexamine the annals and chronicles with a longer vision and broader perspective, but to keep the aforementioned prototype in mind as a checklist. This approach forms the basis of *macro*history.

This is not to reduce the entire body of Chinese history to an uninspiring capsule and label it "Oriental despotism" or "authoritarian tradition." (To my mind, authors prone to use such terminology take too much time to express their own emotional reaction to historical development, at the expense of in-depth studies.) As the following chapters show, once accepting the above generalization as a condition imposed by the physical environment, the historian will see the heroes and heroines on the stage in an entirely different light. Indeed, despots there are too, and their lackeys. But on the whole the story will dispute the notion that the Chinese are completely happy with this setting and wish to perpetuate it. Even in different times and under different circumstances, they sought alternatives, albeit usually without success.

In fact, dynasties collapsed and emperors and ministers died tragically, sometimes taking along with them the women in their lives, because they were unable to live up to the requirements outlined in the foregoing paragraphs. In constructing this study I have found that one can enumerate all the major and minor dynasties, cite the outstanding events, and name personalities of significance, while never abridging their intriguing dimensions and variety, and even branching out to discourse on philosophy and literature without leaving the everlasting conflict. This is to say that a volume built out of the unique features of the China theater can adequately embrace the entire length of Chinese history in an interesting sequence; it does not need to be a collection of anecdotes.

This book proceeds in such a fashion. Most of its contents run in parallel with those laid down by the traditional writers; but additional cases of illustration are also provided. When it comes to the exercising of the historian's judgment, we are our own masters. We alone benefit from the hindsight of the late twentieth century.

Essentially, this is to give a technical (not an ideological) emphasis to Chinese history and to update it to 1987. More than anything else, this perspective enables us to appreciate the enormous scope and profound meaning of the Chinese revolution, now that it is drawing to a close.

The reader must realize that by the end of the nineteenth century the traditional state and society left little to be salvaged. As a result, the Chinese revolution had to run a protracted and embittered course. In the end the bottom stratum of Chinese society had to be uprooted and turned over, pulling everything along with it, until a rational system of land utilization was in place. Egalitarianism, which in the past had been thought to be the utmost goal, happens to be only part of the motivation of the participants. In the end the historical purpose of the revolution is to break up the cellular structure of the villages so that a new state of interchangeability can be attained. Theoretically, at the end of the struggle the entire populace will have some equal opportunity for betterment. For the nation as a whole, nevertheless, the net benefit resides in the hope that soon its affairs can be monetarily managed, thus breaking the handicap of millenniums. Knowing what is likely in the past, I dare say that the final outcome is irreversible. It carries the convincing power of history.

Of course I could not have written this book in several weeks' time. In fact, it took more than several years to produce. Ever since I landed on the West Coast the second time in the autumn of 1952, I have been concerning myself with questions of Chinese history. (My first visit to the United States, to study military science at Fort Leavenworth, took place immediately after my tour of duty in Manchuria in 1946.) Later, for fourteen years as an instructor at SUNY New Paltz, I periodically revised my lecture notes on the basic Chinese history course to keep pace with the latest developments. So, the study and reflection of several decades have gone into this volume.

By definition, any historical work is incomplete. For what it is worth, this little book represents no more than one man's observations of a large volume of events viewed from a crucial point in time, with its natural fallacies and limitations. But at its completion all the joy is mine because I believe that without erudite pretension of any kind, it will be accessible to the general reader, including beginners and tourists.

Aware of all possible inferences, I must say here that my cheerful note about the recent developments on the mainland bears no direct connection with my observations on Taiwan, which appear at the end of this book. Although it is not the role of the historian to make political predictions, under the present conditions I do not see how the "one-country, two-systems" solution offered by the Chinese leaders can turn out to be anything else but a form of confederation. This belief is consistent with my publications on mainland China as well as in Taiwan.

Doug Merwin of M. E. Sharpe Inc. has spent a considerable amount of time improving the presentation of this book, for which I am grateful. But I alone am responsible for its errors and inadequacies.

In conclusion, I take this opportunity to thank the American Council of Learned Societies for supplying airplane tickets for the travel mentioned in the opening paragraph, and the China Fund, which provided the ground support. The opinions I have expressed, of course, bear no connection with my gracious sponsors.

R. H.

October 15, 1987
New Paltz, N.Y.

CHINA
A MACRO
HISTORY

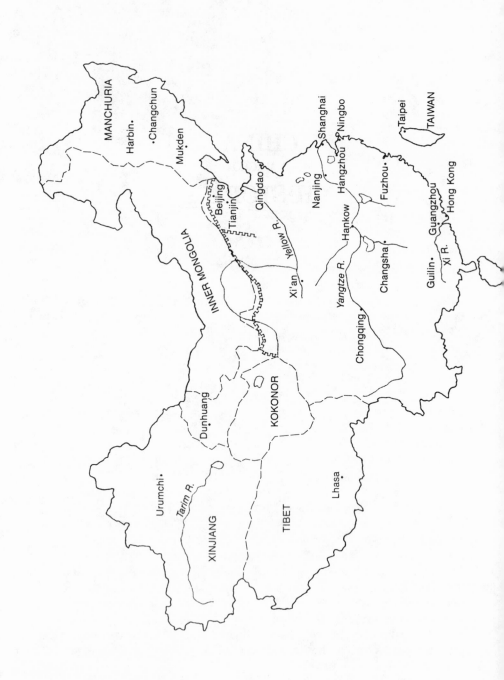

1

Xi'an
and the Loess Land

The city of Xi'an, close to China's geographical center, has become a
point of tourist interest because, among other reasons, as the site of the
capital of eleven major and minor dynasties dating back to the pre-
imperial period, it has remained prominent longer than any other political center in Chinese history, even though the old cities have been lost
to internal rebellions and foreign invasions. Today only their ruins
testify to Xi'an's former greatness.

Several other types of historical site are located to the east of the
present city. Less than five miles away is Banpo Village, the largest
Neolithic ("New Stone Age") site ever discovered in China and 6,000
years old. Evidence from its cemetery has established that it was a
matriarchal community.

No more than twenty miles to the northeast is Huaqing Hot Spring,
where in the eighth century A.D. (compared with the Stone Age a
rather recent date) a Tang emperor's beautiful concubine, Yang Guifei,
is said to have bathed. The then sovereign was a man of artistic inclina-
tions; in fact he was the reputed originator of the Chinese opera. The
woman he loved, who made Huaqing a memorable spot by dipping into
the spring, was an accomplished musician and dancer. But their story
ended tragically. When in 755 a frontier general staged a rebellion and
turned his army against the capital in the name of "purifying the entou-
rage around the throne," imperial troops refused to fight unless something was done about Yang Guifei. Besieged, the monarch allowed his
favorite concubine to be strangled to death. The fun-loving emperor,
now heartbroken, went into exile and ended his reign by abdicating to

his son. The loneliness and remorse of his remaining years are captured by an imaginative contemporary poet, Bai Juyi, whose rhymed lines recount the slow drum-beating and bell-ringing inside the palace compound, where the sleepless Tang Ming-huang, as the retired emperor is known posthumously, watched lightning bugs flicker by and, for another day, autumn leaves piled up in the yard unraked, while he himself sank deeper in a sorrow that nothing in this world could mitigate. The long poem was recited by school boys in China until our own time in the 1920s and early 1930s, to testify that the Chinese educational system even during the imperial period, while armor-plated with moral value, did not completely ignore romance and sensitivity; if it had, the "Song of Eternal Grief" would never have been allowed to pass down to disturb the unsettled minds of the young citizenry of the new Republic. The story of Huaqing Hot Spring and Yang Guifei also reassures us that regardless of ideological indoctrination, the inner reservoir of emotionality basic to human nature is always there, be we Chinese or Westerner, ancient or modern.

Not far away from the hot spring is the place where Chiang Kai-shek was captured during the Xi'an Incident in 1936. In the early morning of December 12 the troops of Zhang Xueliang, the "Young Marshal," stormed the resort headquarters of the Generalissimo to prevail on him to end the "annihilation campaign" against the Communists so that the nation could turn its full force against the invading Japanese. When the coup succeeded, it changed the complexion of Chinese politics and indirectly affected the course of world history as well. To a certain extent we may still feel today the repercussions of this incident of a half century ago. But on that day of "double twelfth," after the small-arms fire had died down, the commander-in-chief of the Chinese Nationalist forces was found by an ordinary soldier and a corporal, alone and unharmed, hiding in a cave in a foothill of nearby Lishan. Today a pavilion stands there to mark the spot where, rather freakishly, history commissioned two such undistinguished agents to perform a theatrical turn of events of such enormous consequence.

As we approach Lishan, we come even closer to history, feeling both the intensity of its influence and its timely relevance. It is general knowledge that Mt. Li, about forty miles from Xi'an, is the burial site of Qin Shi-huang-di (First Emperor of the Qin), whom some historians would not hesitate to call one of the most infamous despots in world history, whose unification of China in 221 B.C. was consolidated by the burning of books which contradicted the state proclaimed ideology and the burying alive of the ruler's critics. His "terracotta army," the sculptured earthenware soldiers and horses and real chariots and weapons that guarded his mausoleum, was unearthed in 1974. Since then thousands of tourists, including three American presidents, have visited the site, and a special exhibit of the figures has been organized to tour the world.

But when we deal with the First Emperor we are touching on China's imperial unification, which postdates the origins of Chinese civilization by thousands of years. The observance of a proper chronological order requires us to deal with several other items of business first. The highest priority goes to the geographical setting of early Chinese culture. So I urge the reader, when en route by train or bus to Lintong County, where Huaqing Hot Spring and the Lishan mausoleum are located, to take a good look at the terrain. The yellow brownish soil, similar to farmland in parts of Tennessee, is an important ingredient in the making of Chinese history. It is easy to spot because in that part of the country the surrounding landscape is often higher than the roadbeds running through it.

As this is being written, we have no absolute evidence whether the development of Chinese civilization was entirely indigenous or was at least in part transplanted from the Mediterranean. In the early decades of the present century, scholars tended to embrace the latter theory. Not only are Chinese archaeological remains dated much later than the relics unearthed in Mesopotamia and Egypt, but the early use of bronze and iron also separates the two theaters by at least 1,000 years. Some scholars speculated that even the Chinese writing system might have been a variation of the hieroglyphic. Certain decorative motifs appearing on prehistorical Chinese pottery were said to bear an unmistakable resemblance to those found in Central Asia and the Near East. Since then, this theory of "monogenesis" has been challenged by a host of scholars from both China and other countries. The Chinese writing system is now held to be unique, down to such fundamentals as the numerals. Pottery wares that are superficially similar should not blind us to the great differences. Chinese metallurgy, even with its primitively developed specimens, shows a unique technological approach that does not suggest imitation. The major food plants in ancient China and the prehistorical Near East point to separate agricultural origins as well. Anthropologists and archaeologists nowadays can even elaborate on the several regional origins stretching from Manchuria to the Pearl River that contributed to China's ancient civilization.

But while the pendulum swings in favor of the theory of the independent origin of Chinese civilization, it does not empower anyone to say for sure that the case is closed. What we can conclude with confidence is that regardless of its origin, native or foreign, this civilization bears a strong mark of geography. Whether the Chinese owe a great deal or relatively little to the early inventors elsewhere does not substantially alter the story. The rudiments of Chinese culture began to show distinctive characteristics as soon as the climate and soil of the eastern Asian continent had an opportunity to act on the food plants and thus affect the destiny of its residents, and it has remained so ever since (see below, chapters 2 and 3). For this reason, the loess land is particularly noteworthy.

The development of radiocarbon techniques after World War II has helped to date many Neolithic sites in China to 4000 B.C. and earlier. Written Chinese history, however, doesn't go back nearly so far. The earliest "dynasty" on record is a ruling house called the Xia, which, if verifiable, would extend the upper ceiling of Chinese history to about 2000 B.C. But until today nothing has been found by archaeologists to establish the Xia's indisputable existence, despite many interesting stories about it. Skeptics never accept such tales as authentic history; they have been arguing that if such a dynasty existed, some written references should have been found along with the artifacts. Those who have faith in early historiography are not discouraged by the lack of such solid evidence. Some of them believe that written Chinese could have dated back to 2000 B.C., but because the earliest specimens of writing were done on silk and bamboo, they are likely to have perished. The current version of the Xia is a part of the written history; it has survived because it was passed down to us by oral tradition and by the work of numerous scribes who successively copied it down, at first in books made of bamboo sticks. Neither side can sustain its argument with finality.

As things stand today, the first page of Chinese history that has archaeological backing bears the relatively late date of 1600 B.C. at the founding of the Shang dynasty, the two capital cities of which, along with a number of the burial sites of its kings, have been excavated. Not only has its writing survived, but it is engraved on tens of thousands of animal bone fragments called oracle bones.

The major Shang sites are located in today's Henan Province, until recent days not an area of general interest to tourists. Historically the entire region is referred to as the "Eastern Plain," forming a westward axis with the loess tableland on which Xi'an occupies a prominent position. The designation of the Shang as a "dynasty" is not a misnomer, as the genealogy of the ruling house exists and the succession of the kings is known to have taken place by and large from brother to brother and, on fewer occasions, from father to son, always within the extended family. But otherwise the Shang appear to be a people who, with their mastery of bronze technology, assumed overlordship over many other peoples on the strength of their military superiority and religious cohesion. The extant bronze objects of the Shang, with few exceptions, are weapons and sacrificial vessels. They were produced in centralized manufacturing plants under state sponsorship.

Many Shang characteristics would have marked it as being closer to other cultures on a similar standing rather than as being distinctly Chinese. For example, although it was a patriarchal society, the Shang allowed its aristocratic women a degree of freedom and equality with men not attained by the daughters of China many centuries and even millenniums later. The Shang people were cheerful and robust, and they consumed large quantities of alcoholic beverages. They practiced human sacrifice and felt no qualms about it, as they routinely and unsentimentally recorded such deeds on the oracle bones. They were able to dispatch an army of 3,000 men on a marching expedition of 100 days. And this army could be augmented by forces contributed by Shang vassals. Sometimes they waged war for profit. The burial sites of Shang kings featured a series of pits one inside another, huge on top and progressively smaller as they were executed downward. Buried along with the remains of the kings were chariots and horses and human beings, some of them decapitated and arranged in formations. The pounded earth steps leading downward suggest elaborate rituals at the funeral services.

We believe that the Shang people, while versed in agriculture, maintained a strong pastoral tradition. In their 500-odd years of history, they moved their capital more than half a dozen times, and hunting is often mentioned on the oracle bones. Near modern Anyang, where the last Shang capital was located, archaeologists have discovered bones of wild animals in great variety. Food production, on the other hand, seems to have been relegated to slave labor; in one pit alone stone sickles have been found by the thousands.

Engravings on the oracle bones indicate that the Shang kings had a special concern for the weather. Calendar making was an essential function of the royal court, and in fact, all the Shang kings were named after the index divisions that formed a calendar cycle. In these respects the Shang dynasty begins to connect with agrarian China. Yet the strongest link between the Shang and the subsequent Chinese cultural tradition is the writing system found on the oracle bones.

Originally, these pieces were scribed for divination, but most of those extant today were reproduced by the Shang archivists as a permanent record. Thus large numbers of them have been unearthed, yielding a great deal of information about a nucleus state on the threshold of becoming a significant civilization. Specialists have counted some 3,000 different characters on the bone surfaces, and of these close to 1,000 have been decoded. This ancient writing system, seemingly yielding ᴧn infinite number of variations, can sometimes be read in part by the untrained eye of a modern East Asian because, pioneered by the geniuses of a primitive era, it has always retained an enduring quality and value that can be universally appreciated. The guiding principles of this system are surprisingly few, as the following sketches illustrate.

English equivalent	Pictogram "sun"	"moon"	Ideogram "the east"	"sacrifice"	Homophone "also"	"to come"
Appearing on the oracle bones						
Modern Chinese equivalent	日	月	東	祭	亦	來

On the left is the pictogram. The sun is portrayed with a circle, the moon a crescent. Once the graphics are in place, no further explanation is needed. Evolving beyond the pictogram is the ideogram. An example is the sun rising behind a tree, which denotes the east. Another is the concept of sacrifice, which is represented by a bird turned upside down being lifted by two human hands into a tripod vessel. For ideas and notions that cannot be presented graphically, a device called the homophone is used. In spoken Chinese the word for "also" is pronounced *yi*, close enough to that for the armpit, the figuration of which on the oracle bones therefore, by sound association, conveys the ideas of "besides" and "alone with it." There is no easy way to illustrate the concept "to come." But since the word is pronounced *lai*, the diagram of a food plant called "*lai*" serves the purpose. It may be noted that all the above symbols, developed at the dawn of the Bronze Age, are still in common use in the Chinese writing system.

Generally speaking, extensions, partial adaptations, approximations, and modifications of the aforementioned devices have enabled the Chinese to work out a broad range of some 20,000 of these picturesque characters. Adopted by the Japanese and Koreans as well, written Chinese is undoubtedly one of the most influential languages in the world. Its aesthetic value arises from its poetic quality; a certain amount of imaginative association bonds the writer and reader together, down to every basic unit of thought. Permitting the Shanghaiese who speaks Chinese in a dialect of soft sounds, like French, and the Cantonese who pronounces the words with hard sounds, like German, to remain culturally conversant with one another, the contributing effect of the writing system toward China's national unity cannot be easily measured. But within its strong points comes its weakness. It turns every line of thought to the same process of combining the square scripts, be it a note of condolence or a laboratory analysis. Auxiliaries serving as prepositions and conjunctions are few. Abstract concepts can only be laboriously presented, usually by overstretching the meaning of the solid elements, thus converting the perceptible into the conceivable. The monosyllabic language furthermore demands an equal number of characters to keep appointment with the tones pronounced. A convention practiced by the literati is to omit some parts of speech, which, while making the writing elegantly terse, inevitably impairs its usefulness as an instrument of precise communication.

Now let us turn back to history. Around 1000 B.C., when the bronze technology had reached its zenith and the vocabulary on the oracle bones had peaked at some 1,000 characters (most of the other 2,000 characters, scholars now speculate, are proper names and variations on characters already deciphered), this Shang culture was replaced by that of the Zhou, a new power that had arisen in the Xi'an region. For millenniums to come, the influence of the masters from this loess land was to overshadow in many respects the achievement of their predecessors on the Eastern Plain. The city of Xi'an, presiding over a region that is not the richest or the most accessible, neither now nor in China's middle ages, was destined to play a more prominent role in Chinese history than its geographic position seems to promise. A far-reaching analogy would put Texas and Oklahoma, historically, ahead of Massachusetts and Pennsylvania in prestige and influence. The concept of "geographical determinism" is important in Chinese history. It sustains the sharp differences to this day between Chinese culture, a product of the Asian continental land mass, and that of the United States, with the latter's preponderant trans-Atlantic tradition.

2

The Second Sage
and the First Emperor

It may come as a surprise to many to learn that in terms of personal persuasive power and overall influence on China's traditional statecraft, Mencius may have been more prominent than Confucius, even though he is known to have studied under a disciple of the Great Master's grandson and subsequently has been honored as the "Second Sage" by Chinese emperors and scholars. In his delightful book *Three Ways of Thought in Ancient China*, Arthur Waley chose Mencius to represent the Confucian school vis-à-vis the Taoists and the Legalists.

We have no accurate dates for Mencius' life; but we know that he flourished in 300 B.C., more than 700 years after the Zhou dynasty was established, which is mentioned in passing in the last chapter of the book *The Discources of Mencius*. His birthplace in today's Shandong Province is some 700 miles east of Xi'an.

Mencius lived in one of the most unstable periods of Chinese history: during the waning days of the Zhou dynasty, the ruling house fell into oblivion; its vassal states were caught up in incessant wars of annexation, which were to extinguish all but one of them, the Qin. Mencius first went to Qi, one of the dozen states that had survived the struggle up to this point. He was given audience by the king, who had just won an astounding victory over an adversary on the northern frontier, the Yan; his attempted annexation of the latter was about to provoke interven-

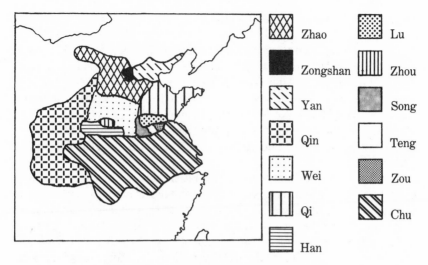

China During the Warring States Period

tion by a coalition of rivals. But Mencius gave the king of Qi no counsel on strategy or diplomacy; he neither supported the annexation nor urged a retreat. He did mention public opinion, which might lead the modern reader to suspect that if he had had his way, Mencius might have advocated some form of plebiscite to allow the Yan people to decide the issue for themselves. His aloofness from political reality made him unwelcomed in the king's court, so he moved on and offered his services to other states. But preaching the same "kingly" way, he had no success in those rival states either.

Yet, not even his most enthusiastic admirer could describe Mencius as a champion of democracy in the modern sense. Focusing on the administering of millions of peasants by the hereditary lords, the Second Sage summed up his concept of government with the statement that "those who perform manual labor are to be governed, and those who toil with their minds will do the governing." Even though Mencius sometimes may have come close to the idea of a "general will" of the people, or, to stretch the interpretation slightly further, "popular sovereignty," he made it unmistakably clear that their right to self-determination was not unconditional. Strictly speaking, it was limited to the right to survival. He defined the general entitlement of the people as "sufficient to eat in good years and escape from extinction in bad years." The minimum standard of living he envisioned was summarized as "those who have reached fifty may wear linens and those who are seventy may eat meat." In other words, charity on a broad front instead of the self-gain of the individual was exalted in the mind of Mencius the political thinker. As a philosopher he developed the theme of universal compassion to the point of indentifying it as the essence of human nature.

Most striking from the historian's point of view is the fact that while advocating his type of statecraft, Mencius, like Confucius before him, credited its origin to King Wen of the Zhou, some 700 years before his time. Along with the *Analects of Confucius*, the *Discourses of Mencius* became a part of the state-sanctioned canon in imperial China and the standard for the civil service examinations until their discontinuation in 1905. Thus it is an important component of the "vertical stem" of Chinese history.

The concept of government by heart is hardly startling; nor is it exclusively Chinese. But it is unusual that such an approach, whether it was actually effected or not, was advocated by Chinese rulers almost continually for 3,000 years and became a vital part of the rhetoric of public affairs in lieu of a constitutional law. To call it the Chinese character does not tell the whole story, for it had the force of climate and geography behind it. This link is more evident when we review certain sections of *The Discourses of Mencius* along with the major events 700 years prior to his time, back to the founding of the Zhou dynasty.

Extant material does not give us a clear indication of the origin of the Zhou people. The short account of their common ancestry, like that of other primitive peoples, is shrouded in legend and fantasy. Nevertheless, it persistently traced their roots to agriculture. An early ancestor of the tribe, a man by the name of Qi (not connected with the state of Qi mentioned above), is said as a child to have taught himself to grow food and hemp and then as an adult to have served as the minister of agriculture under a sage-like king in prehistorical times. Only toward the end of the Shang dynasty does the credibility of history begin to accrue to the account. By this time the Zhou was one of the tribal states under Shang suzerainty, with an agrarian base in the Wei River region around modern Xi'an. During the reign of the last Shang king, the Zhou, either by overbearing power or by impartial arbitration, had won the allegiance of a number of states that were supposedly subordinate to the Shang. The extension of Zhou influence into the Han River region leading to the Yangtze Valley in particular threatened the southern flank of the Shang on the Eastern Plain. Clashes between the Shang and Zhou ensued. The Zhou chief of state, Xibai, was for a time imprisoned by the Shang but later was ransomed off.

It was one of Xibai's sons who finally organized an eastward expedition in collaboration with a large number of rebelling Shang vassals to terminate the Shang overlordship and replace it with the Zhou dynasty. This took place either in 1027 B.C. or 1122 B.C., depending on which school of chronology one chooses to follow. The reader is reminded that only after 841 B.C. is the chronology of Chinese history confirmed by external sources; the natural phenomena mentioned in the chronicles as occurring after that date can now be unquestionably verified by records of other parts of the world. Most of those antedating that year involve some degree of guesswork and cannot be cited with absolute certainty.

The heroic figure who became the progenitor of a royal house that was to last for 800 years, however, never claimed to be the dynastic founder. That honor was given to his father, Xibai, who was posthumously proclaimed King Wen, or the "cultured king," in commemoration of his humility and statesmanship. His son, the leader of the military expedition, whose personal name is Fa, is in turn known to history by his posthumous title, King Wu, or the "martial king." The moral lessons that sons should never make claims so grand as to overshadow their fathers and that virtue and the doctrine of harmony must triumph over military exploits became a tradition ever after, although more often the doctrine was given lip service rather than substantiated by deeds.

We have reason to believe that the Zhou was inferior to the Shang in bronze technology. With the fall of the overlordship on the Eastern Plain the brilliancy in metal design and craftsmanship seems to have been permanently lost. But with the rise of the new rulers from the loess land, China developed a large body of classical literature, some portions of which still make interesting reading nowadays. Primogeniture now replaced the Shang practice of fraternal succession. Religious differences between the two cultures were sharp. The animism of the

China Prior to Qin Unification

Xia (?)

ca. 1600 BC

Shang

1027 or 1122 BC

Western Zhou

771 BC
722 BC —
Spring & Autumn Period

Eastern Zhou

481 BC —

403 BC —
Period of Warring States

Imperial
Unification of the Qin

221 BC —

Shang disappeared with the emergence of the Zhou, and even though ancestor worship continued, the earlier beliefs and expectations that made individual ancestors responsible for their descendants' successes and failures across a wide range of activities, from winning a war to nursing a troublesome tooth, were replaced by the honoring of lineage origin and the guaranteeing of its perpetuation as an obligation of posterity. Some writers have suggested racial differences between the Shang and the Zhou. But if an ethnic difference existed, it could not have been profound, as the written language does not show a notable break with the dynastic change. More convincing is the explanation that the culture developed in the loess land had a greater agrarian influence. The loess terrace, as some scholars reason, may have been the birthplace of China's agriculture. The long list of plants cited in a collection of folk songs dating from the early Zhou seems to give credence to the claim.

In any case, the Zhou founders proved to be the greatest system-builders of China's formative age. The Duke of Zhou, son of King Wen and younger brother of King Wu, is credited with being the chief architect of the state institutions under the new dynasty. To this day historians have reached no consensus regarding his overall design. But there is little doubt that the duke's organization was schematic. The preconceived mathematical concepts usually came with geometric patterns. Sweeping yet simple, the audacious designs were superimposed on a vast country before a single land survey was made or a census taken to test their feasibility. If today such a system were to be imposed on the United States, the uneven shore lines of Michigan would be ignored; in organizing the state we would endow it with boundaries as straight and neat as those of Wyoming. In the idealized pattern of Zhou practice the site of the United States capital, embracing the District of Columbia, would be located on a map at the geographical center, conveniently equidistant, say 1,500 miles, from Maine, Florida, Oregon, Texas, and Arizona. It would be surrounded by a belt of intermediate states, to make Maryland, for example, in direct contact with the Ohio Valley. Moreover, all the subdivisions within the states, including the counties and townships, would be perfectly square in shape. In practice such a plan, as it might be envisioned by a bricklayer, could never be carried out completely; nevertheless, inconsistences could be tolerated at a time when space was abundant and population sparse. Conceptually, this approach would quickly put the masses of a large country in order.

The Zhou system, called *fengjian* in Chinese, is always rendered "feudal" in English. The similarity between European "feudalism" and *fengjian* exists only in some aspects, and rather more in spirit than in substance. Generally speaking, against an agrarian background they both entrusted local government to the hands of hereditary lords. The territorial lords under the Zhou king were commissioned from the kin of the royal house, descendants of the vanquished Shang, and chiefs of other tribal states already in existence. They were divided into five ranks according to the size of their domains, which were in theory standardized. Their functions and duties to the king varied by the distance of their fiefs from the royal capital. They were supposed to reside within nine belts of land, which formed huge square frameworks concentric with the capital city. In practice, no such territorial division could be drawn on the map. Nor had Xi'an, the capital, actually been situated at the center up to this time.

Aside from such bold but unrealistic concepts, however, many innovations of the Duke of Zhou can be verified, sometimes even in detail. The paradox is not difficult to explain: The overarching principles of state-building are expected to bring forth an ideal perfection in conforming with the Natural Law. While deviations are as a rule accepted, the lower echelon nonetheless must at first strive to achieve the projected symmetry and balance to the best of its ability. For that pressure is constantly exerted from the top. In the long run, however, it is fitting that China is becoming a country of political thinkers under the influence of a bureaucratic management that habitually gives a priori recognition to form rather than to substance. What started as a technical necessity has become Natural Law itself after prolonged usage.

Another example of the Duke of Zhou's innovations was the alignment of his type of feudalism with kinship relationships. In every fief the family temple of the lord functioned as a kind of territorial shrine. The patron ancestor held the entire population together to form a pseudo-kinship. (A legacy from this arrangement is that today dozens of Chinese surnames trace their origin to those tribal states.) Within each unit, not only was the position of the lord hereditary, but also, his councillors and ministers always came from the designated noble lineages, who took possession of estates within the fief mandated at the founding of the dynasty. Those nobles assumed military leadership as well. In the early phase of the Zhou, the warrior-administrator caste was separated from the general population.

Under the Zhou, the cultivated fields were supposed to be arranged according to a "well-field system." A "well" consisted of about forty acres of land in a perfect square. By a division of three on each side, the entire field was gridded into nine equal parts of about four and a half

The "Well Field System"—the ideal and a possible application. The schematic design is a product of the drive for standardization. This approach was to have a profound effect on Chinese politics for 3,000 years to come. It implies a doctrine that the infrastructure of a nation and society can be artificially created. It also leads to a tradition that the form conceived from the top weighs heavier than the substance at the operational level.

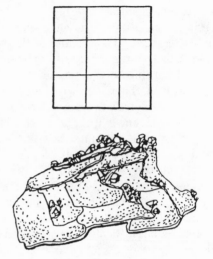

acres each. Eight peasant families occupied the peripheral subdivisions and jointly cultivated the center square, which was the lord's demesne. The arrangement, not necessarily carried out precisely as described, seems to have been in effect in wide regions. Evidently, in those days the peasant populace regarded their unpaid labor on the lord's demesne to be a public obligation. A lingering effect of this practice in the current Chinese language, somewhat curiously, is that the same character is used to mean both "the public" and "lordship."

To say that the Zhou introduced feudalism to China may be misleading. Rather, with *fengjian* the new dynasty installed a mode of government that was congenial to the spread of agriculture at the time. The alignment with kinship relationships contributed to its stability. The ideology of peaceful coexistence, which many centuries later was to be labeled "Confucian," owed a great deal to King Wen and the Duke of Zhou, as Confucius himself admitted. The devotion to ritual and the obsession with form rather than substance, as previously mentioned, were to be passed on to agrarian China for millenniums to come. Indeed, the Zhou did not take hold of China for 800 formative years without leaving a permanent imprint. Its enduring influence is such that for historians it is often difficult to determine whether a characteristic under discussion is that of the Zhou or that of the Chinese.

But at the top of a league of agrarian states in a sprawling country, the house of Zhou exercised effective overlordship for no more than 250 years. During the early centuries new fields were opened; "barbarian" tribes that continued fishing and hunting as their major methods of gathering food were converted and brought within the pale of civilization. From its vassals the Zhou collected tribute, and the arbitration of disputes by the court was effective. But by the early eighth century B.C., if not earlier, these positive attributes were gradually slipping away. In 771 B.C. the Zhou capital at modern Xi'an was ransacked by an invading tribe, which also killed the king. When the crown prince resettled in the east, the dynasty, now known as the Eastern Zhou, was set for a long period of decline. In the meantime, the royal domain fell into the hands of the Qin, nominally still a Zhou vassal.

Traditionally, this era of diminishing royal power is presented in history in two distinctive but not chronologically connected segments. They are the "Spring and Autumn Period" (722 B.C.–481 B.C.) and the "Period of the Warring States" (403 B.C.–221 B.C.), to conform to the time span of two classical history works. *The Spring and Autumn Annals* is a state chronicle; the *Strategy of the Warring States* is a collection of anecdotes at the court level. Both are brilliantly composed.

During these two periods a social revolution which took centuries to reach a conclusion evolved. Population growth had made the earlier Zhou arrangement, which tried to limit everything to a fixed quantity so as to maintain a constant relationship among all things, unworkable under the new circumstances. The "no man's land" between and among the states had vanished; further expansion of those states brought them to armed clashes. Their external problems also had a tendency to be entwined with internal controversies and vice versa. The Zhou king, already deprived of his own territorial base to sustain his military power, found his orders no longer heeded by the vassal states. To make things more difficult for the royal house, tribute from those states stopped coming.

But the story is not entirely one of decadence and decay. Obviously, social mobility accelerated the changes, at first working within the greater and lesser nobility lineages, thus making the status quo difficult to maintain, and then breaching the barrier that separated the commoners from the nobility altogether. Productivity expanded. Bronze coins began to circulate. Education advanced so far that toward the end of Eastern Zhou, scholars from the plebeian class began to frequent the courts of the contesting states to give counsel to the lords, who, as was the fashion, now called themselves kings. The Eastern Zhou, especially the Period of the Warring States, is sometimes referred to as an era in which "one hundred schools contended." The richness and diversity of political philosophy reached such heights that the achievement, as if to have overtaxed China's brain power, was not to be repeated for the next 2,000 years.

Aside from the Confucian school, the Taoists and Legalists were the most prominent schools among the so-called "hundred," which actually numbered no more than a score. The Taoists had little respect for mundane authority: "Until all the sages are dead, there is no hope of ending the most flagrant banditry." Their acceptance of cosmic unity and readiness to return to primitive simplicity were reinforced by their resistance to the curtailment of freedom, either through enticement or through cohesion. Taoism therefore gave comfort to pantheism, romanticism, and not the least anarchism. Those sentiments, however, provided no immediate cure for the current political turmoil except to turn wise men into recluses. Later, Taoism inspired poets and painters over the ages, favored limited government in peacetime, and supplied a leveling ideology for peasant rebels on numerous occasions. The Legalists may have come close to the eighteenth century positivist school of jurists in the West. They held that law reflected the sovereign's will, unhampered by convention or any conventional sense of morals. But Chinese Legalists put themselves in a far worse light because their platform, proclaimed at a time when China was struggling desperately to achieve unity, sanctioned only the awards and punishments of despots whose idea of justice was usually embodied in martial law.

How can we account for the great turmoil of the Zhou age? How can we explain the great contradiction of this era, that on the one hand there was the entreaty that rulers and statesmen must have hearts as gentle as that of Hans Christian Anderson, and on the other there was the argument that the end justified all means, springing from a super-Machiavellian political reality that contrived the rooting out of opposition by burning books and burying dissidents alive, and that all this happened hundreds of years before Christ?

If a single development in Chinese history sets it far apart from other civilizations in the world, it is the imperial unification of the Qin in 221 B.C. The political maturity that this feat required—after all, it came not long after China's Bronze Age—fixed the pattern of centralization that was to be followed for millenniums. The record is startling.

It is said that when King Wu crossed the Yellow River to put an end to the Shang dynasty, some 800 vassals of the Shang joined forces with him. Even though we cannot say for sure that each of them represented a tribal state, the number is an indication of the multitude of autonomous units then extant. During the Spring and Autumn period, 170 states were mentioned in the chronicles. By the time the all-out war of annexation was under way, the Chu, the power in the south, eliminated forty of these. By the time of Mencius, only about a dozen could still be plotted on a map. Among them only seven were powerful enough to be reckoned with. But the process of reduction continued inexorably, until all the barriers of the former Zhou feudatories were razed and the territory, ruled by one man, stretched over a good portion of the eastern Asian continent.

The 550 years of the Eastern Zhou also saw the nature of warfare change drastically. During the Spring and Autumn period, armies were small, engagements often lasted only one day, and a sense of chivalry usually prevailed. The devotion to rituals by the belligerents kept warfare artistic and in conformity with the feudal code of ethics. Such civility disappeared without a trace during the Warring States period; as the states grew to a size similar to today's European nations, wars were waged with no less ferocity than those known to modern man. Toward the end of this period, opposing armies of close to half a million men each were often mentioned. Field operations followed by sieges could last for months. Some of those states apparently achieved the level of total mobilization; in one instance at least, a king ordered all able-bodied males over fifteen years of age to report to a frontier town. The numbers of war dead and the atrocities committed against prisoners in this age, exaggerated or not, would cause a modern reader to shudder. Confronted by such a gruesome record, one begins to wonder whether or not the reputation for a peaceful disposition that many writers have attributed to the Chinese is deserved.

China's imperial unification under the Qin is a major milestone in world history. No parallel to the gigantic spiral movement toward it, accelerating in both speed and intensity, has occurred elsewhere in the world. Many of its background factors are beyond our ken, but with the aid of modern science we can try to pin down its fundamental causes with some degree of confidence. This we shall attempt to do in the next chapter. Clarification of this point, we hope, may help to explain why the kind of universal compassion preached by Mencius, so markedly bland, should receive so much enthusiastic support over such a long period of time. There are, perhaps, certain factors that connect the Second Sage with the First Emperor which even they themselves were unaware of.

3
Soil, Wind, and Water

The yellow brownish soil that the tourist sees from Xi'an to Lishan is on the southeast fringe of the loess land. Its extra fineness, sometimes almost like flour, suggests that originally it was wind blown, having been deposited over a large area several million years ago. Its depth ranges from 50 feet to 700 feet. The lower portion could also have been formed by the crushing pressure at the end of the Ice Age. Perhaps a large amount of the original soil was carried away by water and redeposited to the east, where it also took a great length of time to accumulate to its present thickness. This phenomenon affects Chinese history for a number of reasons. Being uniformly fine, this loess soil invited the working of it with primitive tools, such as wooden plows and wooden hoes. The nation-building of the Zhou, teamed with its effort to spread agriculture, apparently was facilitated by this soil property. A consequence was that 1,000 years before the Christian era, China had already attained a degree of cultural homogeneity, the cell structure of her society being aligned with a concomitance of farm production on relatively small plots and kinship cohesion. This is confirmed by contemporary literature, not decisively from any single entry, but with corroborating references from a variety of sources.

Yet the loess was to decide China's fate in a different way. The middle section of the Yellow River, running a north to south course for nearly 500 miles, dissects the loess land. It also receives several tributaries flowing out from the interior. The combined result is an unusually large amount of silt in the Yellow River's current. While in most rivers a silt content of 5 percent is considered high and that in the Amazon can reach 12 percent during the summer, the Yellow River has established an observed record of silt content of 46 percent. One of the tributaries on one summer day produced an unbelievable 63 percent. The Yellow River therefore constantly tends to fill up its own channel and break its dikes, causing incalculable loss of life and property. This inherent

Loess Land

danger is exacerbated by the fact that the volume of water flowing in the Yellow River varies widely between the flooding and dry seasons. Logically, only a central authority, preferably upstream, which could mobilize all the resources available to deal with the problem and command the concerned parties effectively and fairly would be in a position to provide the needed security against the constant threat. When the Zhou king was unable to carry out this function, the resultant void exerted greater pressure for a stronger center. Natural forces were driving China toward national unity.

An entry in the *Spring and Autumn Annals* discloses that in 651 B.C., in the absence of Zhou leadership, a league convention was convened by the powerful Duke of Qi, who led the subscribing principalities to pledge, among other things, never to execute waterworks detrimental to the interests of the other states and never to impose a grain embargo in time of famine. This Guiqiu Convention was cited by Mencius some 350 years later, but he immediately lamented that the contending states in his day ignored those vows that affected the well-being of the population so much. As if to underline its importance, the *Discourses of Mencius* mentions water control eleven times. At one point the text explicitly condemns the practice of discharging flood water into neighboring states. It would be difficult for us to dissociate the condemnation from the omnipresent threat of the Yellow River and the origin of the problem, namely, the loess in its current. In another context, Mencius suggested that security and stability would come when national unity was achieved. Those links now work together like a chain. The ultimate lesson we can learn from the ensemble is that geography exercises a decisive influence on history when the latter is reviewed in depth and the former is examined in a broad scope.

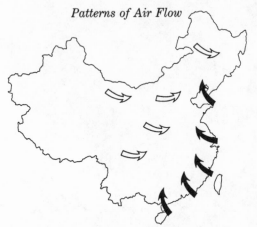

Patterns of Air Flow

The reference to grain embargoes deserves further comment. Rainfall in China is highly seasonal, with 80 percent of it coming in three summer months, during which time the prevailing wind direction changes. Moreover, monsoon rain in China is cyclonic; the moisture-laden air blowing from the general direction of the Philippine Sea has to be cooled to yield rain by the low pressure centers drifting toward the east and northeast. The livelihood of many millions therefore depends on the synchronization of these two sets of variables in the atmosphere. When the two kinds of current meet frequently over a given area, there will be flood and inundation. When they constantly miss each other, extremely dry weather and droughts are the likely results. Early historians, unaware of the meteorographical mechanism, left warnings in their writings about a serious crop failure every six years and a general famine every twelve years, which they held to be inevitable. Prior to the founding of the Republic in 1911, over a span of 2,117 years China's dynastic histories registered 1,621 floods and 1,392 droughts serious enough to be officially noticed; this averages out to 1.42 disasters annually throughout the span of time.

In the *Spring and Autumn Annals* we encounter many instances in which opposing armies raided each other's crops across their mutual boundary, and the cutting off of food supplies in time of famine led to war. In the *Discourses of Mencius*, famine and starvation are cited seventeen times. On one occasion, perhaps in 320 B.C., the king of Wei, whose territory embraced both banks of the Yellow River, told the Second Sage that in times of serious crop failure he had to relocate the populace across the river in large numbers. By this time the state of Lu had expanded its territory from its original authorization by five times, and neighboring Qi, by ten times. It is not difficult to imagine that the larger states in those days had a clear advantage over the lesser ones. In times of natural disasters they alone had effective resources at hand to provide relief; therefore they were likely to gather a greater following in the wars of annexation. While the princes waged wars of aggrandizement, the common people were struggling for survival. The competition was turned into a spiral drive with

aggregated commit-
ments from both.

There was one more
meteorographical factor
that sustained the cen-
tralization movement.
The rainfall at a particular place over a number
of years might fluctuate;
the average annual
yields in wide regions of
China, however, follow a
definite pattern. This is
easy to understand. The

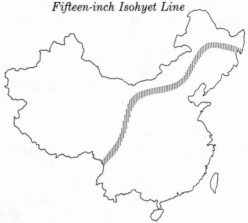

Fifteen-inch Isohyet Line

moisture in the air currents is apt to evaporate faster as it moves inland, if it has not already been condensed to give rain on the coast. Of interest to us here is the so-called 15-inch isohyet line ("iso" means equal, "hyet" means rain), which skirts around the heartland of Manchuria from the northeast, runs parallel with the present Great Wall in the middle, and curves southwestward to separate Kokonor and Tibet from China proper. The territory to the southeast of this line, where an annual rainfall of fifteen inches or more can be counted on, fits the description by Lattimore: "Agriculture teems in China, and mankind swarms." In contrast, he refers to what lies to the north and west as, "over thousands of miles of territory men neglect agriculture altogeth-er, they do not live directly off vegetation of earth but interpose a mechanism between it and themselves." This is his charming way of saying that those people are nomads. They roam about with their cattle seeking water and graze in a generally arid area. There is no way to convert a pastoral economy to a planters' economy.

The record of 2,000 years of struggle between the agriculturists in China and the cattlemen beyond the pale is one of bad feelings and very few fond memories. Especially when pressed by bad weather, the war bands on horseback naturally were inclined to pillage the farmers who had a half year's savings. Occasional raids could lead to large-scale invasions, and preemptive wars launched by the defenders cried out for reprisal.

Chronologically, mounted bowmen had first appeared on Assyrian reliefs as early as the ninth century B.C. But "full nomadism" and cavalry tactics developed much later, marking time before reaching East Asia. Finally, by the third century B.C. the threat of nomadic incursion had become serious enough to justify the incorporation of the separate earthworks erected by the several northern states into a continuous barrier, a feat that alone would have earned the First Emperor a place in history. This development testifies again that national defense favors centralization. The exposed frontier roughly coincidental to the 15-inch isohyet line, being the longest in the world and burdened with tortured memories of not only the fighters on the front but also the womenfolk at home, is the third geographical factor dictating China's agrobureaucratic management under a strong center.

With all these factors in view, we can see that no less than the Legalists, Mencius, who missed the reign of the First Emperor by less than fifty years, had reason to argue in favor of a central authority. Just as Qin Shi-huang-di was about to carry out the imperial unification by brutal force, the Second Sage was preaching good will and moral inducement. Historically they were addressing the same set of problems.

In the short term, Mencius seems to have lost out. By the time he urged the lords of the Warring States to return to the humanism of King Wen, the Zhou *fengjian* had been revised beyond recognition. The well-field system had been abandoned. The hereditary nobility as a warrior-administrator caste had been replaced by the bureaucrats. Because the kings were able to appoint magistrates to manage the local districts, they taxed the peasants directly and conscripted them into their armies by the thousands. The mood of competition was further advanced by a growing commerce which, though in its infancy, thrived because of the extraordinary effort of certain prominent individuals involved in interstate politics. This was no longer an ordered system in which everything fell into its proper place, in which public affairs could be handled with etiquette and compassion. The wave of wars of annexation continued, until there was only one declared winner.

Yet in the long run Mencius, like Confucius before him, foresaw China's destiny as a large agrarian community set up against certain mathematical principles yet tempered by humanism. The body of lofty sentiments called Confucianism therefore had a place in such a setting. In the *Discourses of Mencius* we find that the Second Sage was in disagreement with two philosophers slightly younger than he. One, Yang Zhu, advised everyone to adhere to his self-interest. He apparently felt that moral exhortations, pressing individuals to act against their own wishes, only led the public to further confusion. So he said that he himself would not contribute even one hair to advance the world's well-being. The logic that everybody should follow his natural instinct to seek pleasure and avoid pain comes close to that of the type of "possessive individualism" prevalent in the modern West. Taking an opposite position, the other, Mo Di, expounded the idea that Heaven commanded everyone to love his fellow men, impartially and without ritualistic pretensions. With such a compelling vision in view, no effort was too demanding. In practice Mo Di and his disciples risked their lives in a vain effort to avert the war of annexation.

Mencius had no kind words for either man. Yang Zhu's devotion to self-interest, he charged, would eliminate the need for the ruler. Mo Di's universal love, on the other hand, would negate the uniqueness of the father. Carrying his rebuke to an uncompromising extreme, he admonished: "Only fowls and beasts exist without rulers or fathers!" This intolerant tone may come as a surprise to the modern reader. It can only be understood in historical perspective.

Toward the end of the Warring States period, iron tools had been introduced. The resultant increase in productivity brought social sophistication to the top layer of society. Yet for many centuries to come China remained a large agrarian nation with a homogenous base on the bottom, and writing by scribes was still done on bamboo sticks until the invention of paper in the first century A.D. The demand that the empire act as an integral whole, outlined above, was at no time relaxed. Under the circumstances, there was no better way to build up a cell structure within the peasant population than by promoting kinship cohesion. A corollary to this was to have a hereditary ruler as the father image. Good will toward one's fellow men had to be differentiated to accommodate the familial principle. The idea of man as an individual, either oriented to self-interest or propelled by unconditional altruism, might appeal to the modern reader; it was, however, impractical for ancient China. For one thing, it would have created serious problems in legal matters. Even twentieth century China, let alone the China of the pre-Christian era, lacks the judicial competence to handle the civil rights of every individual. In fact, for the entire imperial period the nation maintained a basically unchanging penal code that upheld a tight-knit social order based on kinship affinity and defended good conduct within its ability. What rights the individual was entitled to had to be conditional to this social fabric.

Modern jurisprudence is a very expensive institution, and it did not develop overnight. In the Western world, it was at the end of the medieval period that the feudal lords, unable to control the urban centers, granted the burghers municipal immunity, a franchise from which civil liberty eventually blossomed. At the beginning it was an unplanned arrangement. Only in the past two centuries has there been a conscious movement to extend civil privileges to the entire population. Only in the past several decades do we see such a degree of fulfillment. It is an irony of history that in China this stage of development never occurred, not because of any conscious move against it, but because it was never an issue. As the European Sinologist Etienne Balazs puts it, Chinese officials never lost control over the cities. In fact, the power of the mandarin remained strongest within the city walls.

Apparently, when the Confucian administrators enacted laws that put men above women, the aged over the young, and those who had the status of the educated elite over the unlettered, they felt that they were acting according to Natural Law. For a great number of years, the calm and orderliness that emanated from this system commanded admiration abroad. It was only in the early nineteenth century when the commercial interests of the West became established in force along the China coast that the Confucian style of statecraft, projecting an ideal perfection, more a fiction than a reality, yet taking the minimum rather than the maximum satisfaction of the populace as the norm, quite suddenly appeared to be a cheap form of government that was neither solid nor flexible. Once the weakness was exposed, what was inefficient was also charged with having been immoral.

The juxtaposition among Yang Zhu, Mo Di, and Mencius may help to explain the vertical stem in Chinese history. But, of course, the story does not end here. It has a long way to go. Its unfolding will lead to many surprises and reversals. Our introduction so far has given the impression that when anything of significance happens to China, it is likely to occur on a vast scale. The panorama of excitement and drama of the many vicissitudes in China's history, along with the unavoidable failures and blunders, is stunning.

4
Behind
the Terracotta Army

Scholars have reason to feel grateful to the commune workers in Lintong County who in the spring of 1974, by sheer good luck, brought to light the terracotta army on guard at Qin Shi-huang-di's mausoleum where it had been buried twenty feet under the loess soil for 2,200 years. If the find fails to answer all the historian's questions regarding China's imperial unification, it provides clues to several crucial points. The most important is that the evidence speaks of an unmistakable Chinese character, distinct from that of early civilizations elsewhere.

In recorded history, the ancestry of the royal house of the Qin is cited in the "who-begot-whom" fashion of the Old Testament. As the chronicles enter into the Warring States period, the entries begin to envelop major events of history with fanciful legends. Even this portrait of Qin Shi-huang-di seems to have been executed by a caricaturist, who must have had the image of the hawk in mind, for the upper lip seems to be represented by a beak. The great historian Sima Qian, who wrote only about a hundred years after Shi-huang-di's time, recorded the emperor's origins as follows: About 250 B.C., a prince of blood from the Qin, following the practice of those days, took residence in the royal court of Zhao as hostage to guaran-

Qin Shi-huang-di

tee the armistice between the two states. Despite the arrangement, intermittent frontier clashes occurred. So the prince's position was insecure. Being one of the score of sons of the Qin heir apparent, he did not receive much attention from home. A rich merchant by the name of Lü Buwei, however, noticed that the situation could be worked to his own advantage. It so happened that the Qin heir apparent had just elevated his favorite concubine to be his wife. She was influential but childless. Lü Buwei at first made friends with the neglected prince in the hostile court by means of fancy gifts and flattery. With more luxurious gifts and more abundant compliments he went on to tour the Qin capital, this time serving as an envoy from the prince. He convinced the wife of the Qin heir that in order to protect her future she should adopt the prince now serving as hostage in the Zhao court, because of his character and his aloofness from domestic politics. The scheme worked, and the overlooked prince upon his return to Qin and the death of the king was himself installed as heir apparent.

A minor detail was that while still in the Zhao capital the prince was introduced to one of Lü Buwei's concubines, a dancer of great beauty. He took her from the generous merchant without knowing that she was already pregnant. Within a year she gave the new heir apparent a son, who thirteen years later became the King of Qin. Another quarter of a century later he was to rule China as the First Emperor. His natural father, the shrewd merchant, acted as a counselor until he fell into disgrace.

China's imperial unification in 221 B.C. is a major milestone in history. Without question this unusual deed had to be carried out by extraordinary persons. But the peculiar circumstances that set those figures in motion were more than incidental episodes. As we have already observed, some of the background factors took several hundred years to develop.

The conversion from the Zhou system to a state structure that put the entire population directly under the command of a single king administering through a bureaucracy was by no means a Qin invention. The Qin was no pioneer. But while other states moved toward reorganization piecemeal, the Qin introduced a program to effect sweeping changes that were coordinated beyond any compromise. The steps taken included the total abolition of the aristocracy, the introduction of a system of merit appointments, dismantlement of the well-field system, taxation by acreage on transferable landownership, military service by conscription, and promotion of food production and the textile industry at the expense of all other pursuits. As the records show, these measures had taken effect about a hundred years before Shi-huang-di was installed as the Qin king. The ultimate centralization that consciously made the state a kind of collective personality of all the royal subjects amounted to nothing less than a "totalitarian system." Indeed, the Qin was a police state. It differed from a modern totalitarian state only by the fact that the latter forcefully converts a society that has already been pluralized to serve its single-minded purpose. The ancient state of Qin, on the other hand, seems not to have completely separated itself from its natural course of growth and development. Although it geared up to face wartime circumstances, nationalism played no part in Qin conquests. All the important advisers who gave counsel to the Qin kings were alien, and under Shi-huang-di's unification, in no instance was the citizenry discriminated against because of state origin.

Legalism, which supplied the ideological underpinnings of the streamlined state of Qin, holds that man's nature is evil. Goodness, however, could be generated by concerted action directed by the state. In this sense the Legalists sometimes sounded very much like Henrich von Treitschke, and it is their "modern" outlook that fascinates Western readers. Their concept of law gave no consideration to tradition, custom, ancient privilege, conventional ethics, kinship preference, or even compassion. It reflected the sovereign's will, codified, comprehensively and precisely written, and universally and impartially applied. Insofar as they valued nothing materialistic except the power and wealth of the state, the Legalists could not hold to any jurisprudential concept even remotely akin to the civil law of the modern Western tradition, but at that time, several hundred years before the Christian era, their ideas must have had a great deal of egalitarian appeal within the contemporary context. The Legalists, too, saw themselves as adherents of Natural Law. Their vision that once the laws were proclaimed the ruler could rest at the hub of the wheel from which the bureaucratic spokes radiated is not an entirely inaccurate picture of the Chinese system of bureaucratic management that was to prevail for the next two millenniums.

In any case, in the long run although politically China matured early, there was a price to pay. Taking form in the pre-Christian era, the state institutions appeared streamlined on the surface, but lower layers were crude and undeveloped, especially by latter-day standards. Until very recently, China has lacked a judiciary apparatus substantial and independent enough to be compared with similar institutions in the West. The reasons for this reach far back. The Confucian concept of law, inseparable from the familial principle, confused justice with personal sentiment. Legalist law, on the other hand, could easily be applied as an administrative tool but not much else.

Classical historians have pointed out that in its contest for control of China, the Qin enjoyed a geographical advantage over its competitors. On the east it was protected by rivers and mountains. From the passages within those barriers the Qin could invade neighboring states at will while remaining immune from reprisal (see map p. 11). The territory lying to its southwest could be annexed and absorbed because the aborigines there offered little resistance. Since the war of annexation was evolving, historically, toward a unified imperial rule, a power from the far side with long-range goals was bound to fare better than the central states, which were caught in a confusing and uncertain web of intrigues and rivalries with their neighbors. This tendency became more pronounced in the last decades of the struggle when these states, with little success, in preparation for the Qin onslaught tried desperately to work out some form of alliance. Rarely mentioned is the fact that the Qin also benefited from its economic backwardness. Its undiversified agriculture provided the internal cohesion that made mobilization easier. This was an age when numbers counted; military technology, being more or less in equilibrium, did not confer on any contestant a qualitative edge over the others.

Shi-huang-di's career followed that of his forerunners. The standard strategy was incessant incursions across borders. Armed migrations followed. When possible, the early Qin strategists demanded that fortifications vital to the frontier defense of potential enemies be surrendered or razed, at times not hesitating to resort to slaughter to reduce the male population of service age in an opponent's territory. Diplomatic maneuvers, especially those designed to split the nexus of Qin's rivals, softened the resistance. Very rarely was a battle fought that was not beyond Qin's borders. We have strong suspicions that the Qin legions were often turned loose to live off the enemy. In this connection, several major natural disasters that seemed to bolster Qin's cause occurred after Shi-huang-di was installed as king. There was a famine in 244 B.C. The next year a locust pestilence affected the western portion of China. In 235 B.C. drought struck. In both 230 B.C. and 228 B.C. famines were again cited in the annals. Nevertheless, the military triumphs of Shi-huang-di were impressive. Within the decade prior to 221 B.C., five of the six rival kings were captured, and the remaining one surrendered. All their capitals were taken. The last state to fall was the Qi on the east coast. The Qin offensive went by way of the state of Yan to turn the northern flank of the Qi. When that battle concluded, the Qin ruler proclaimed himself emperor.

The unification was cemented by deeds. Boundaries were redrawn to divide China into thirty-six commanderies. After all the hereditary lords were eliminated, each commandery was jointly administered by a civil governor, a military commander, and a censor-in-chief. The Chinese writing system, beginning to manifest regional diversity during the Warring States period, was unified by the proclamation of a Qin script. Units and measurements were likewise standardized, as was the width of axles on carriages. To root out local interests in the provinces, 120,000 prominent households were relocated to take up residence on the outskirts of the capital. Weapons except those in the possession of the imperial army were confiscated and recast into twelve gigantic bronze statues, which stood in front of the imperial palace to reaffirm the emperor's resolution that war was forever proscribed.

In 213 B.C. it was decreed that certain books be burned. A reader-in-waiting, a good Confucian, suggested that the emperor pay attention to the ancient models of governance. When Shi-huang-di referred the matter to court discussion, the Legalist chancellor countered that the practice of allowing men to indulge themselves in antiquity to give opinions on current affairs would ruin the state. He went on to suggest that the prohibition of private learning altogether would protect the Qin reform from "seditious libel." The burning of books was part of this program; other measures included the death penalty for citing classical works in daily conversations and applying historical examples to criticize current policies. The condemned books included histories of non-Qin origins and all philosophical and classical works aside from those in the possession of the imperial academy. Exceptions were made only for references on medicine, divination, and agriculture. With the emperor's approval, the order took effect in thirty days.

The next year brought the infamous "burying scholars alive." The emperor had recruited, along with regular academicians, groups of astrologers, alchemists, and other kinds of practical scientists. Two of the men commissioned to seek elixir, having failed to produce the medicine, spread the word that Shi-huang-di's impetuous temperament was unfit for longevity. The enraged ruler sent his guard on a house-to-house search within the capital. The two principal offenders were never found, but 460 men were rounded up either for maintaining connections with the fugitives or for having something to do with the craft. They were buried alive.

Many traditional Chinese historians, compelled by custom to either praise or condemn historical personages, have found themselves unable to exercise the option in the presence of a man of such giant proportions as the First Emperor of the Qin. How could his grotesque atrocities be condoned? Yet how could his contribution to the nation's unity, conceived with such majestic vision and carried out with so much skill and courage, be passed over without a word of appreciation, if not admiration? A thoughtful reader may be troubled by the savage acts committed by the emperor and his followers, and yet, at another passage, be touched by the many personal risks the First Emperor took and the dauntless determination with which he sought to fulfill a purpose that was above and beyond the scope of an ordinary man's vision.

The accounts in the recorded history portray the First Emperor as vain and, at times, even whimsical. Given the general level of understanding in his time, the accounts of his superstitious tendencies may well be true. Nevertheless, once he is said to have dispatched 3,000 prisoners to deforest a mountain after he was told that the goddess in control of the area had been responsible for the strong wind that had impeded his river crossing. At least on this occasion he was more defiant than fearful of supernatural power. His adaptation of black as the imperial color was epochal in his day. The inscriptions on the stone tablets he erected indicate that next to his concern for the eternal peace of the realm, he greatly valued sexual morality, which he regarded as essential to the well-being of the populace. He had more than twenty sons and at least ten daughters; but except for his promiscuous mother, the chronicles remain absolutely silent about the women in his life. The First Emperor traveled extensively, visiting not only the urban centers but also the great mountains and rivers, the lakes and the high seas. He toured the capital city incognito at night. Although proud of his military exploits, Qin Shi-huang-di is not known to have ever commanded troops personally. On the other hand, he was a tireless worker. He set quotas for the amount of documents, by weight, that he must dispose of daily, not resting until his work was done. On issues of state affairs he always consulted his advisers first; but the final decisions were always his own. Perhaps the most remarkable thing about Qin Shi-huang-di is that for twelve years his iron-fisted rule never caused a major incident, this over an immense country that had been ravaged by war for decades, and indeed for centuries.

He left a position that no one could fill. Immediately after his death, palace conspiracies and machinations set the emperor's chief advisers, chamberlains, and sons to plotting against one another. Within a year popular uprisings erupted in the commanderies, and in another three years the Qin fell and all the close relatives of Shi-huang-di and all the key personnel on his staff perished.

The archaeological find of 1974 does not provide clues to Qin Shi-huang-di's legitimate or illegitimate birth; nor does it sustain the argument that he was a good or a bad man. So far the excavation has only unearthed a portion of the outlying area of his burial place, but already it is clear that the scale of the design is dazzlingly impressive.

This site is an enclosure of over three acres. It is estimated that no less than 7,000 life-size earthenware soldiers equipped with real weapons, real chariots, and pottery horses are protecting the resting place of their master. The entire scene is marked by its grand scale on the one hand and its dedication to details on the other. The figures of the soldiers seem to have been copied from live models; no two of them are alike. Their facial expression shows endless individuality.  They all wear the same hairstyle; yet in each case there is a slight variation in the way that the hair is combed, the whiskers are trimmed, and the braids are knotted. Their caps are decorated with patterned dots; their belts have metal hooks; their armor jackets are sculptured to indicate leather straps serving as fasteners; and their shoes have cleats on the soles. Their armor varies from that of the foot soldier to that of the cavalryman, notably with the omission of the shoulder piece on that worn by the mounted warrior to permit more freedom of movement when on horseback. The armor of the officers is more elaborate. The metalwork is refined, with even the smaller straps featuring decorative designs. The poses of the earthenware statues are diverse; they are standing at attention, kneeling down to man crossbows, driving chariots, poised for hand-to-hand combat, each at the battle station called for by the overall tactics. In sum, what is represented is an entire division of Qin infantry, flanked by a formation of chariots and a squadron of cavalry, ready to go into combat at a moment's notice. While the scale of this display is impressive, specialists speculate that more soldiers, horses, and chariots may be positioned on the southern flank of this division. Or, even more impressively, entire divi-

sions of the same terracotta army may be deployed on the other three sides of the emperor's burial chamber, which would quadruple the scale of the present discovery.

According to historian Sima Qian, the construction of the First Emperor's mausoleum took thirty-six years and engaged 700,000 artisans. Also recreated in the subterranean chamber was Qin Shi-huang-di's entire court, complete with the palace buildings, and representations of the empire's major mountains and rivers were modeled from quicksand. Armed mechanical crossbows were strategically placed inside the

tumulus to deter grave robbers, and numerous artisans were buried alive inside the tomb because they knew too much.

These accounts may never be verified, but even now, visitors can make solid historical inferences from what they see. If Qin Shi-huang-di had been totally convinced of the power of the supernatural, wouldn't he have been persuaded to substitute size for numbers of his guards? One may wonder why he didn't choose to protect his tomb with superhuman figures scores of feet high, similar to the huge Nubian statues now overlooking the Aswan Dam, or create multi-headed, multi-limbed monsters similar to the deities of the Hindu tradition. And if he had been completely convinced of the effectiveness of military rule, he might have valued uniformity more than variety. The earthenware figures could in fact have been reproduced en masse from stereotypes, similar to the identical images of foot soldiers recurring in long files on the terrace relief of Darius' Hall of Audience, or even to the lifeless figures on the Arch of Constantine.

One can almost see the philosophers, artists, and craftsmen rubbing shoulders with squads of sorcerers and contingents of army officers, all working together to design the underground project, the layout and execution of which could never have been achieved without an exhaustive exchange of ideas and the coordination of skills. In this sense the terracotta army stands as a historical document corroborating the written record on the extraordinary levels of mobilization in the Warring States period and giving credence to the so-called hundred schools of political thinkers of the era. It is further evidence of the vertical stem in Chinese history: some 2,200 years ago, many of the outstanding features of the Chinese state and society were already in place. Here is a system that involves a certain amount of make-believe on the top, to the extent of blurring the differences between rationality and irrationality.

Although we cannot subscribe to the Legalist doctrine that individuals should be compelled to do good for the whole community and punished for acting to the contrary, this vast array of baked clay sculptures convincingly impresses us that a national life purpose could be created by the will of the state. The Machiavellian concept of "universal egoism" cannot simply be put aside just because it is evil. It may be appropriate that Arthur Waley chose to call this entire school of philosophers "realists."

The visitor to the array of baked clay sculptures may wonder, how-

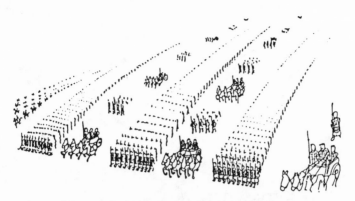

A possible parade formation of a division of the Qin army

ever, why for all the ingenuity and magnificence demonstrated by the project, and the organizational strength behind it, the technical capacity never realized its full potential by moving China to a major breakthrough, as the Renaissance did in Western Europe. The lack of follow-through may be understood in the perspective that while arts and crafts always have creative potential, their fruition demands a social impetus. Michaelangelo had to demonstrate his talent to the Vatican. Rubens prospered because of his connections with royalty. The misfortune of the anonymous artists of the Qin is that their work, collectively executed, had to be dedicated to the ruler whose own portrait was painted with a beaked lip, and whose museum was his own mausoleum. Yet, what happened to these anonymous artists is not totally unjust. Their effort did not turn to dust. Some 2,200 years later their masterpieces, cleaned and restored, have been brought into the sunshine to give presence and feeling to an important turning point in history.

5

The First Empire:
Establishing the Standard

For all practical purposes, when Shi-huang-di died the Qin dynasty vanished; but his achievement of imperial unification was not to be undone. Within a decade there emerged a new dynasty, which endured for more than 400 years. The Han, divided halfway between the B.C. and A.D. eras and with a population roughly estimated to be close to sixty million at the height of its prosperity, is often compared to Rome in the West, as it controlled a territory equally as vast and remained in being until the decline of the Roman Empire. The Chinese empire, however, maintained an internal cohesion that was unknown to the West.

The new dynasty is idealized by Chinese writers as marking the first time that commoners took up imperial roles. The dynastic founder, Liu Bang, was a minor police officer under the Qin. Both chancellors, Xiao He and Cao Cen, had been county clerks. A general, Chen Ping, had at one time worked as a butcher. Another, Han Xin, begged for food in his youth. Qing Bu and Peng Yue had risen from the ranks of brigands. The plebeian composition of the new imperial court, however, only reflected that the territorial lordship had been so thoroughly uprooted that for the national reconstruction it was neither necessary nor even possible to rally behind the old aristocracy. It was by no means a sign that China was ripe for social revolution. For thousands of years to come the nation was unable to install a form of governance truly representative of the large and homogeneous agrarian base; certainly it could not be at this early stage.

Having inherited the broad and leveled base of the Qin, the imperial organizers of the Han demonstrated their acumen at making amends for the excesses of their predecessor. Yet, pursuing a policy that was essentially "forward three steps, backward two steps," they worked toward a centralized bureaucratic management that took several generations to reach its fulfillment and that eventually emerged as the prototype of China's imperial rule for ages to come.

An immediate problem faced by the new dynasty was that the sprawling empire could not be governed entirely from the center. A solution was found by introducing a "zebra form" of provincial composition. In certain areas the Qin commanderies were to remain in place. In other districts a new hereditary lordship was installed. The Lius—the emperor's brothers, uncles, and cousins—were made regional princes; handfuls of generals and chancellors who had performed outstanding service became marquises. They held fiefs that dovetailed with the territory directly managed by the central government. This juxtaposition kept the two kinds of domain at peace to avoid the Qin over-centralization for the short term, yet without leaving a breeding ground for regional contention reminiscent of the Warring States in the long term. The arrangement was not intended to be permanent. Before the first Han emperor's reign was over, many of the marquises had already been found at fault and removed from their positions. Further depletion of their ranks was a task for the first empress and the succeeding emperors. In 154 B.C., close to a half century after the founding of the dynasty, a move to sharply curtail the power of the territorial lords provoked a general rebellion, which was put down. Thereafter many of those principalities were abolished. The surviving ones suffered not only by having their domains reduced in size but also by their internal administration being taken over by the imperial government. The consolidation of central power reached a high point under Liu Che, the fifth emperor, who is usually referred to by his posthumous title of Han Wu-di. His reign from 141 B.C. to 87 B.C. was not only the longest in the dynasty but also the most consequential.

Liu Che proclaimed the first ideological platform for imperial rule, which was generally summarized as "the promotion of Confucianism to the disparagement of all other schools." In reality, he and his advisers extended the coverage of Confucianism long and wide enough to embrace all the theories and practices useful and vital to the centralized bureaucratic management. Confucian doctrines of self-restraint, mutual deference, humanistic sensitivity, kinship cohesion, and devotion to rituals were adopted as a comprehensive code of behavior for the bureaucrats. The teachings of Mencius, which held that the state had a stake in the livelihood of the populace, were similarly endorsed without reservation. But the curb on mercantile interests in deference to food production, a Legalist principle, inevitably became a part of Wu-di's officially sanctioned ideology, as did the practice of state monopoly on major commodities such as salt and iron. Reliance on the penal code to discipline the governed remained intact.

Certain beliefs, either unsanctioned or not directly mentioned by Confucius, were also included in this package. Wu-di, the emperor himself, performed the mystic sacrificial services on the high mountains to seek communion with the deities. His court erudites expounded a theory that the five material agents (wood, fire, earth, metal, and water) retained certain corresponding values with the four directions plus the center, with the five principal colors, with the pentatonic musical scale, with the five key personal virtues, and even with the five governmental functions; for example, fire belonged to the summer, the color of which was red, and it remained the agent of the Ministry of War. This concept was anchored in the belief that every "thing" in the universe, be it a natural phenomenon or a social occurrence, belonged to some visible or invisible scale and therefore carried a certain inner rhythm that could be mathematically manipulated. Its origin can be traced to an ancient classic, the *Yijing*, or the *Book of Changes*. The pseudo-scientific approach to problems, often bordering on superstition, revealed the fact that learned men of the age were under great pressure to quickly assess a mass of data embracing both the knowable and the unknowable. Yet, the Han courtiers also persistently applied their vision of poetic association to drive home the message of sound government based on ethical harmony. For one thing, they went so far as to correlate politics with weather. In this way they rationalized the absolute power of the imperial throne yet at the same time tempered it, giving confidence to the bureaucrats by endowing them with a feeling that Natural Law was within their grasp, thus enabling the hereditary monarchy and literary bureaucracy to work as a team. Although this mixing of cosmology with political science seems to have served a purpose, the drawback of this formation, a cult of the state that is confusingly called Confucianism, is that once it was set up it remained virtually immovable for the next 2,000 years. Indeed its effect lingers on even today.

The conservative character that many Western observers attribute to the Chinese can in part be explained by certain basically unchanging features in their environment, which have dictated an enduring structure for their state and society. Today few tourists would contemplate a trip to China without a visit to the section of the Great Wall at Badaling. The original wall constructed by Qin Shi-huang-di, running beyond the 15-inch isohyet line (see p. 23), went to ruin centuries ago. The present brick structure was rebuilt in the fifteenth century, with new watchtowers added in the sixteenth century when gunpowder was already making such masonry fortifications obsolete in many parts of the world.

The sight of the continuous barrier, thousands of miles long and repeatedly renewed and added on to, is a reminder that China's frontier problem has existed almost as long as Chinese civilization itself. Its connection with Liu Che, Wu-di of the Han, is that this unusual monarch, who came to the throne at the age of fifteen and whose fifty-four-year reign coincided with the zenith of Han power, made an audacious and relentless effort to terminate the nomadic problem once and for all. Despite many victorious campaigns, his goal was never realized. Wu-di died in 87 B.C., and by then the severe strain put on the state coffers by the Xiongnu Wars was becoming a major contributing factor in the decline of the Former Han, as the earlier half of the dynasty is called.

The First Empire

Qin	□	221 BC 206 BC
Former Han		202 BC ... 8 AD
Later Han		25 AD ... 220 AD

Xiongnu is a general designation for the Altaic-speaking people who became a major threat during China's early imperial period, and who were to be succeeded in the centuries and millenniums to come by at least a dozen other nomadic peoples of similar or different ethnic backgrounds. The early organizational maturity of the Xiongnu might have had a bearing on China's imperial unification, and vice versa. By the time the name was mentioned in the Han records, apparently the Xiongnu had already formed a confederation of twenty-four tribes, extending their influence over a 1,500 mile front from the fringes of Manchuria to the grasslands in Kokonor. In 200 B.C. they are said to have besieged the Han dynastic founder Liu Bang in today's Shanxi with more than 300,000 mounted warriors. The number may be an exaggeration, but there is no doubt that they could turn out 100,000 men for a major campaign, not necessarily assembled as one body, but grouped into a number of smaller battle formations over a large area that could be strategically coordinated. Being nomads, they enjoyed an advantage over the Chinese in what the military specialists referred to as "the coincidence of combat conditions with living conditions." That is to say, while Han China had to go through the cumbersome process of mobilization—inducting, training, equipping, transporting, and supplying its troops—its foe in the north could skip most or all of these steps. Its male population lived on horseback; their weapons were their tools. They never lacked mobility.

The wars between the two sides were atrocious owing to the harsh conditions of the deserts and steppelands on which they were fought. Once the opposing armies engaged each other, there was no turning back, especially for the Han. Although the defeated might be wiped out, the victorious were also decimated. Escape was hardly possible. Few prisoners were taken and still fewer were exchanged. Usually those who surrendered had to give service to their enemy, with women and children meeting the same fate as the warriors. The entire livestock of the nomads could be netted as war booty, and their reprisals against the planters in the south, when they could lay their hands on them, were by no means more lenient. The Han campaign can be seen as a skirmish in the long rivalry between the two cultures that stands in history as a permanent stalemate. This outcome found its expression in a large body of Chinese literature, some pieces jingoistic clamoring, others by and large venting war-weariness in myriad poetic ways.

Aside from an inspection tour to the front in 110 B.C., Wu-di absented himself from the battlefield. But he personally directed the offensives against the Xiongnu, organizing the orders of battle and allocating horses and soldiers to his commanders. After each engagement the emperor himself decided on their rewards and punishments.

In a typical campaign 100,000 cavalrymen took to the field. Since the infantry support and supply troops ran to several times that number, a total strength of close to a half million men was the general rule. Divided into three to five columns, the army would search for the enemy, and a time and place for rendezvous were designated in advance. They usually operated within a range of 500 miles in the hostile territory. Although on occasions no enemy was encountered, usually fierce fighting took place. In the campaign of 99 B.C., Chinese battlefield casualties ran to 60 to 70 percent; few survivors returned. Even in the campaign of 119 B.C., which was a Chinese victory, of the 140,000 horses involved in the action, less than 30,000 returned. During Wu-di's long reign he launched eight such campaigns. Other expeditions were sent to north Korea, to China's southwest corner, which knifed into today's Vietnam, and to Kokonor to fight the Tibetans.

What was the total cost of those campaigns? Although Sima Qian's claim that it took more than sixty-four hundredweight of grain from the interior to deliver one hundredweight to the battlefield cannot be taken as literally true, it does suggest the extent of the logistical problem. Moreover, Wu-di's strategy was to consolidate the frontiers and then, once the threat of the enemy was removed, relocate the population on a large scale to secure the territory; this of course added to the costs. As a result, a new range of fund-raising devices were put to work, including a property tax on merchants, a license tax on boats and carriages, commutation from punishment to fines, a state monopoly on wine, salt, and iron, and government participation in trade. All these measures, together with the conduct of the war itself, pushed the empire's centralization further. And Wu-di's personal control over the army, as we shall soon see, had a profound effect on Han court politics.

Did Wu-di break the dynasty's backbone by carrying out his great military campaigns? The evidence does not allow us to conclude this. At the height of his Xiongnu wars, there is no sign that China's prosperity was affected. This contradiction reveals a fact that has an enduring interest to students of Chinese history: China is the only nation in the world that has on record permitted the central government to tax the individual peasant household from the pre-Christian era to the twentieth century. This tax base, very broad and extremely fragile, differs from anything in the historical Western experience. The situation is best illustrated by Li Kui, a statesman of the Wei during the Warring States period. When Ban Gu wrote *The History of the Former Han* in the first century A.D., he still found the case relevant to taxation and government finance in his time. Because it is pertinent to this discussion, here is what Ban reports Li as saying:

> A farmer in a household of five works on 100 *mu* of land [about 11.4 acres by the measurement of those days]. Each *mu* produces 1.5 hundredweight of grain. Total harvest 150 hundredweight.

> Land tax at 10 percent, total 15 hundredweight. After tax yield 135 hundredweight.

> Food, 1.5 hundredweight per person per month. For the household of five, 90 hundredweight for the year. Remainder 45 hundredweight. At 30 copper cash per hundredweight, worth 1,350 cash.

> Deducting 300 cash for community sacrificial and festival services, available for household expenses 1,050 cash.

> Clothing, 300 cash per person, 1,500 cash needed. There is a shortage of 450 cash.

> Incidental expenses for sickness and funeral services, as well as tax surcharges for military campaigns, not included.

Li Kui's solution for the problem was governmental assistance in marketing the produce, purchasing the foodstuff when there was a surplus and offering it for sale in times of shortage, thus providing relief to the producers. During Wu-di's reign this policy was implemented under the direction of Minister of Revenue Sang Hongyang, who had a businessman's background, to make an extra profit to help defray war expenditures. The same device was to be attempted by China's managers of public finance many times again in succeeding dynasties.

The passage attributed to Li Kui was in fact typical for the entire imperial period, as enduring as the Great Wall. The numbers might vary in different times, but essentially the same story persisted as long as the historian can remember. An inevitable consequence was that the agrarian population was driven to work on marginal land and, as the new fields were opened up, to heighten the intensive farming. Despite the idealized freedom from manorial control, each peasant, in addition to his status as a self-employed laborer, was also a small businessman and therefore subject to the usury and cruelty of a very restricted local market. When the government attempted to take over marketing, it ushered in a new range of activities that the regular staff on the literary bureaucracy could not handle; nor were there even adequate laws to assure their proper functioning. Fundamentally, government participation in trade created many problems involving variable quantities, and this upset the agrarian mode of governance, which held every item as a fixed sum. The note of disharmony was to resonate tragically many times in Chinese history. It is worth noting that attempts made by subsequent dynasties to commercialize a part of the governmental operation always met strong resistance. None went very far or had an enduring effect. In the present case, Sang Hongyang's violent death ruled out the possibility that his effort would succeed.

Given the extent of political centralism, it is understandable that the bureaucrats were always concerned with the problem of tenancy. Since public office derived its strength from the amount of food and manpower collected from the pool of small self-cultivators, landlordism always meant an erosion of this tax base. As the above case illustrates, it is also obvious that the prime producer was unable to provide an extra share for the landlord. A point that Chinese writers failed to recognize, however, is that the case itself had been a product of the centralized management. Their argument in favor of small self-cultivators as opposed to landlordism mixed administrative considerations with humanitarian concerns. While egalitarianism without organizational sophistication does not reflect clear economic thinking, in view of the need for a broad and general administration in the background, nor can we call it a simple "mistake." Suffice it to say that the tax structure was tied to land tenure, and both were dictated by the uniform control from the center. And the entanglement remained a permanent feature in the macrohistory of China.

In the reign of Han Wu-di, the unbearable extraction was applied in this context. It was brought up by both Sima Qian and Ban Gu. Because the Han dynasty endowed the provincial governors with sufficient power, they could select their subordinate officials. But those in charge of the local districts could never maintain such close contact with the governed as the feudal lords did in their fiefs. The system stipulated a land tax that was supposed to be one-fifteenth (less than seven percent) of the crop yield, and a head tax of 120 copper cash for each adult. And the universal conscription called each able-bodied male to an annual frontier duty of three days, commutable at paying 300 cash. This level of exaction was not exceedingly high in terms of the national wealth of the Han empire. But the taxation was applied horizontally to the populace— to a man who owned five *mu* of land no less than to a man who owned 500 *mu* of land. And in the rural areas, the tax laws could not always be administered in an orderly way. During the reign of Wu-di, the collection was said to be "many times" over the normal quota. (See p. 41) An indication of the volatile situation was that in 108 B.C., during an imperial inspection trip, many provincial officials were found at fault in providing services and supplies, and two governors committed suicide as a result. It seems that although maximum pressure had already been put on the districts, it was not enough.

After Wu-di, the vigorous frontier policy was abandoned. Fortunately, not much later, the Xiongnu also dissolved their confederation. There was another Chinese expedition to the steppelands in 72 B.C., but in 55 B.C. the Xiongnu split into five groups and fought among themselves. Subsequently their southern branch accepted Chinese suzerainty, which permitted the Han court to reduce the frontier garrison even further.

A legacy, however, had grown out of the military campaigns in the ascendency of imperial in-laws. A very strong-willed man, Liu Che was also very jealous of his own power. His private life was marked with a certain weakness for women that led to many controversies. In his management of military affairs he was overly generous toward his favorite generals and overly severe in punishments meted out to the others. Fundamentally, with the Xiongnu wars he had accumulated in his own hands a great deal of power that could not be institutionalized or delegated. It is much commented on that Li Guang, a popular Han general who commanded the respect of the imperial troops and the nomadic foes alike, was never rewarded. In his last campaign he was forced to detour from a regular route and in doing so got lost. When the grand commandant, Wei Qing, who was the empress's half brother, threatened to report the case to the throne, Li, in anguish, chose to end his life by his own hands. On the other hand, the emperor's generosity to Wei Qing was such that three of the grand commandant's sons, still in infancy, were made marquises on account of their father's military

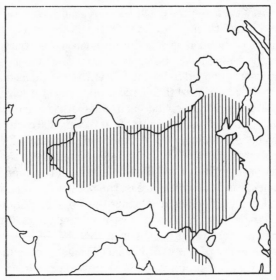

The Han Empire

merit. Another general, Huo Qubing, who was the empress's nephew, was always well regarded by the throne. The emperor ignored reports that while Huo's soldiers were starving in the field the general's kitchen train returned from the front with surplus delicacies on it. Only Huo Qubing's early death prevented his promotion to grand commandant. That position eventually went to his half brother Huo Guang, who had never seen action on the battlefield.

After Wu-di's death, Grand Commandant Huo Guang served as regent for the next emperor, an eight-year-old who later reigned for thirteen years but died without issue. The regent then consulted the empress and selected a prince of blood to be the successor. After twenty-seven days he found that that man did not meet his expectations, so he had him removed and replaced by another descendant of Wu-di, this time a young man of eighteen. The new emperor was observed to be in discomfort when he had to ride in the same carriage with the regent.

Yet, Huo Guang had not become the unchallenged authority in the Han court without a struggle. In 80 B.C. he had the court faction opposing him purged, executing many prominent figures, including Sang Hongyang. The extant account of the events, apparently based on the Han court record, charges the vanquished with treason. The conspirators are said to have attempted to dethrone the reigning emperor and to replace him with another prince, their discontent being traced to numerous petty rivalries and household intrigues.

On record, Huo Guang was popular among the courtiers trained in the Confucian tradition. His regency was marked by a retrenchment from Wu-di's militancy. During the two decades when he was in office, taxes were remitted or reduced, and peace negotiations were begun with the Xiongnu chieftains. In 81 B.C. the court sponsored a public debate on the state monopoly on major commodities, and as a result, that on wine distillation was abolished.

There is no evidence that either Han Wu-di or Huo Guang understood their own roles in history. Indeed, full understanding is difficult to arrive at even thousands of years later. Behind the lives and deeds of these men is the rarely discussed fact that China's monarchy was an impossible institution. It was neither divine nor secular, but both. It was neither irrational nor rational, but both. It was neither Confucian-humanistic nor Legalist-methodical, but both. At the dawn of the imperial era, the occupant of the Chinese throne was already called on to administer a population of sixty million with the aid of some 130,000 bureaucrats. His tools were few, but his approach to problems, forced to cut through many levels of inconsistency and uncertainty, had to remain decisive.

A sympathetic reader may envision the son of heaven as the Son of Heaven because he was drafted to handle a situation in which, to put it analogously, the lower Mississippi could at any time change its course and run into the sea in Florida, a drought or locust pestilence could lay waste to the entire harvest of Kansas and Iowa, and in the north, all the way to the Canadian border, would be huge expanses of desert with few oases. From the position of being the First Farmer on the Land, Han emperors issued declarations showing their concern for the people's livelihood. We should not take the gesture as pretension, since drawing subsistence from the income of small self-cultivators, they had no reason to feel otherwise. But the organizational order that they set up to carry out the function featured, again to yield to metaphor, a pyramid constructed upside down, that is, its fidelity to the original design diminished as it moved away from the source of power, which must be retained at the top. The differences between reality and the projected ideal perfection could be large.

The semireligious setting of the court at Xi'an strengthened the position of the emperor as the final authority on earth; his arbitration carried the force of divine judgment. From this practice emerges a tradition that in power politics technical problems are treated as moral issues. This usage is not lacking present-day applications. But insofar as the individuals occupying the top positions were prone to human frailty, intrigues and contrivance could run rampant within and outside of the palace when there was a change of command, especially one that involved a reversal of policy.

Huo Guang died peacefully in 68 B.C. But two years later, still another charge of conspiracy claimed the lives of his wife and son, along with many relatives and family associates. The chain of events did not even end there. Imperial in-laws continued to play a dominant part in court politics. The position of the grand commandant had ceased to be that of a field commander. Customarily it was occupied by the reigning emperor's father-in-law or maternal uncle, who, more a politician than a general, overshadowed both the civil bureaucracy and the cloistered sovereign. This trend, once established, continued to gather momentum, until it precipitated Wang Mang's usurpation.

Wang Mang is one of the most curious figures in Chinese history. He is variously depicted as a usurper, the greatest hypocrite, and a manipulator of public opinion, yet an idealist, a reformer, and even a revolutionary. Circumstances suggest that he might have possessed some substance of all those qualities, but no simple characterization suffices. Fortunately, the issues he dealt with, which affect our interest in China's long-term development, can be discussed without a detailed biographical focus.

The nephew of a Han empress, Wang Mang married one of his daughters to another emperor. Before he became regent in 1 B.C., three of his uncles and one cousin had occupied that position consecutively for twenty-eight years. In view of the morbidness of the Han court at that time, his takeover probably would have been better received by historians if he had succeeded in revitalizing the empire. But because he failed, his high-sounding pronouncements only made his controversial career appear to be even more hopelessly quixotic and his manipulation offensively unforgivable.

The situation he faced is clear enough: Because of the broad agrarian base on which the dynasty was founded, the Han government by its own constitution had to work earnestly in a public spirit. But after being in existence for over 200 years, the palace and the aristocracy, called by contemporaries "the inner court," involved itself in numerous insidious matters and sometimes acted to counter the "outer court," whose rank and file were recruited by merit, some of them taking the Confucian sense of sound government very seriously. In the countryside there was a tendency for the taxable land and manpower to fall into strong local hands, and therefore be rendered unreachable by the revenue collector. The phenomenon is referred to by the Chinese as *jianbing* (takeover by annexation), and it was to remain a perennial problem for the imperial government for over 2,000 years.

Since the land tax was collected from every *mu* of property and the poll tax from every head, in theory the change of ownership (including persons sold as household slaves) should not affect the total amount of tax yield. But here the problem was that as administered in the rural areas and in ancient times, the tax registers could never be regularly revised to reflect the changes. The same problem existed in the Roman Empire. No matter how methodically the original data had been obtained, in time all of them turned into inelastic regional quotas. The Chinese, who assessed taxes on individual households, constantly found population mobility and property transfers causing the loss of revenue, especially when the new titleholders maintained connections with governmental circles. For the local officials, an easy way out was to assign the uncollectibles to the remaining taxpayers and demand that they make up the difference; this, however, generated further absconsion and tax evasion, thus turning the ever-worsening situation into an accelerating spiral. A nominally light tax, because of the way it was administered, could in fact become unbearable. Excessive taxation moreover incited banditry. Ultimately, large-scale write-offs had to be put into effect, which seriously dampened the bureaucrats' own morale.

We are uncertain as to exactly how bad the situation was before Wang Mang took over. But at one time he mentioned a tax rate set at fifty percent of the crop yield. Even if this is hyperbolic, the circumstances leading to the exaggeration suggest that the situation was serious.

Yet, whatever spurred him to action, Wang Mang did not proceed to his reform in any deliberate manner. He took the conceptual approaches in the Chinese classics for granted, imagining that a pyramid could indeed be inverted. He expected that his exercise of the sovereign's will in Xi'an could carry to the far corners of the empire. He made an equally hasty retreat when things did not work out to his expectation. The usurper-reformer toiled ceaselessly. His economic programs included nationalization of agricultural land and indentured laborers, starting with the immediate prohibition of their sale. For monetary reform he introduced a complicated currency system which monetarized cloth and even cowrie shells; they were made interchangeable with the precious metals and bronze coins according to specified rates. Under his direction state monopoly widened and governmental participation in trade enlarged its scope, to embrace even banking. As circumstances demanded him to become ruler in substance as well as in title, Wang Mang proclaimed himself emperor in A.D. 9. He repacked the top aristocracy, but little was done with the civil service proper. Sometimes, different names were employed to effect changes for their own sake. To enforce his programs he resorted to the extensive use of the secret police.

The Wang Mang story has nevertheless sparked the imagination of many Western writers who cannot help but marvel at the "liberal" policies enacted by the Chinese in this early age. In doing so they too, like the frustrated reformer of so long ago, have ignored the background differences between a modern Western state, in which everything can be mathematically managed, and a traditional Chinese bureaucratic structure, in which it could not.

Needless to say, Wang Mang failed. When his economic programs stalled, peasant rebellion broke out. At the same time, a number of war bands rallied behind Liu Xiu, a ninth generation descendant of the Han dynastic founder. Wang Mang was killed in A.D. 23. Two years later when Liu Xiu proclaimed himself emperor to "restore" the Han dynasty, Xi'an was still in the hands of peasant rebels. Flying banners in red instead of the yellow of the Former Han, the new "Later Han" regime installed its capital at Loyang, thereby to have some historians refer to it as the "Eastern Han."

6

Literati
Turned Warlords

One disadvantage of writing a macrohistory is that the narrator is compelled to confront violence as his first item of business. If the subject covered is Europe in the present millennium, the historian might pick up the Crusades immediately after the Battle of Hastings and carry on, in a breathless fashion, with the Hundred Years' War followed by the War of the Roses, and wars of the rising national states after the religious wars. The nature of human history being such that the vital turning points are marked with rousing battle cries, it leaves the writer little choice. Chinese history is no exception. Yet, instead of dwelling on the extent of the bloodshed, I suggest a look at the brighter side: For China, while the upheavals may have been more torturous, the relative stability that affected the mass of the population also endured longer. The two halves of the Han dynasty, for instance, lasted some 200 years each, virtually the entire history of the American republic.

Cultural and materialistic achievements during this period of peace were remarkable. For one thing, education advanced. The national effort to promote scholarship started with the Han. An imperial university was established by Wu-di, and toward the end of the pre-Christian era, the enrollment had already reached 3,000. When Wang Mang was regent, he reportedly constructed a dormitory that had 10,000 compartments to house an equal number of students, a figure that is more than likely an exaggeration. But the founder of the Later Han, Liu Xiu, was one of those university students, as was his adviser Deng Yu. An-

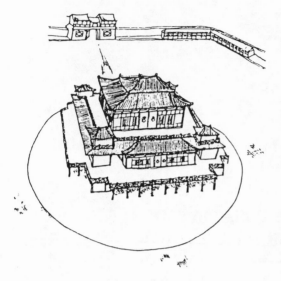

other classmate, Zhong Chong, eventually became the imperial tutor of the heir apparent. Moreover, half a dozen of the top generals were noted for being highly learned men, further evidence of the spread of scholarship. In A.D. 59, the second emperor, Ming-di, lectured on ancient history at the new imperial university at Loyang; the open session is said to have attracted a crowd of many thousands. In the second century A.D. this university had 240 buildings comprising 1,850 rooms. By the middle of the century, although we have no idea how it was administered, this institution had 30,000 students either enrolled at or affiliated with it. At the same time, private learning advanced apace. It became fashionable for renowned scholars to gather 500 or more disciples around themselves; the most accomplished had 3,000 followers.

Enrollments of such magnitude are a measure of the general prosperity of the time. Although traditionally the Chinese dated the invention of paper to A.D. 105, many years later, texts of the classics were still being copied on silk fabrics at great expense. Travel and maintenance of so many scholars undoubtedly required a concentration of wealth. When by the Western reckoning B.C. was turning into A.D., we are told, Xi'an was a metropolis of close to 250,000 inhabitants. The population of Loyang ranked next, with slightly less than 200,000.

Indeed, it is a disappointment that today nothing stands on the sites of those old cities to testify to their past glory. China does not have a Parthenon or a Coliseum to show off to visitors. There are no Gothic cathedrals or medieval guild halls. China's ancient buildings, constructed with timber, have long since perished. Fortunately, recent archaeological discoveries have enabled us to reconstruct the magnificent designs of the old cities. Each gateway in the city wall of Xi'an, for example, consisted of three entrances in a row; the extant wheel-ruts reveal that four carriages or carts could pass through each of the entrances simultaneously. The remains of the foundation of a ceremonial building give the impression that the architects of those days, while shunning height, were preoccupied with dimensions in their designs, achieving grandeur through symmetry and balance. The devotion to geometrical harmony as a part of Natural Law marks a conceptual approach not fundamental-

Stone inscription found inside a Han tomb

Stone inscription found inside a Han tomb

ly different from Stonehenge yet points to a fairly advanced civic life. A cluster of buildings, terraced, was usually encircled by a moat.

While bronze objects, lacquerware, and clay models help to illuminate the narratives of written history, scholars of the Han dynasty are especially delighted with the large collection of bas-reliefs unearthed from several ancient tombs. Those stone engravings on the walls of the mortuary chambers were intended for the deceased, as they face inward toward their remains. The absence from the artwork of religious themes such as angels, saviors, and redemption surprises us. Instead, historical episodes, legendary figures, tales of mythical origins, and scenes of everyday life are illustrated. It is the last category that interests us most, as it is the most authentic source of social history. From this and other sources we have a general idea of Han daily life.

The upper class in those days wore robes with long sleeves, and their headgear in the form of a kerchief was ubiquitous. They sat on floor mats to hold banquets, play musical instruments and games, and conduct lectures. A two-seat carriage was a common contrivance of transportation. Hunting and fishing were acceptable pastimes of gentlemen. The theater remained undeveloped, even though entertainers skillful at dancing and singing were abundant. The well-to-do were also amused by jugglers and magicians, and some of the scenes of merrymaking maintain their appeal to this day.

The common people wore pajama-like garments and shorts while working. Sometimes, but rarely, a knee-length overcoat was added. While the single household remained the basic economic unit, agricultural work constantly required cooperation among neighbors. Millet, wheat, and rice were the major food crops. Women attending to silkworms were almost universal. Iron forging and salt production remained two principal state industries even though, during the Later Han, the governmental monopoly on them was abolished. Commerce was prominently represented by single-family stores engaging in retail trade, as is still the case in the inland cities in the twentieth century. Although not included in the bas-reliefs, we know that conditions of poverty were commonplace. Han emperors frequently issued edicts mentioning natural disasters and crop failures. Some of the destitute eventually ended up as slaves, as cases of selling wives and children are mentioned often in the sources. Most of the slaves became household servants, and thus did not contribute significantly to the national economy. The consensus of modern scholars is that the total number of slaves probably never exceeded one percent of the population.

Following the empire's military conquest, China's cultural influence reached past the Yalu River to portions of Korea, and to parts of Vietnam as far south as the Gulf of Tonkin. Pockets of unassimilated subcultures, however, remained along the China coast. About 200 years ago a golden seal was discovered on the northern tip of Kyushu, a major island of Japan, which indicates that the Han had conferred vassal status on a Japanese chieftain. Similar seals of the same design and stylized engraving have been found in many parts of China. A lacquer piece unearthed from a Korean tomb about a half century ago bears the signatures of two artists and a date of manufacture corresponding to A.D. 4. Another piece carrying the same two names and the date 2 B.C. was discovered near Ulan Bator, the capital of the present Mongolian People's Republic.

During the Later Han, the Xiongnu no longer remained a serious threat. In fact, two Chinese expeditions in A.D. 73 and 89 are supposed to have pressured the nomads into waves of western movement, which, as some historians suspect, might have had something to do with the eventual appearance of the Huns in European history. More costly to the Later Han government were the protracted campaigns against the Tibetans in the west, facing Kokonor, and intermittent fighting went on during the entire period. It is less noticed than the Xiongnu wars in the Former Han because the Tibetans failed to organize a unified command. Their frontier incursions lacked penetrative depth. In turn, the Han counteroffensives were comparatively limited in scope.

China's expansion to the northwest was aided by the daring personal adventures of brilliant men holding imperial commissions. As early as 139 B.C. in the Former Han, Wu-di sent an officer to seek alliances with the states in Central Asia in order to "cut off the right arm of the Xiongnu." Although this purpose was not achieved, the Chinese made initial contacts with the Indo-European-speaking peoples in that region. This effort was renewed during the Later Han by General Ban Chao, brother of historian Ban Gu. From A.D. 73 to 102 Ban took handfuls of followers on his missions, at their height comprising only about 1,000 volunteers. His method was to take advantage of the promised imperial power behind him, undoubtedly luring the oasis states with lucrative trade and tempting awards. He then utilized the forces of nearby states to subdue those still lying ahead to push his westward conquest like a tidal wave to the Caspian Sea. On occasion he commanded legions numbering 25,000 men at one time and 70,000 at another, all contributed by the native states west of the Pamirs. Yet in the long run Ban Chao's contribution to commercial and cultural contacts were more enduring than his military exploits. The territories that he conquered could never be held permanently. On the other hand, the camel caravans that came to ply his routes of conquest have since then made deeper imprints in history with their tracks. Along with the transcontinental trade, China was enriched by the importation of new fruits and vegetables and musical instruments from other lands.

The above sketch makes it clear that in the second century A.D. the basic ingredients of the Chinese empire that were to go on for many centuries were already in place. And by then the imperial order had also stretched to the remotest frontiers that its power could make it reach. That being the case, one may wonder why so many vicissitudes were yet to come, so many cycles of collapse and regeneration. There is a preliminary answer in the vision of macrohistory: The accumulation of agricultural wealth since the rise of the Han dynasty, once reaching a plateau, could be neither checked nor institutionally consolidated. This was by no means a temporary oversight that could be promptly discovered and corrected. When we seek to explain this today, we fully realize that human history itself marks a continuous effort to supply new insight into past events. Without the records of the next 1,800 years, including the experience of the modern West, we might never be able to interpret the collapse of the Han adequately.

The founder of the Later Han, Liu Xiu, fits nicely the modern definition of "the gentry class." The relationship of his family with the imperial household of the Former Han had been decreasing over the generations. Its aristocratic influence had been progressively diminishing as the forefathers of his lineage, having branched out from the houses of a prince and a marquis, took scaled-down positions as governors, district military commanders, and, as in the case of Liu's own father, county magistrates. The first time Liu Xiu appeared in history, he was a young man versed in farm management. At one time he represented his uncle in enlisting the aid of local officials to collect unpaid rent; on another occasion he sold grain in a district where there was a food shortage. Because of his background and the similar outlook of his close followers, the Later Han government is sometimes referred to as a coalition of the well-to-do. While this observation is literally true, one cannot draw the modern inference that the regime's make-up dictated that it advance gentry interests. There were no legal means to implement such policies. Furthermore, it was not backed up by an ideology adequate to motivate the bureaucrats for such a movement. Institutional arrangements that clearly define the rights of private property and the rendering to them of legal protection are historical concepts particular to the modern West.

To clarify the conditions in China during the early imperial period we must look at the Later Han in more detail.

Even though it is impossible to compress the intellectual history of some 200 years into one paragraph, we can say without reservation that elements of "natural religion" dominated Han thought, perhaps more conspicuously during the Later Han period. The idea is that the universe is organic. The interplay of *yin* and *yang* reveals itself in natural phenomena and in human affairs, which are identical because the same inner rhythms are at work (p. 38). This cosmic unity makes it impossible to separate the church from the state, the spiritual from the mundane. When carried to its logical conclusion, it even makes it difficult to draw a clear line between this life and the hereafter. Since longevity is nothing more than the perpetuation of one's experience on earth without its pain, the terrestrial subjects decorating the walls of the burial chamber should be good enough to give comfort to the deceased, instead of promising salvation and redemption. It was with the same devotion to the cosmic unity that the architects designed buildings to convey the appeal of ideal perfection. Their beauty comes from their wholesomeness.

In the Later Han records we read passages showing that with the arrival of the winter solstice, which marked the shortest day of the year and therefore the turning point for the *yin* to give way to the *yang*, Han officials, in both the imperial capital and provincial government seats, changed into robes of crimson color. Musical instruments were tuned. Earth and charcoal were put on the scale to compare their relative weight as affected by the spirit of the day. The shadow of the gnomon was measured. It is unclear whether this flurry of activity was meant to symbolically publicize the seasonal change, or to actually contribute to the spiritual transition. This may be one of those instances when a ritualistic observance was in itself a fulfillment.

Accepting all these as components of its state cult, the Han, especially the Later Han, could never see itself as solely a worldly creation. To defend the rights and privilege of a special social class would have been out of order. Staying away from such earthly terms, the state nevertheless had an obligation to Heaven for seeing to it that the populace was content and happy. In 54 A.D. when Liu Xiu was urged by his courtiers to sacrifice to Heaven at Taishan to confirm his mandate, he declined on the grounds that the people were not yet in a state of felicity. Two years later, however, he reversed himself and performed the ceremony — a maneuver of dubious merit. What was the criterion of contentment and happiness? And who was to judge? But the ambiguity served a purpose. In a modern perspective, the ideology of the Later Han can be summed up as a political philosophy of the status quo and trying to get along with all sides. Liu Xiu's contest with Wang Mang was short-lived. His empire was actually wrested from the peasant rebels and local warlords, and that campaign lasted over a dozen years. Indeed he and his followers had not lost sight of their family interest, and it was self-defense that had driven them to take up arms in the first place. But Liu's exposure to the Confucian classics and his rural experience also convinced him that the stability of his empire depended on a peasant population whose basic needs were satisfied. These divergent impulses could not easily be reconciled. The preaching on cosmic unity and natural harmony, however, gave him sufficient free play to achieve the purpose of moderation and reconciliation in a more subtle manner. In practice, the founder of the Later Han was concerned with the geomancy of public buildings. He also had a tendency to mix his pedantry with an interest in omens and prophecies. The blessings he was seeking were not for himself in another life but for his empire in this world, and this commitment is recorded in the state archives. Now we can see that the status quo and compromise bear a connection with the "natural religion" and "state cult" mentioned earlier—the kind of Han ideology which both Liu Xiu and his son Liu Zhuang (Ming-di) promoted.

In managing the empire, these two rulers did fairly well with public finance. Their strategy was to set the level of taxation at the lowest level possible; but within the statutory limits they would relentlessly press for its realization. The land taxes, according to the official proclamation, were reduced to one-thirtieth of the crop yield. The monopoly on major commodities, as disclosed earlier, was abolished. Liu Xiu's edicts also provided many ways for the manumission of slaves. The compilation of tax registers started in A.D. 39. The next year more than ten governors died in prison for submitting falsified or inaccurate returns. Both stringent and calculating in particular instances, Liu Xiu and Liu Zhuang are noted by historians for their attention to details. An indication of their success was that the total number of taxable households, having gone through serious declines after Wang Mang, was brought up steadily toward the end of the century. Conditions were not as satisfactory in the second century. But no serious shortage occurred even with the expensive campaigns against the Tibetans and the luxurious life-style within the palace. It was in dealing with private wealth that the dynasty exposed its institutional inadequacy, and this eventually caused its downfall.

The emergence of private wealth in a dominantly agrarian country always presents a problem. It can be instantly transformed into political power, and on many occasions it is compelled to take an active role in politics. Sima Qian testified that during the fighting of 154 B.C. (see above, p. 37), a merchant in Xi'an in three months reaped a tenfold profit from money he had loaned out. In this case, the man had gambled on the victory of the imperial army; but investments could also be made in different ways to cause instability and upheavals. And under certain unusual circumstances, the affluent in the countryside could cause even greater disturbances.

To begin with, rural China was made vulnerable by the large number of small self-cultivators, a phenomenon that reflected a historical pattern (p. 42). Since all of them were small businessmen of a sort, the appearance of a few bigger businessmen inevitably led to imbalance and tension. Under the superficial harmony competition raged. There was a natural tendency for the wealthier and more powerful to displace the poorer and weaker. The government, unable to implement any plan of progressive taxation, would first face the loss of revenue, and then the effort to provide relief to the poor would also suffer. Another factor worth noting is that China achieved imperial unification well ahead of its time; local customs did not have an opportunity to develop and mature. The pattern of small holdings put any meaningful legal service further beyond the reach of the villagers. Thus rarely were cases of indebtedness, mortgage, foreclosure, and dispossession carried out under the orderly supervision of the law. As a rule it was the local ruffians who took matters into their own hands, conveniently under the direction of the rural wealthy. Yet the abuse did not end there. When cases could not be peacefully settled in the villages, rarely could they be handled better in governmental offices. The magistrates who were compelled to review them faced an abiding dilemma. Their Confucian training compelled them to act with compassion toward the poor; yet in the name of law and order they could not ignore the interests of the rich. Frequently they either had to ingratiate themselves with certain influential persons who were behind the disputes or defy them to make a righteous name for themselves. Once the subordinate offices became bogged down in legal inexactitude, the higher offices would soon find themselves in the same predicament. This summary, in its spiral fashion, is a recurring theme in China's agrarian history. The ineffectiveness of the law could only be overcome by a discipline that applied both to officialdom and to the general population alike.

The situation became unmanageable during the Later Han because it was a dynasty of "restoration." The momentum had already built up. The complacency of the status quo and getting along with all sides and the quasi-religious outlook of seeking fulfillment in this world prevented it from moving in any single direction. A laissez-faire policy enabled the empire to recover and rehabilitate itself after the general disturbance caused by the Wang Mang interlude, but in the second century A.D., the further accumulation of wealth in private hands, especially without an adequate outlet except reinvestment in land, disturbed rural tranquility to such an extent as to incapacitate the local government, which was long on ideology but short on administrative skills.

The promotion of Confucianism during the two Han periods, while contributing to ideological cohesion among the bureaucrats, also had an adverse effect. Learned men found few outlets for their talent other than governmental service. Knowledge for its own sake was not encouraged at all. In the second century A.D., Zhang Heng conceived the brilliant notion that "heaven is like an egg and the earth its yoke." The bronze seismograph he designed in A.D. 132, of which now only an illustration of a reconstruction remains, is said to have measured eight feet in diameter. His close contemporary Wang Chong persistently refuted the assumed connections between natural phenomena and human affairs. Neither of these two brilliant thinkers gained a significant following. In contrast, the stone tablets erected in front of the imperial university in A.D. 175, on which were engraved the text of six Confucian classics, daily attracted scholars and students arriving in more than 1,000 carriages. Their thirst was for a knowledge already engraved on the stone surface.

The entry of men versed in Confucian studies into the civil bureaucracy occurred first in the "recommendation system" under Wu-di of the Former Han. Each province was to "elect" a man who was noted for being filial pious and another man for being incorruptible. As the system gradually became institutionalized during the Later Han, a single nominee was supposed to combine the two virtues of *xiaolian*, or "filial pious and incorruptible." In each round of selection one supposedly represented 200,000 people. The choice could hardly be objective. Nor could the nominees be admitted to a deliberating assembly to deal with issues of national interest. They were given individual offices. The process in reality bonded the beneficiaries to the provincial officials who had nominated them, creating private connections that weighed heavier than public functions. The Confucian emphasis on personal virtue in preference to law also had its disruptive effect. The large congregations of students in the metropolitan districts provided forums of public opinion. But their concentration on the moral character of individuals, more emotional than practical, blotted out the last chance to solve problems by an objective standard.

This combination of factors led to an inextricable situation toward the end of the dynasty. Although factional quarrels traced their origins to the local districts, they always exploded in the capital. A pattern had been established: When provincial officials tried to check local ruffians, the most notorious were found to be under the protection of the rural wealthy, who in turn maintained connections with holders of high offices, not infrequently palace eunuchs. Magistrates and governors of righteous reputation were compelled to act. Their summary jurisdiction and prompt executions of the offenders on moral grounds invited reprisals. When that happened, the sacrifices laid down by these virtuous officials themselves, along with their families and associates, were no less than the price paid by the villains. From A.D. 153 to 184, many events that were not to occur elsewhere until modern times took place in Han China. Students by the thousands demonstrated in the streets of Loyang and delivered petitions to the imperial court. Mass arrests ensued; black lists were compiled. Hundreds of political prisoners died in confinement, some of them without any public notice.

Because in its last stage of development the partisan controversy aligned eunuchs on one side against some outstanding bureaucrats supported by students on the other, one gets the impression that this was a struggle of good versus evil. Although this may not be an entirely inaccurate observation for the short term, it obscures certain background factors. Undeniably, the major problem of the dynasty in its last decades was the erosion of the power of local government. The national frontiers remained intact, and there were no policy debates at the national level even when things were clearly out of hand. The capital split because the eunuchs and their cohorts were well received by the upstarts in the countryside but rejected by the established gentry, both represented by the civil officials. Perhaps an imperial ruling of A.D. 135, which permitted the eunuchs to pass on their ranks and estates to their adopted sons, complicated pecuniary matters in the local districts. The charges against them for obstruction of justice, therefore, are logically convincing. But they are not convincing enough to sustain the hypothesis that before then there had been law and order. Indications are that there had not. If there had been, minor infractions would have been nipped in the bud long before they had a chance to grow into major crises. If the rural areas were not already ripe for the picking, it would have been most difficult for agents from the capital to make so many inroads in so many provinces. And when things came to a boil, the civil officials did not seem capable of dealing with the problem. This was reflected by the reaction of the upright bureaucrats. Some of them executed prisoners who had received imperial pardons. Others extended their persecution of their opponents to family members and associates. With the pervasive lawlessness came an ineffable feeling that everything was lost.

In their final showdown in A.D. 189, eunuch Zhang Rang asked Grand Commandant Ho Jin, who sided with the bureaucrats: "You said that we inside the palace are corrupt. Please tell me, Sir, from the ministers on down who is loyal and honest?"

The cynicism is not the point here. But this remark does bear truth not appreciated by contemporaries: Law differs from discipline; it is a social imperative. Unless the lower levels abide by it, the upper levels cannot be expected to take it seriously. Unless it is enacted in tandem with the normal functioning of civil life, it will be most difficult to enforce.

Given the situation described above, the fall of the Han is hardly surprising. Imitating the Qin, the dynasty structured its imperial government in a tripartite system. The chancellor functioned as the head of civil officials. The grand commandant was in charge of the army. A third component, the censorial-controlling branch of the government, was normally led by an imperial secretary. Sometimes different names were used, but this basic organizational structure was not altered. In the later part of the second century A.D., however, the ideal bore little semblance to reality. The chancellorship had lost much of its authority. The supervisory function had fallen on the shoulders of a second-echelon official called the "colonel of censure," who seemed most of the time to be the leader of an "opposition" to the imperial court. The position of grand commandant, in the tradition of the Former Han, was monopolized by the emperors' in-laws. And, following the precedent of Huo Guang (p. 44), the holders of this office were kingmakers. The appearance of a string of child emperors and even infant emperors sometimes happened incidentally but for the most part was owing to their efforts. The eunuchs rose to prominence for several reasons. As confidential managerial staff next to the throne, they were indispensible to the emperor and, when the emperor was a minor, to the empress dowager. Some of them had established reputations as guardians of the immediate imperial family. They also exercised control over the capital garrison, which even the grand commandant could rarely keep under his thumb.

The showdown of A.D. 189 put all pretensions aside. He Jin, a half brother of the empress dowager, became grand commandant in A.D. 184 when a peasant group called the Yellow Turbans threatened the capital. His successful suppression of them added prestige to his power. In this instance he was allied with Colonel of Censure Yuan Shao. Their scheme to purge the eunuchs hinged on their summoning to the capital a division of frontier troops. But eunuch Zhang Rang acted first. Zhang, whose brother had been executed by a former colonel of censure in a contested case, was linked to the imperial family by a daughter-in-law who was none other than the empress dowager's own sister. He managed to lure He Jin into the palace and had him murdered on the spot. When Yuan Shao avenged this deed, he burned the palace and killed all the eunuchs in sight, causing Zhang Rang to drown himself.

The Han dynasty could have come to an end at this point. The arrival of the frontier troops, too late for the showdown, did nothing to restore law and order. On the contrary, their uncontrollable general and undisciplined soldiers only intensified the anarchy. Many bureaucrats abandoned any hope of reviving the central leadership and returned home to organize self-defense forces. By its mandate the throne should have mediated if not regulated the divergent interests between the peasants and the landlords, between the upstarts and the established gentry, between the local governments and the central administration. As it happened, the throne itself became a pawn of a family quarrel, sparking a power struggle that in turn activated all the related social issues. Yet, if in name only, the dynasty hung on for another thirty years. With the emperor a prisoner, and the capital burned down, the population had yet to see what seemed to be a senseless warfare turn the entire countryside into a revolving stage and convert civil leaders into warriors, some of them against their wishes. Even before this happened, men of insight and wisdom had predicted that there would be a period of disorder. But no one had foreseen that China was to lose her symmetry and balance for more than three and a half centuries.

The Battle of Guandu in A.D. 200 is an interesting interlude, not because it solved anything, but because the background of the participants gives us an insight into the dimensions of the struggle. The invading army was led by Yuan Shao, none other than the colonel of censure who has earlier wanted to purge the eunuchs. On this occasion he intended to make himself the overlord of the rising regional forces. His sixth generation ancestor Yuan Liang had started the family fortune as an expert on the *Book of Changes*. After serving as a court academician, Yuan Liang passed his specialty onto his grandson Yuan An. The latter, on the strength of scholarship and recognized righteousness, rose from being a county magistrate to being a provincial governor and then a grand minister. From then on, not a single generation of the household was omitted from the highest court distinction, until those who claimed to be office subordinates and former disciples of the Yuans crowded every province. When Yuan Shao raised the standard, the family protégés and their associates contributed a fighting force that was said, probably with exaggeration, to be 100,000 strong. Food was delivered from north China on 10,000 carts. Opposing him was Cao Cao, whose background was more complex. His foster grandfather was a eunuch and the emperor's reader-in-waiting. But Cao himself received the nomination of *xiaolian*. In the early stages of his career he went along with the bureaucrats and established a reputation for being capable. He built up his army from Yellow Turbans who had surrendered, and fed them with the produce from his own military farms. His declared aim of restoring the Han central authority was one of the most controversial issues of the period.

Cao Cao emerged victorious from the battle of Guandu, but the Han dynasty was not revived. Until the reappearance of a unified empire with the rise of the Sui dynasty in the late sixth century, China was going to witness many short-lived dynasties and experience the invasions of the barbarians.

7

Prolonged
Disunity

Chinese historians regard the disappearance of a unified empire from the fall of the Han in 220 to the rise of the Sui in 581 as a long period of forlorn hope and endless chaos. This is true to a point. One could describe it by saying that it was like the effect of the Thirty Years' War on Germany being amplified and prolonged tenfold. In certain parts of north China, sadly, depopulation did occur. Bronze coins, which had come into existence in the late Zhou and been widely circulated during the Han, totally vanished in some areas during these later centuries. Without a central authority to handle relief, one could imagine the miseries when large-scale natural disasters struck wide areas, for example, the great drought of 309, when the major rivers became fordable, and the epidemic of 369, which exacted heavy tolls along the north bank of the lower Yangtze.

Yet, the label "Dark Age" is hardly adequate. Indeed, although warfare was incessant in these centuries, large-scale engagements and decisive battles did not occur very often. If they had, the reunification would have taken a different course than what actually happened (see Chapter 9). Clearly this was not another Warring States period. After four and a half centuries of imperial rule, China was no longer the same combination of competitive states grown out of feudal matrices. Gentry influence, which had diffused the rural power during the Later Han period, also made general mobilization difficult if not altogether impossible. The records show that in the period of disunity armies were often made up of hired mercenaries.

The presence of non-Chinese elements added to the complexity. Referred to by traditional Chinese historians as the "five barbarians," they were Tibetan and Altaic-speaking peoples, the latter including proto-Mongolians and early Turkic war bands. But in some cases even specialists are uncertain about the classifications, much less able to sort out the mixed fighting hordes. Nevertheless, along with a handful of Chinese adventurers, these several ethnic groups established sixteen kingdoms in north China from 304 to 439, some of them coexisting or slightly overlapping, others directly succeeding one another. Initially, as roving barbarians, they inevitably appeared to be destructive. But once they began taking their kingdoms seriously, they also began to develop education and promote agriculture. Two of the "barbarian" states actually reconstructed portions of the Great Wall to protect themselves against other nomad invaders who might follow in their footsteps to disturb their own empire-building.

In the last phase of this era, the Sinicized barbarian states in the north and the "exiled" Chinese dynasties in the south fought seesaw battles that went nowhere. Trade relationships were established and envoys were exchanged. Yet there was no expressed wish that the situation should become permanent and the separate states retain the territories that they now occupied. The guiding force behind government, in the north as well as in the south, was political philosophy, not geopolitics. There was neither the rhetoric nor suitable boundaries to set up separate states within a realm that was so culturally homogeneous. Only the universality of an imperial order could keep the bodies of bureaucrats together ideologically—a fact that can be observed in the extant annals.

When Cao Cao tried to reestablish a central authority during the last days of the Later Han, he succeeded within the territory marked as the Wei on the map on the next page. But he failed ignominiously in his effort to subdue the southern portions of the empire; nor did his descendants have much success. This story, with its geopolitical twist, will be of interest to the tourist and the present-day student of history alike.

At that time the Shu Han stood to the southwest, encompassing today's Sichuan Province and the surrounding areas. An empire within an empire, it had sufficient manpower and natural resources to sustain a prolonged war effort. Yet despite its size it was well protected by mountain barriers on all sides. In recent years many foreign visitors have seen the breath-taking scenery of the Yangtze Gorges guarding its eastern gateway. Actually the precipitous cliffs dropping directly into the river appear even more awesome when the boat sails upstream, as the slower pace allows the sharp vertical edges to delay dramatically the unfolding of the next vista, which heightens the suspense as one

Jin Invasions

moves through the impossible ravines. During the civil war in the third century not even the most audacious general dared to assail this natural barrier; nor during World War II did the Japanese, who came within striking distance of the eastern entrance.

The third state, the Wu, was a state of water resources. A naval power, it too fortified its major cities along the Yangtze. Present-day Nanjing (called Jiankang or Jinling in the past), for instance, was a Wu creation. When it was built, the city was protected by a stone wall that stretched to the river bank to incorporate it into an impregnable fortress. Today, portions of the wall are said to be still visible near the downtown area, which is now located quite some distance from the waterfront owing to the shifting of the river bed over the centuries.

Thus the three states were locked in a stalemate, the Wei with its cavalry, a northern speciality, having the edge. Finally in 263, more than a half century after Cao Cao attempted to eliminate Wei's rivals, Sima Zhao, a Wei general, was able to break the deadlock by organizing a surprise offensive through Shu Han's back door by making an extended detour through an uninhabited area in the mountains. The annexation of this southwest kingdom was achieved swiftly. In a little more than a year Sima Zhao died, and his son Sima Yan, following the example of the Cao family ahead of him, declared the transfer of the mandate of Heaven from the Wei to his household. The proclamation of the Jin dynasty in late 265 occurred in a ceremony in which the "retiring" imperial Cao family conceded and peacefully handed over the authority. This ritual, imitating the Wei takeover of the Han, would be copied by four more short-lived dynasties during this period.

The Jin conquest of the Wu was organized on a long-term basis. Military farms were established to assure food supplies. The building of ships, undertaken in the territory previously held by the Shu Han, took seven years. When it was completed, the commander, General Wang Seng, who had the reputation of doing things in a big way, was already seventy years old. His mammoth war junks were said to be 600 feet long and able to carry 2,000 troops with a number of horses. For their part, the Wu defenders installed underwater obstacles and set up barricades over narrow spans of water with iron chains anchored to rocks. General Wang sent huge rafts out ahead of his armada to sweep away the obstacles. As for the iron chains, he fabricated torches out of firewood, each no less than 100 feet long and scores of feet in diameter and soaked with sesame oil. The intense heat generated by these torches melted the metal obstacles and enabled Wang to sail down the Yangtze to Nanjing to receive Wu's surrender in the spring of 280.

These exploits, of such heroic proportions, appear in official history. Although unable either to verify or to deny them, we can observe from the deeds a fateful outcome. The Jin, with its claim of legitimacy, appeared to be the only house during this period of three and a half centuries that managed to eliminate all its rivals. With its seizure of Nanjing in 280, it apparently was on its way to realizing an imperial order in its full dimension. But hope was dashed only a decade later as events in north China began to rock the foundations of this promising dynasty. In 291 a domestic quarrel started within the Sima family, and the involvement of the imperial princes spread the strife from the palace to the countryside. A civil war ensued. Non-Chinese war bands within and beyond the Great Wall chose this occasion to rise up. By 317 both Xi'an and Loyang had been sacked. A prince in residence at Nanjing proclaimed himself emperor to continue, nominally, the dynasty now known as the Eastern Jin. But it never again controlled much more territory than the southern half of China. In 383, on the north bank of the Yangtze, the army under this feeble government in exile managed, to everybody's surprise, to turn back a combined invasion force led by a Tibetan general and with vastly superior numbers. Yet the Eastern Jin failed to consolidate the victory with a sustained drive to the north. It merely hung on at Nanjing, as did the four succeeding dynasties that each in its turn claimed to be the ruling house of the whole of China. In reality they held the southern part of China together until the emergence of the Second Empire in Chinese history under the house of the Sui.

When we first survey the history of this period, we may see it as being long on romance but short on logic. Many unusual men and women left their mark on history with their heroism and their folly. Yet there is no clear sense of what all the deeds were about.

As we have seen, it started with the fall of the Han. This has been attributed to the rise of eunuch power, the uprising of the Yellow Turbans, and the mistake of mobilizing unruly frontier troops. But as it happened, a full-scale civil war broke out only after the eunuchs had been purged, the Yellow Turbans had been successfully suppressed,

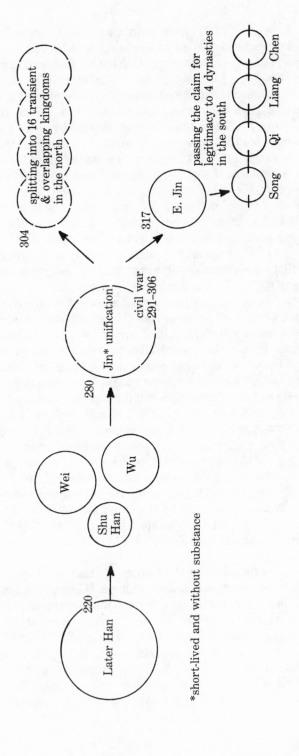

splitting into 16 transient
& overlapping kingdoms
in the north

304

Jin* unification

civil war
291-306

280

E. Jin

317

passing the claim for
legitimacy to 4 dynasties
in the south

Song   Qi   Liang   Chen

Wei

Shu
Han

Wu

220

Later Han

*short-lived and without substance

China Toward a Long Period of Disunity

and the frontier troops had ceased to be a problem. The same could be said about the internal disturbances of the Jin. At first all the blame seemed to fall on an evil empress. She was said to be vain and treacherous; one historian even insisted that she was ugly as well. It was her scheme to deprive the empress dowager of her authority and to remove the heir apparent (not her own son) that invited the intervention of the princes of blood, who by the Jin system acted as provincial authorities no less than court counsellors. But the disturbances that spread over many parts of the empire turned serious only after the empress had been destroyed and all the alleged wrongs appeared to have been righted. Nor had the ensuing battles, with more than a quarter of a million men taking to the field, appeared to be an inevitable aftermath to a family dispute that had originated from the women's quarters.

Modern scholars have advanced a theory of "key economic areas" to probe for a more fundamental cause of the prolonged disunity. They hold that some large food producing areas, better connected internally than externally, caused the regional governments to slip away from the firm control of the center. The originality of this theory cannot be denied. It is convincing enough when applied to the failure of Cao Cao to unify the three kingdoms; it is also useful in explaining the success of the Eastern Jin in turning back the Tibetan general's invasion in 383. But it makes less sense in the face of evidence that the geopolitical difficulties obstructing unification could indeed be overcome, by the military ingenuity of the Sima leadership, for example. Nor does the theory adequately answer the question why the internal rebellion under the Jin had to break out within the territory adjacent to the capital, while the newly conquered areas lying in the far south remained peaceful and intact.

In the absence of more adequate explanations, we may have to give the traditional emphasis on *jianbin*, or the gentry's annexation of the small plots of the self-cultivators (p. 46), more thought. Land tenure indeed had been a serious matter throughout. More than social justice, the pool of small taxpayers had provided the simplicity and homogeneity essential to bureaucratic management in rural areas. When the Han court promoted filial piety and incorruptibleness as guiding principles for its governance, clearly it derived its strength from cultural cohesion instead of managerial complexity. Such an organization could be subverted by landlordism. The reader must keep in mind that in the countryside, taxable households would be difficult to hide but the acreages of land and the total numbers within the households, including bonded servants, were not. An actual decrease in taxable households therefore was always accompanied by a loss of revenue. An inevitable consequence was that governmental services, such as relief for the poor, local defense, and maintenance of irrigation works, had to be cut back. Moreover, gentry dominance was bound to change the character of local government; it challenged the imperial rule that orders always uniformly came from the top downward. We have already observed that during the Later Han the erosion of the local government had caused great instability.

When the Cao family took over from the Han and the Sima family from the Wei, the immediate danger of a total collapse was averted; but the fundamental cause of the crisis remained unrectified. The imbalance could be seen from the ordinances issued by the ruling houses. The Wei declared that it wished to recruit men of managerial ability to participate in its government, regardless of their virtue. The Jin tried to limit landholding for individual households. Both attempted to free themselves from the clutches of the local gentry, who, no matter who they were, usually had a claim for righteousness. Neither dynasty had much success. Suffice it to say that the surface tranquility of north China was precarious at best. Only under strong dynastic founders did it manage to hold on. Once they were gone, the ripples sent out by petty quarrels within the palace compound were all it took to incite the restless elements in wide regions to join in, to amplify and transform the original dispute among the princes into a series of military campaigns over several provinces that lasted for sixteen years (291–306). The fact that the fighting was more a melee than a significant struggle with definite war aims suggests a breakdown of social order of a vast dimension.

The timing of adding barbarian ingredients to the melting pot, toward the end of the aforementioned sixteen-year period, is another point deserving attention. The first to raise the standard was Liu Yuan, a man of mixed Xiongnu and Chinese ancestry. Setting up his headquarters well within the Great Wall in 304, he was able to gather to himself 50,000 fighting men in twenty days. As a former Xiongnu commissioner under the Jin, he had the advantage of being able to recruit the nomads along the borders, as some of the tribal units had already been incorporated as auxiliaries into the Chinese defense system. Other individual barbarians who answered his call had been bondsmen and farm laborers in Chinese households. In fact, another emperor-to-be, Shi Le, who made the claim fifteen years later, had been sold as a slave in his youthful years. The participation in the civil war of the Jin princes gave his military career a start. These examples expose the dangerous instability of Jin China in the early fourth century; indeed, invasions by whole tribes of nomads occurred in this period. But overall it was the dissolution of China's imperial order, one that was based on a cultural cohesion among large numbers of small self-cultivators, that enticed the

war bands to participate in the scramble for power. There is less substance to the story that a "barbarian inundation" swept away an empire.

Yet the impact of those horsemen on Chinese history is far from
minor. As the disorder became endemic, rural communities organized
self-defense forces and erected fortifications under local gentry leadership—a practice whose origins trace back to the second century A.D.
and the rise of the Yellow Turbans. In the fourth century this phenomenon had become widespread in north China. In about 350, within six
prefectures in today's Shanxi Province, there was a league of 300 such
autonomous self-defense units. In the late fourth century, the territory
west of the Yellow River was said to be dotted with 3,000 of them. The
cell structure of the formations comprised only clusters of villages. But
a league of these units might boast a membership of as many as 100,000
households, Chinese and non-Chinese included. As a rule an overlord
was elected by the leaders of the subdivisions. The powerful local clans
who assumed leadership roles within the self-governing units supplied
elite troops and created an atmosphere of aristocratic presence. Had
this trend been allowed to continue, a new form of feudalism might have
taken root in China, or at least Chinese history in the later centuries
would have paralleled that of medieval Japan. But mobile warfare over
a large region, which favored huge bodies of fighting men, settled the
course in a different fashion.

Major battles in this age were rarely fought by less than a quarter of
a million men, with at least three foot soldiers to every cavalryman. The
demand for numbers prompted the transient states under barbarian
rulers to raid the self-governing units organized by the gentry. They
either sent their governors to take over or pressed the leagues for
substantial contributions in manpower and military supplies—in either
case depriving them of their semi-formed local autonomy.

This brought China to a low point in the fourth and fifth centuries.
An imperial system emphasizing universal self-restraint and mutual
deference had come to a dead-end. As an alternative solution, local
autonomy based on property holding might have transformed gentry
landlordism to manorialism. Neither was the second choice allowed to
become a reality. Moreover, when the military governors took over the
local units, the cell structure within them was not destroyed. Thus
landholding could not return to the pattern of small plots owned by self-
cultivators, and without fulfilling this prerequisite a centralized bureaucratic management could not again rise. To the frustration of the
contemporaries, the sixteen transient kingdoms of their day left only a
"barbarian" imprint on history. Probably they never realized that given
another chance, the fragmented empire could indeed be restored to its
former splendor and even better. But it took time.

8
When Historical Components Sprawled Far and Wide

Lü Meng

Cao Cao

Guan Yü

For most Chinese, the universe operates harmoniously. If something goes wrong, someone must be responsible. For the period of prolonged disunity, the Chinese have found a villain in Cao Cao (right). Even Qian Mu, perhaps the greatest among those who have carried China's historiographical tradition into our time, has not forgiven Cao's deeds as a usurper. The reason is understandable. Under the imperial system, Natural Law worked its way from the top downward. When the ruler was said to hold the Mandate of Heaven, it implied that he alone embodied universal virtue and wisdom. In practice, details of conditions on the lower levels could not always be ascertained. It is even doubtful that the divergent interests over the enormous realm could ever be reconciled. But, holding the mystic power of the throne, the emperor remained an effective arbiter. All he expected from the learned bureaucrats was a degree of make-believe. Armed with the tenets of self-restraint and mutual deference, there was no dispute they could not resolve and no technical difficulty they could not overcome. Cao Cao's sins were not limited to his attempt to solve practical problems with raw power, but also, being an outspoken man, he did much to puncture the widely accepted myth. He was supposed to have said: "If

Heaven blesses me, let me be King Wen." This was a reference to Xibai, or the "cultured king" of the Zhou (p. 13), who had continued to remain submissive to the Shang so that his descendants could finish it off with ease. When Cao Cao died in 220, his son Cao Pi lost no time in fulfilling his father's intent by declaring himself Emperor of the Wei dynasty and compelling the last Han ruler to transfer the Mandate of Heaven. Forty-five years later, the Sima family did exactly the same thing. Sima Zhao became the ruler in all but name; his son Sima Yan formally replaced the Wei with still another dynasty, the Jin.

We cannot go so far as agreeing with Professor Qian that "a nation is the product of spirit"; but his observation that any regime of substance has to stand on some theoretical foundation is indisputable. Inasmuch as in ancient China technical difficulties in governing the immense territory necessitated the acceptance of a hereditary monarchy as a repository of values, Cao Cao, Machiavellian in deed as well as word, could not escape the condemnation of generations. In the Chinese theater the prescribed makeup for his role has always been a coating of chalk to reflect his treachery and craftiness; only the edges around the eyes are given a touch of black to animate quick wit.

Although the Chinese theater was first mentioned in the Tang dynasty and developed into a commercial form of entertainment during the Song, it did not assume its present guise of "Peking opera" until at least 1,000 years after the period of disunity; yet even today Cao Cao and his contemporaries continue to be the most frequently staged characters. Among this group the most admired hero is Guan Yü (middle), a general who appears with a distinguished red face. In real life Guan was arrogant and indiscreet. Against common sense he fought a two-front war, and his rashness to action without giving a thought to retreat cost him his life only a month before Cao Cao's death. Yet for millenniums the Chinese have worshiped this fallen hero as no less than a god of war, not for his generalship but for his moral strength. Guan Yü is said to have been true to his every word, and his chivalry was "heavier than a mountain." Some secret societies still venerate him as a patron saint.

To slightly redress the balance, the stage also presents a hero of a different kind. Lü Meng (left) was none other than the opposing general who laid the trap for Guan Yü and delivered his head to Cao Cao. Again the characterization is exaggerated—the mysterious facial makeup does not necessarily bear any physical semblance to the man. Lü started as a warrior with an anti-intellectual outlook. Only at the urging of his patron lord did he, at first reluctantly, take up reading. Yet in the process something in the literature caught his fancy; he became absorbed in it and so went through a quick intellectual transformation.

His colleagues were amazed by his conversion overnight from an unlettered soldier to a sound strategist. The butterfly mask over a pair of alert eyes therefore is intended to convey the inner dynamics of a complex personality. Plain for all to see, Lü Meng possessed something extra that Guan Yü lacked.

But how can the student of history benefit from these vignettes? I would urge the present reader to consider how sociologists distinguish the "little tradition" from the "great tradition." In this case, while the informal and less coherent cultural elements corroborate the "highbrow culture" to an extent, they deviate from it in many other ways. Only through this more relaxed and more entertaining format can the ideas proposed by the philosophers and statesmen be conveyed to the masses. The extensive coverage of this period by the Peking opera, a popular form of entertainment, was aided by the publication of a volume of fictionalized history in the sixteenth century, which goes all out to dramatize and romanticize these events. By bending toward the little tradition it enables a larger audience to relish an argument not essentially different from Qian Mu's: A nation is a spiritual being. In times of insecurity and disorder the characters of individuals require a closer and stricter scrutiny. Obviously, the playwrights, no less than historians of the traditional school, felt confident in applying an unchanging moral yardstick to measure individual characters. Their opinion is so unanimous that their report can be presented in colored designs—with red, black, and white.

Official historians, who represented the great tradition and whose function was to mete out praise and condemnation, of course did not hesitate to blacken the black and whiten the white. Under their aegis, never before and never after the period of great disorder and insecurity have so many "imbecile and perverted" rulers appeared in the annals. Liu Ziye was a teenager who occupied the southern throne for eighteen months. The chronicles report that he was once approached by his half sister, a young woman called Princess Shanyin: "You and I differ in gender; yet both of us are born of the same father. Now look: You have palace women counted by the thousands; but one husband is all I have! What kind of inequality is this?" He therefore provided her with thirty male concubines. Sima Zhong was the unhappy Jin emperor during whose reign civil war broke out and the barbarians gained ascendancy. On being told that people were starving he is supposed to have countered his informant with the question: "Why don't they eat minced meat?" A third emperor, also a teenager, spent his time designing a floor with gold foil on it that was patterned after the lotus, a Buddhist symbol for bliss. When he let his favorite concubine, a Lady Pan, walk on it, it was said that her every step brought forth a lotus blossom. All three emperors were murdered. Liu Ziye might never have escaped moral censure if he had actually authorized male concubinage in an age when the superiority of man remained a cornerstone of society. But as it happened, his misdeeds were revealed by his murderers after the assassination. The denunciation went so far as to include in his biography a reference to his poor handwriting as extra evidence of his unworthiness. The question of sexual inequality, whether it was raised by the princess as quoted or not, sounds incredibly ahead of its time for China in the fifth century. We cannot accept Sima Zhong's remarks on minced meat without suspicion; it comes too close to Marie Antoinette's cake. Nor can we seriously believe that Xiao Baojian, the third murdered emperor, committed a misdemeanor by bringing forth his floral patterned design. Instead, we are struck by his originality. His creation, even as described, inspires a Chinese vision of the lovely young woman on Botticelli's canvas *The Birth of Venus*. It should have won him artistic recognition rather than be seized on as evidence of a tyrant's debauchery.

In these instances and many others the viewpoint of the traditional historians deserves more attention than the historical facts that they tried to present. With the episodes and anecdotes they made this point: Chinese-style absolute monarchy worked two ways. While all proclamations from the imperial court embodied the virtue and wisdom of Natural Law, the occupant of the throne was also held responsible for every kind of unhappiness of the population. Unless the people were satisfied, the emperor could not relax—a doctrine that Mencius expounded with vigor and persistence.

The repeated failure of the throne in the age did not necessarily reflect a degeneration of imperial blood. Rather, it was a manifestation of the fragile constitution of the state at that time. Imperial control had retreated from the wide reach of cultural influence to the area of palatial discipline. As the sphere of action narrowed, more pressure was felt on the top. More burden had yet to be shouldered by the southern court. Professing to be legitimate, it should have done better than the northern barbarians.

A check of the circumferential conditions verifies the sequence of events. The obsession with recovering North China favored a military government in the south under men of strength. But no adequate support came from the lower level. The powerful clans driven to the south after the fall of Xi'an and Loyang by now had developed their estates in stretches of land surrounded by mountains and lakes. Relatively secure within their holdings, they remained apathetic toward Jiankang, the seat of the exiled government. Following the practice of the Jin (see above, pp. 65), the succession states in the south dispatched their princes of blood to be provincial governors in the strategic areas. Lacking sufficient grass-roots support in their posts, their princely offices only made them vulnerable; they fell prey to the ambitious men surrounding them who happened to have real strength. The coups at the provincial level were no less sordid than those at the national level. Ultimately, the rapid turnover of dynasties in Jiankang differed little from the instability in the north. Neither was able to restore an imperial order and a bureaucratic management. Yet a state of balance necessary for feudal decentralization was also missing on both sides.

An atmosphere of forlorn decadence pervaded the southern capital, soon to be called Jinling. The affluent, denied proper outlets for both their talent and their wealth, turned snobbish and self-indulgent. Social status, now amply relished, was traced to north China many generations back. The composition of genealogies became fashionable under the circumstances. Men began to wear facial makeup. Scholars developed a "parallel style" of prose-writing; as a rule, the symmetry and balance laboriously arrived at was prized more than the central message and logic of the essay. The city was called "gilded and powdered"— in fact a Chinese "tinsel town."

But this period of forlorn hope was also a period of rebirth. Certainly Confucianism was not completely dead. If it were, how could the history of this period of prolonged disunity subsequently be written in such a fashion as to accommodate the batteries of moral praise and condemnation to pass even the most rigid standard? Where did the historians find the source materials and derive their inspiration?

Unexpectedly, the most substantial contribution to the regeneration of the Chinese empire had to be made by the so-called barbarians—out of respect hereafter we shall refer to them as non-Chinese or minority groups. That story belongs to the next chapter. Here we wish only to note that this was not to be the only time in Chinese history that the minorities played a decisive role in reviving an imperial order. Dynastic configuration of the Chinese type always involved a schematic design of some kind (see below); moreover, the state had to incorporate the mass of the peasantry. Owing to their primitive simplicity and lack of prior commitment, the invaders from the steppeland were more suited to performing this task; it took time, however, for them to become acquainted with the agrarian milieu and things Chinese.

Also overlooked by contemporaries, the renewed interest in Taoism and the infatuation with Buddhism in this age had much to do with the broadening of China's intellectual horizon for centuries to come. Confucianism is a social discipline. During the time of disorder when its application was narrowed, scholars sought alternatives. The so-called "Seven Sages of the Bamboo Grove" of the late third century epitomized this trend. The group included an uncle, a nephew, and five close friends. Among them was Liu Ling, who always traveled on a mule cart with a jar of wine and was followed by a servant carrying a spade with the instructions to bury him on the spot, wherever and whenever death should occur. The air of abandon was not the only message they sent forth though. In fact, several of the seven served in the Jin government, one became an army officer, another was later executed. What they were turning their backs on was the rigid decorum and pretension of the age. Against the background of the intellectual narrowness of the Later Han, their embracing of the Taoist purity and oneness and emancipation was a quest for salvation.

China's turning to Buddhism is a complex and intriguing story. The range of endorsements and critiques of the alien faith gives us some idea of the magnitude of its impact. Those who defend China's "rationality and integrity," among them Dr. Hu Shih, deplore the importation of the other-worldly doctrine, as it makes heaven appear in thirty-three floors and hell in eighteen layers. But those who are convinced of its stimulating effect point out that even just the concept of *karma* may have induced the Chinese to think more of causes and effects as revealed by Natural Law than the Han dogma of symmetry and balance, which equated virtue with color and sound pitch. In any case, the sending of monks to India and the reception of great masters from other lands did more than give comfort to the soul. The benefit extended to philosophy, literature, education, science, music, sculpture, painting, and architecture. Some specialists point out that it was while translating the Sanscrit literature that Chinese scholars mastered the mechanics of phonetics, which eventually blossomed into the richness of Tang poetry. The scope of the influence is so vast that some recent Chinese publications have declared that Buddhism is "an integral part of Chinese culture." One historian, Lei Haizong, goes so far as to say that Chinese civilization after A.D. 383, or the year the Jin army turned back the Tibetan invasion, had become "Tartar-Buddhist."

Tourists who visit the "rock temples" at Yungang, Longmen, and Dunhuang are struck by the diffuse manner in which Buddhism penetrated Chinese life. At first sight, the honeycomb pattern of the grottos on the sandstone cliffs is not impressive. But exciting things await the visitors who step inside. At each of the sites the statues and images of Buddha count in the tens of thousands. The largest, at Yungang, has ears that are about nine feet long. The smallest measures less than an inch in its full length. And in between, life-sized figures are numerous. There are wall murals, polychrome paintings on the ceilings, reliefs on

the pillars, sculpture in the round in the cliches. All three sites originated in the period of disunity. But the artwork at Dunhuang on the Silk Route maintains more continuity with subsequent dynasties than the other two places. There the visitor may conduct a chronological survey of Buddhist art over a millennium. The exhibit at Longmen was augmented by additional works during the Tang. Even at Yungang, basically a creation of the fifth century, one project stretched over four decades. Fairy tales along with historical and religious themes provided inspiration for the artists to create smiling and grinning faces, trembling fingers, and taut muscles. Students of history are rewarded by glimpses of ancient costumes, drapery and textile designs, musical instruments, and even physical anthropology. At Longmen there is a grotto dated 575 with all the herbal medicine recipes available at the time engraved on its walls.

Nevertheless, at all the sites one thing is definitely missing. There is no such thing as an overall plan or a unified sense of dimension. Even though some of the projects were initiated by empresses and emperors to honor their parents and to bring blessings to themselves, the artwork had to be framed within the weather-beaten rocks, making the spectacular view simultaneously an eyesore and a nightmare—and in sharp contrast to the "Bible of the stone" neatly installed on the facades of the cathedrals of Chartres and Amiens. Yet the open-air exhibits reveal Buddhism's true character as a religion for men of the countryside. It could reach believers no matter what their monastic order was, if any. Its theological essence could be seized as a formula for quick salvation; yet it could also be retained as a theme for metaphysical speculation by intellectuals. Its very multifariousness created a dilemma for Chinese rulers for a long time to come. They all wanted to utilize its universal appeal as an ideological instrument for governance; yet they were afraid that its other-worldliness, when carried too far, would work against that social discipline called Confucianism.

Have the years of prolonged disunity become lost centuries in Chinese history? It depends on how you look at it. The components of history, missing a central focus, seem to sprawl far and wide; yet there is no lack of logic for the events that occurred between the year 220, when the Later Han finally collapsed, and the year 589, when the Sui unification found fulfillment. What was involved certainly went far beyond the virtues and wickedness of a handful of men whom the traditional historians took pleasure in praising and condemning, and whose faces the playwrights took equal pleasure in painting black or white. We have already observed the negative side of the story. With the next chapter we will move on to the proceedings of reunification. But let me pause to quote Liu Yuxi, a poet of the ninth century. He had so much to say about the Jin conquest of Nanjing in 280 (p. 64), which brought a temporary and illusory national unification:

Wang Seng's fleet had come down from Yizhou,
Those war junks were multi-decked.
Oh, Jinling, with its majestic aurora,
Had to ruefully put away its imperial designs.
The iron chains, a thousand fathoms long,
Had slipped down to the riverbed.
Now flying on the stone wall were rows of banners.
They signaled readiness to surrender.

How many times have we
Turned sentimental because of past events as such?
Yet, regardless, the same mountains are still guiding the same span of water
On its eternal run, as icily as ever.
This is a day that we can settle down anywhere within the Four Seas.
We see on this spot the deserted ramparts,
　　Standing there,
　　Desolately,
　　Amidst autumn reeds.

9

On the Road
to Reunification

The Tabas were a prominent clan of the Xianbei people who played an important role in China's reunification. Scholars are not entirely certain about their ethnic composition or origin. They seem to have spoken a pre-Turkic language, but there were also pre-Mongol and pre-Tungusic words in it. According to Chinese historians, when the Tabas arrived on China's northern frontier in the late third century, the tribe had just evolved from a primitive communal society. It still had no housing, no written language, and no law code. And probably nor did they, before the tribesmen made contact with Chinese traders, possess any private property.

In the second century the Tabas and other Xianbei groups had started their migration from Manchuria. In 258 a league convention was held at Holingeer in today's Suiyuan, at which the Tabas confirmed their leadership position over thirty-six tribes. In the early fourth century they boasted that they were able to put 200,000 archers into combat. Nevertheless, their whole population seemed to be only about 600,000 persons. It was unlikely to have exceeded one million. In 310 a Taba leader entered into an agreement with a Jin general who needed his help to drive out other nomads. The Xianbei tribes made 20,000 cavalrymen available to this general; the Chinese in turn authorized the Tabas to settle in today's Shanxi, on a belt of land about 100 miles inside the Great Wall. This marked the first time that the tribes had an agricultural base.

When the joint venture proved unsuccessful the Tabas temporarily slipped into oblivion. The later fourth century saw the ascendancy of the Tibetans, who held most of the non-Chinese groups in submission, the Xianbei people included. It was only after the failure of the Tibetan attempt to overrun the south in 383, already noted above (p. 65), that the Tabas reasserted their independence. In 386 their leader, Taba Gui, proclaimed himself the King of Dai, later redesignated as Wei. This is one of the many early Zhou states that the rising dynasties a millennium later chose to name themselves after, mainly for occupying the same geographical areas. Some are even duplicated. Following traditional Chinese historians, we will refer to the state under discussion as the Northern Wei or Taba Wei. In 399 Taba Gui elevated himself from king to emperor. Until it split into two parts in 534, his creation lasted for 148 years and produced twelve rulers, a record during the period of turbulence. Subsequently, the dynasty was not counted among the sixteen transient kingdoms.

During the early stage of empire building, the Tabas, as a minority group not sufficiently advanced in culture, concentrated on extending their agricultural base with captured manpower. In 391 Taba Gui inflicted a crushing defeat on a Xiongnu tribe. The Wei annals claim that 300,000 horses were captured along with four million head of cattle. The ruling nobility of the vanquished, along with their families, 5,000 persons in all, were put to death. The surviving tribesmen were sent to the Yellow River bend near today's Baotou and forcibly converted to agricultural workers, the state seeing to it that land and farm implements were distributed to the captives. This process was repeated with other tribes until the early fifth century. In 398 the Tabas moved 100,000 Koreans and Murongs (another Xianbei tribe) to their capital district in today's Datong, where they were given tools and draft animals. The settlement of Kalgan in 413 was under the personal supervision of a Northern Wei emperor.

In the capital district the Tabas organized themselves into eight departments to supervise the agricultural workers, the farm units being state owned and state operated. As early as 404, an official report indicated that within the eight departments persons could no longer be distinguished by their tribal origins. In 440 an imperial decree demanded all households that possessed draft animals to make them available to those who did not have them. The government went so far as to work out a conversion formula to allow the latter households to pay back the former with labor. From these incidents we can see that if the agricultural workers had started out as state serfs, they gradually became independent self-cultivators. Some of the Tabas who had been sent to supervise them might have made themselves large landowners; but they did not divide the bulk of the estates or turn the majority of the population into their tenants.

It was the ability to tax the agricultural population directly that enabled the Northern Wei to extend its control over a large area. At first it dispatched army officers to register the newly absorbed population and, as an interim arrangement, collected textile materials from them in lieu of regular taxes. But in 426 it was decreed that all taxation matters were to be handled by the civil government. Numerous commissions and agents were abolished. This could not have been attempted unless obstructions in the middle echelons, such as clan and gentry influences inside the Chinese population and the skeletal tribal structure remaining among the non-Chinese elements, had been neutralized. The annals of the Northern Wei of the early fifth century are crowded with entries noting local leaders surrendering with the populations under their control, typical examples being 5,000 households in one case and 3,000 in another. Apparently the tendency toward local autonomy that had been developing since the Later Han had finally been broken. Wherever the Tabas did not conquer they could apply pressure to win over. The fact that their dynasty was able to shield the northern frontier against a new menace, that of the Avars, and was ready to distribute relief in time of famine must have enhanced their influence. The depopulation of parts of north China also made their work easier. But their initial decision to create a logistical base with farm labor under their own exclusive control, cruel but ingenious, was the pivotal factor.

Before its own demise in the sixth century, the Northern Wei managed to register some five million tax-paying households consisting of no less than twenty-five million persons. This was an extraordinary achievement, especially during the time of turbulence.

The most important legislations of this alien dynasty were proclaimed in the late fifth century. A salary schedule for all the bureaucrats was announced in 484, implying that before that date governmental finance was still geared to decentralization. Taxation took the household as an accounting unit. Households were classified into nine grades ranging from the upper-upper to the lower-lower. The average household was assessed with twenty hundredweight of grain, two bolts of hemp cloth, and other impositions including silk and silk wadding. In reality, all this could only be taken as a general standard. The taxable income within the households varied widely; even the numbers of households did not necessarily correspond to the actual situation, as contemporary records acknowledged that sometimes as many as fifty households registered as one. The central government could only demand that the proceeds from the households of the three top grades be delivered to the capital. Those quotas being derived from rough estimates, the actual maneuvering within the districts was up to the provincial and local officials. The new announcement marked an effort at tightening up the operation.

A year later the decree on the Equalization of Land Utilization (*juntian*) was proclaimed. It took the position that all the land belonged to the emperor; individuals derived the right to use it at the sovereign's pleasure. Without elaboration, the edict authorized the "granting" of forty *mu* of land to every male subject over the age of fifteen, and half of that amount to every female. Additional allowances were made for draft animals and slave labor within the household. All this was to ensure the planting of staple crops, and all reverted to the government upon the death or retirement of the grantee. Land set aside for hemp, mulberry trees, fruits, and vegetables belonged to a different category. It was also rationed to the households according to the number of persons in them. But acreages in this latter category could be inherited or even transferred under certain restrictions.

This statute stands as a milestone in Chinese history. With only numerical adjustments and revisions, this *juntian* edict of 485 was later copied by all the succession dynasties and through them passed on to the unified empires of the Sui and Tang; it remained in force as an institutional arrangement until the late eighth century, a period of close to 300 years. Similarly, the Northern Wei taxation and militia system was also a prototype for institutions of later dynasties.

Readers of these edicts and statutes often ask: Was the land grant a promise or a fulfillment, an entitlement or a limitation? How much of the program was carried out? Did the local officials on the one hand actually assign the plots to the landless peasants, and on the other confiscate the acreages from the large landlords whose holdings exceeded the per capita allowance? A precise answer to these questions will always evade even the most competent historians. An understanding of the whole issue must be reached from the circumferential evidence and through reasoning. Essentially, any imperial program of substance had to be broad in scope. When it was carried out by the bureaucrats in the rural areas, the uniformity of the standard usually exceeded the general feasibility to suit every situation. The provisions of course required that all persons in charge enforce the program to the best of their ability. Wherever a clause became impracticable, however, the data could be manipulated, and laws could be compromised or discounted. In other words, there was always a bottom line of resistance to universal enforcement that no effective police power could break, and monetary control as a tool to assure general compliance was not available in those early days. The sympathetic reader may at this point realize that this legacy weighs heavily on Chinese administrators in modern times.

Within this context the *juntian* of the fifth century onward cannot be regarded as a failure; as for the primary purpose of creating an infrastructure on the basis of a large pool of self-cultivators to pay taxes and to answer the call for military service, it was an outstanding success. Unlike the paper schemes of Wang Mang's reforms, it was pushed through by a nascent military power during a time when restitution and rehabilitation were looked forward to by all quarters as a deliverance. In practice, the proclamation of 485 never took the position that an entitlement was a guarantee. It included an "escape clause" that in those districts where land was insufficient for allocation the acreage allowance could be lessened, or the unsatisfied peasants could apply for resettlement in other regions. The nationalization of agricultural land provided a legal basis for the bureaucrats to apply maximum effort toward implementing the sweeping reform. State ownership was not seen as a primary aim in itself.

The extant documents confirm this observation. Large landowners existed in this period as the exception rather than the general rule. Tax evasion remained an insoluble problem. For example, records show that there were an unbelievably large number of unmarried taxpayers as compared to an unbelievably few married persons when the law significantly burdened the latter in favor of the former. But the same evidence testifies that the goal of increasing the tax registration was for the most part accomplished. The fragmentary eighth-century land registers found in two frontier posts do not contradict this generalization.

Another measure the Taba state of Northern Wei implemented to break the local clan influence was to initiate a communal organization of its own. The 486 decree called for every five taxpaying households to form a neighborhood, every five neighborhoods to form a village, and every five villages to form a communal association. Leaders in charge of those units were appointed by the local officials. In this way the government maintained a channel of command to reach the general populace. The revised tax schedule, meanwhile, took each household of a married couple as the basic accounting unit, against which an annual liability of two hundredweight of grain and one bolt of cloth was assessed. Clearly enough, the enactments on communal organization, taxation, and land tenure were interlinked. Their combined effect restructured an empire, conceptually, from the bottom up.

Chinese writers, when dealing with this chapter of history, take delight in emphasizing China's cultural influence, the mighty pull of which ultimately induced the tribesmen to follow the civilized manners and moves of the Middle Kingdom. Of course, bureaucratic management of agrarian masses was an indigenous device. It could not have been invented by the nomads. The enormous gap between the two modes of life helps explain why the Tabas took so long before they mastered the techniques of managing their Sinicized empire.

When the proclamation of 486 took effect, it was exactly 100 years since Taba Gui had made himself the King of Dai. The establishment of an imperial university at Datong and the sacrifice to Confucius by the Northern Wei had also been on the record for several decades. By this time, against a background of a series of intermarriages, the imperial family itself had become more Chinese than Xianbei. For the major reforms in the 480s, the most vital decisions were made by a Chinese woman who has come down in history as Empress Dowager Wenming, née Feng, the titular grandmother of the reigning emperor. Her adviser was Li Chong, a prodigy versed in the classics whom she had promoted from the secretarial ranks. It was only after the empress dowager's death in 489 that the emperor took over the reins of the government. But once in control, Taba Hong further amazed his contemporaries and later historians alike by an enthusiasm for Sinicization that knew no bounds. In 494 the imperial capital was moved from Datong to Loyang, a city that had to be reconstructed from ruins. The Xianbei costume was proscribed. Next came the prohibition of the use of the Xianbei language. Persons under thirty must immediately speak Chinese; only those above that age were allowed some time for practice and adjustment. Officials who violated this rule risked demotion and dismissal from governmental service. Intermarriage always pleased the sovereign. As a matchmaker, the emperor demanded that every Taba prince take as his wife a daughter of a distinguished courtier of Chinese birth, the emperor himself to announce the pairing off from the throne. The last remaining Xianbei identity, plural syllable surnames, were seen as unbecoming. So the emperor substituted the Chinese "Yuan" for the Xianbei "Taba." He appointed a committee of four to work out a system which eventually converted 118 non-Chinese surnames into those that sounded more familiar to the natives.

Were all the steps taken by Yuan Hong epoch-making? Only superficially. They either confirmed trends that were already in progress or added symbolic ostentation to them. The major contribution of the Taba clan to China was the creation of a new homogeneous peasantry base, which had proven indispensable to any working imperial order. In providing the groundwork, Yuan Hong's ancestors had shown perseverance and patience. It was precisely their avoidance of instant ascendancy and quick profit that had enabled them to escape the fate of the Tibetan leadership and of the sixteen transit kingdoms, the last four of which their state absorbed. Empress Dowager Wenming's and Li Chong's reforms became feasible because of the broader preparations that went before. Yuan Hong, capping the success, actually helped to undermine it.

The reconstruction of Loyang brought a gaudy display of wealth. The favor shown to the Chinese gentry families by the throne caused a great deal of antagonism among the Xianbei nobility. It also worked against the policy of neutralizing the powerful clans in the rural areas. Yuan Hong himself died in 499 at the age of thirty-two. But not long after, unrest on the northern frontier, discontent among the non-Chinese army commanders, and palace coups and intrigues plagued the Northern Wei for a generation until the state split into two parts.

From the perspective of microhistory, not even a separate volume could present the unmanageable details of this period with clarity. But with hindsight close to one and a half millenniums later, the general trend is quite clear. Toward the mid-sixth century, the infrastructure of a regenerated empire was already in place. The bulk of the agricultural resources and the peasant manpower could be mobilized to sustain an imperial drive. What was lacking was a disciplined bureaucracy, or a similar homogeneous body on the top not spoiled by vested interests. At this moment the actors on stage hardly understood their own doings.

The split of 534 occurred when a Northern Wei emperor, afraid of the army officers who could dethrone and execute him, fled to Xi'an to seek protection from another general, only to be murdered by this man. With this the Taba state in fact ceased to exist. Nevertheless, the military men in the east and the west each competed to install his own puppet emperor. The Eastern Wei then lasted sixteen years and the Western Wei twenty-three years, neither possessing much substance, of course. The east was dominated by the Gao family, who eventually replaced the Tabas with a Northern Qi dynasty. In the west the Yuwen family was in control, and they in turn eliminated the puppet regime of their own making to proclaim a Northern Zhou dynasty. The Gaos were of mixed Xianbei and Chinese blood. They tried to pacify the non-Chinese nobility without offending the native gentry. The Yuwens traced their ancestry to both Xiongnu and Xianbei origins. At this moment they also denounced Taba Hong's Sinification to rally the support of the non-Chinese elements.

In reality, those policies and platforms had ceased to be the most crucial issues. While all this was going on, the Taba taxation and household registration system was beginning to pay off. With it, universal conscription could be put into effect. There was a competition for general mobilization. Both the non-Chinese nobility, who claimed their hereditary privilege on the strength of their tribal affiliation, and the large Chinese households, who built up their local influence by extending a protective umbrella over the general population, had lost their commanding position and with it their ability to tip the balance. The tension between these two groups had been largely responsible for

China's disunity over three and a half centuries. When their power diminished, the reintroduction of imperial bureaucratic management was not far off.

Under these conditions the west had an advantage over the east. The entry of the Yuwen family into the region is dated only 530. While claiming Xianbei supremacy, the territory was, however, noted historically for its receptiveness to steppeland influence. The nobility was by and large a mixed stock. The state had already announced the restoration of the non-Chinese surnames that Yuan Hong had converted by decree. In the absence of people bearing those names, the Yuwens used them as badges of honor to award Chinese officers who provided them with outstanding service. The power vacuum allowed the Western Wei, and later the Northern Zhou, more freedom of action. Entrusting its state planning to a scholar by the name of Su Chao, the Western Wei built up a bureaucratic order by using for its blueprint the *Rituals of the Zhou*, a book that was itself noted for its free construction and schematic approaches to problems. Clearly, in the western region there were fewer vested interests standing in the way of unification.

With the entire stretch of history of the Taba state in view, we can also see a definite pattern in the making. On the road to reunification the driving force started from the north to reach the south, and subsequently from the west to absorb the east, or as a whole from the inland sector and economically less developed areas to absorb the regions more accessible to water transport and laden with more internal complexities. The requirement of homogeneity and broadness in organization enabled the Xianbei people to assume the leadership role. Once they relocated their capital at Loyang, however, they also constructed fancy gardens and tall buildings. Given our own life-style, there is no need for us to adopt the traditional viewpoint that luxury and soft living per se have to debase man's character. But in the context of empire-building in the sixth century, Yuan Hong's Sinification program clearly damaged the organizational simplicity which the Taba leadership still needed.

The endless palace coups and plots that dominated several decades of the mid-sixth century, therefore, allowed the divergent elements at the top to purge and purify themselves. Compared with the events that had led to the period of prolonged disunity, the central theme was reversed. Previously, before the fall of the Later Han, the erosion of local government caused instability in the court. Now, on the road to reunification, a considerably integrated countryside demanded a streamlined government at the top to deliver an imperial rule of substance.

The man who read the message correctly was Yang Jian, Duke of Sui and later founder of the Sui dynasty. Yang inherited his father's posi-

II.
In 534 the Northern Wei split into two parts. The Western Wei settled its capital as Xi'an. The Eastern Wei moved to Ye, near modern Anyang.

E. Wei

W. Wei

V.
Having taken over from the Northern Zhou in 581, the Sui annexed the Chen, the last of the transient dynasties in the south. Reunification was achieved in 589.

Sui

Chen

I.
The Northern Wei, having eliminated the last of the 16 transient kingdoms in the north, moved its capital from Datong to Loyang in 494.

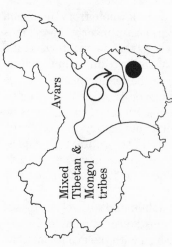

Avars

Mixed Tibetan & Mongol tribes

III.
In 550 the Gao family took over from the E. Wei to form a Northern Qi dynasty. In 557 the Yuwen family took over from the W. Wei to form a Northern Zhou dynasty. The latter achieved a bureaucratic management of the population more effectively than the former.

N. Qi

N. Zhou

IV.
Yang Jian, the founder of the Sui, assisted the Northern Zhou in annexing the Northern Qi in 577.

N. Qi

N. Zhou

Duke of Sui

China on the Way to Reunification

tion as a leading military commander serving under the Northern Zhou dynasty. His daughter was married to the heir apparent of the Yuwen family. In 577 he accompanied the Yuwen emperor on the military campaign that terminated the Northern Qi. The next year the emperor died. Yang Jian's son-in-law ruled for two years and then followed his father to the grave. No one can say for sure what happened in Xi'an during these three eventful years. Had Yang Jian acted in self-defense, or did he act in a premeditated way to terminate the Yuwen household? The fact remains that before he proclaimed his Sui dynasty in 581, fifty-nine Yuwen princes had met violent deaths.

Truly Machiavellian, Yang Jian could weep in front of his retinue when he was shown the coarse food of the people, which contained bits of edibles mixed with inedible husks. His bureaucrats wore cloth robes. An early practitioner of "sting operations," he let his undercover agents offer his own officials bribes and sentenced to death those who yielded to the temptation. The founder of the Sui has been sufficiently praised and condemned by historians in the past. His type of cruelty and his moral tone being nothing new to us, we pick up the pieces of information here merely to show how far China had to go to create a disciplined bureaucracy at the rebirth of an empire.

Only by understanding this background can we appreciate the fact that once the groundwork was laid, military operations that accomplished the reunification itself were relatively simple matters. A civil service familiar with rural affairs provided the best personnel procurement program and commissary supplies that a peasant army could ask for. With these and the concomitant numerical superiority, victory was assured. In 577 the Northern Zhou mobilized some 150,000 men. This force drew out the Northern Qi army to meet it near today's Linfen in Shanxi Province. Despite the sieges and maneuvers, the crucial battle lasted for less than a day. At the end of that day it was all over for the eastern kingdom. Yang Jian's conquest of the Chen, the last of the four transient dynasties in the south, took about two and a half months during late 588 and early 589. It is said that 518,000 troops were dispatched. The Chen never put up anything more than a token resistance near the capital of Jiankang (today's Nanjing). It must have been difficult for even the participants themselves to understand that this was the way to end a period of disunity that had troubled China for more than three and a half centuries.

10

The Second Empire: A Breakthrough
That Failed to Materialize

The early Tang dynasty in the seventh century marked the most splendid and satisfying period in the history of China's imperial era. Confidence continued to build as the nation increased its prestige abroad and brought its domestic institutions to near perfection by the standard of the day.

It was a period of system-making. The *juntian*, or the organization of land utilization introduced by the Taba Wei (p. 81), was renewed. Nationalization of agricultural land therefore remained in force. Under the Tang every able-bodied male was eligible to receive 100 *mu* of land. Eighty of those would revert back to government control upon the grantee's retirement; but the remaining twenty could be passed on within the family as inheritance. A census was taken every three years. With the acreage allocation came a streamlined taxation system. The obligations consisted of three components, payable as a package by each household under the allotment plan. It involved a grain payment of two hundredweight, a bolt of silk fabric twenty feet long, and corvée service of twenty work days. The rates appeared to be remarkably low against the full allotment of 100 *mu* of land. Because of these provisions the population registration continued expanding for over a century. The increased receivables at the state granaries and warehouses contributed to the era of good feelings.

Conscription coalesced with the population registration. A selective service provided soldiery for the militia, which could be called to interior and frontier duties according to complicated but regularized procedures. Since an average district enrolled 1,000 militiamen, it seemed that the 634 military districts should be able to mobilize a half million men on short notice.

The Xiongnus and Avars who had long troubled China's northern frontier were gone. Now the most powerful groups of nomads active on the borderland were the Turks, whose tribal designation was for the first time noticed by historians. But in 630 a Tang general inflicted a crushing defeat on them. Thereafter the Chinese emperor, at the request of several tribes, assumed the position of "heavenly khan" over them. The Uighurs, another Turkic-speaking people, tendered their submission without a fight. The Tibetans were pacified when the Chinese Princess Wencheng was married to their king. Before the mid-seventh century, the Tang had made direct contact with India and Iran. Only the Koreans were able to defy the Chinese high-handedness for a prolonged period. The struggle went on until 668, when Pyongyang was finally occupied by Chinese forces.

The Second Empire

Sui	581 – 618
Tang	906
Northern Song	960 – 1126
Southern Song	1127 – 1279 AD

The central government of the Tang was organized into six departments: personnel, revenue, rites, defense, justice, and public works. Not yet a true prototype of a cabinet, with its division of labor it was nevertheless characterized by method and order. A major departure from the administration of the Han was that the government from the Sui onward, which hereafter we shall characterize as "the Second Empire," assigned local officials to the lower echelons. The recommendation system was discontinued. The Sui began to conduct civil service examinations open to all candidates. The Tang followed the practice with some consistency, even though the triennial examination, that is, the organization of the metropolitan and provincial examinations into regular three-year cycles, did not appear until the Song. A social impact of the open-examination system was the breaking of the domination of governmental offices by the powerful clans. The standard literature requirement in preparation for the examinations probably helped stimulate the invention of block printing in about A.D. 600. An unhappy consequence, however, was the tightening of the bureaucratic grip on Chinese life. The Tang had 18,805 positions within its civil service proper. The government payroll, to include local auxiliaries, clerical assistants, and army officers, carried 368,668 salary recipients—an alarming figure in the Middle Ages when China's total population was perhaps approximately 50 million.

The early Tang continued the internal expansion of China. The development of the south, stimulated during the period of disunity, continued to absorb the energy of the Second Empire. The short-lived Sui dynasty was noted for its ruthless efforts at canal construction. When a project was organized, the mobilization of the work force did not spare women and children. Sometimes hundreds of miles of new channel were completed by millions of laborers in several months' time. Sizable cities were abandoned so that the residents could be relocated along the new waterfronts. Those new channels connected the Yangtze River with the Yellow River and eventually extended to the north China plain. This relentless drive in public works with no regard for human cost, as well as its unsuccessful campaign in Korea, caused the Sui to fall as quickly as it rose. But the network of artificial waterways executed by Yang Guang, the brilliant second emperor of the Sui who had so much talent but so few scruples, was to benefit the following dynasties in no small degree. Although during the Tang revenue arriving from the south was yet to constitute a substantial portion of the state income, the new north-south trunkline facilitated interregional migration, which eased the pressure on certain overpopulated areas. The enterprising spirit associated with the southward movement endowed the era with feelings of progress and promise. It was during the Tang that Guangzhou (Canton) and Zayton (modern Quanzhou) became important seaports. Early Chinese settlements on Taiwan appeared in the seventh century.

Inspired by visions of grandeur, the Sui and Tang reconstructed Xi'an as a planned city in a checkerboard pattern. Five miles in one dimension and six in the other, its walled enclosure 1,000 years ago was about eight times the size of the modern city. Its main thoroughfare, running north to south, was 500 feet wide. When in the eighth century the Japanese borrowed the design to construct their new capitals at Nara and Kyoto, they not only followed the general pattern on a reduced scale but also found the Chinese name of a main avenue attractive enough to be reused twice in their own metropolises.

The Tang was cosmopolitan. The imperial Li family claimed a traditional aristocratic Chinese lineage of long standing. But during the period of disunity the ancestors of the Tang emperors served under several alien dynasties and frequently married into families of non-Chinese origin. And the practice of intermarriage was not even discontinued after they secured the imperial throne. Perhaps this mixed ethnic background gave substance to the emperor's claim to be the heavenly khan. When the prestige of the Chinese empire was high, Indian princes in the Indus valley acknowledged its suzerainty. A usurper in Assam was arrested and delivered to Xi'an for punishment. Embassies arrived from Korea and Japan. The Chinese capital was visited by Syrians, Arabs, Persians, Tibetans, and Tonkinese. The im-

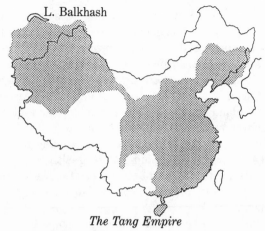

The Tang Empire

perial university enrolled students from many of those foreign lands. Among them the most enthusiastic were the envoys of Japan. Some Japanese, cultural attaché's of a sort, lived and studied in China for decades. Upon their return to their homeland they played an important role in organizing Japanese state institutions and in so doing made their country culturally a replica of Tang China. From the bronze coinage to women's hairdos, from interior design to the game of *go*, Japanese culture has ever since borne an ineradicable continental imprint. Korea and Vietnam followed the same pattern with reduced intensity.

Religious toleration came with the high watermark of security and self-confidence of the Tang. When the Buddhist scholar Xuanzhuang returned from India in 645 after an absence from China of sixteen years, he was interviewed by Li Shimin, the second emperor of the dynasty. Enormously pleased, the sovereign then made available living facilities and the editorial and clerical assistants that the great traveling monk needed to translate the 657 Sanscrit texts that he had brought back. A Taoist temple was built by the dynastic founder in 624. The proselytization of Nestorian Christianity was authorized by an imperial edict dated 638. Zoroastrianism received less notice. Nevertheless, its church in Xi'an was given official blessing and its clergymen treated as equivalents to holders of the fifth and seventh ranks of the civil service.

What happened to this period of splendor and satisfaction? Put in its simplest terms, it may be said that the ideal state did not endure because, gradually, the central leadership became indolent and irresponsible. Palace attendants increased to uncontrollably large numbers. Toward the mid-eighth century, musicians and performers alone counted more than 20,000. Palace women were probably twice that number. The bureaucracy not only expanded its membership but also multiplied its pay scale. Emperors and ministers degenerated in character. Practically everything described earlier was now reversed. In 751 the Chinese army was defeated in central Asia by a league of Arabs. Even a Thai state in the southwest forced Tang forces to retreat. The Tibetans revolted. The ninth century saw the further development of warlordism within the frontier army commands. Peasant rebellions erupted in the inland provinces. The eunuchs, who had aroused little attention earlier, now wielded power within the capital, enthroning and deposing emperors. At the same time, the growing influence of Buddhist monasteries and their accumulated wealth finally alarmed the state. In the 840s came a series of measures of persecution; an edict of 845 set out to destroy 4,600 temples and forcibly secularize 160,500 monks and nuns.

The reversal was complete and thorough. Some historians suggest that the Tang dynasty can be divided into two distinct parts. It seems that An Lushan's Rebellion in 755, close to the chronological mid-point, serves as an appropriate dividing line. That would give us a period of grandeur and prosperity, which lasted for 137 years, to be followed by a period of ruin and disorder, which lingered on for 151 years.

Of course, an empire of accomplishment could not have turned decadent overnight; nor could it have been sent careening downward by a freakish event. The fact that a serious rupture seems to have broken a major dynasty's continuity in the mid-eighth century suggests something else not yet accounted for. At this point, in the interest of macrohistory, we temporarily leave An Lushan and A.D. 755 to go back to the founding of the Tang dynasty in 618 in order to establish the needed range of vision.

Among China's prominent monarchs, Li Shimin may have the most personal appeal. In the last years of the Sui, when rebels and bandits took possession of many parts of China, he persuaded his father, Li Yuan, Duke of Tang, to proclaim himself emperor. At that time Shimin was only sixteen years old. From then until he was twenty-four, he mostly fought to secure the dynasty and regain peace. He had compassion and curiosity. He was fearless and tireless. Often he directed battles personally and sometimes appeared in front of his troops with several mounts to negotiate with the enemy commanders. As a political leader he gathered around himself a group of learned men of broad vision. Even though most of the Tang institutions followed the Sui design, the operating procedures were derived from Li Shimin's management, which covered a reign of twenty-three years. In the opening paragraph of this chapter we mentioned that Tang institutions reached near perfection by the standard of the times; most of the credit should go to the youthful ruler who was the dynastic founder in all but name. An outstanding feature of the central government of the Tang was the division of labor, which gave the impression of some form of checks and balances. A council of state encompassed the six ministerial departments, which carried most of the work load. A design board initiated edicts, proclamations, and policies of significance. A review board examined state papers, raised questions, and called for inquiries. Together with the Tang practice of dividing the realm of law into four broad departments, i.e., the penal code, administrative statutes, office procedures, and operative bylaws, the organization showed sufficient neatness to fit the regenerated empire. When the Japanese transplanted those institutions to their land, they called the whole system "government by law" (*ritsuryo seiji*).

But an alert reader will have no difficulty in seeing that these are not the kind of checks and balances that we are accustomed to nowadays. No component of the Tang government represented the divergent interests of the constituencies, and therefore an independent judiciary could not have emerged from such a matrix. No matter how enlightened Li Shimin was, his government was perforce a form of absolutism. Only with the discipline of Confucianism did the Son of Heaven create some inner checks within himself. Li's annals disclose that one day, after meeting his courtiers, he returned to his quarters angrily mumbling: "One of these days I'm going to kill that old farmer!" The empress asked him who he was talking about. It happened to be Wei Zheng, an outspoken adviser who, with the indulgence of the emperor himself, had repeatedly contradicted him in public. On this occasion the empress saved the day by changing into ceremonial robes to congratulate the sovereign for having so devoted a counsellor who was willing to risk his life to give him loyalty. The episode nevertheless indicates that the rationality of the Tang institutions had a narrow base. More personal than institutional, it basically represented the will of the emperor.

Yet it was not that the Chinese were by nature averse to representative government. We have already noted that the Han had tried, through its recommendation system (p. 57), to spread its recruitment of officials to wide geographical regions. Technically, however, a deliberative assembly could not have been attempted when the bulk of the population was composed of farm households who owned several acres of land each, and there were many millions of those. To accept proper qualification above that level would have confirmed *jianbin* (p. 46), or the reduction of self-cultivators into tenants, which in the past had robbed the empire of a homogeneous tax base and rendered the bureaucratic management unworkable. A period of prolonged disunity had been its consequence. The Tang, having institutionalized the civil service examinations and consolidated the power of appointment, found Confucian morality more than ever an essential guideline to its governance.

But government by virtue always implies a form of despotism. When the emperor must maintain a front of moral perfection, it makes the throne a most dangerous seat to occupy, and conversely, any sense of rivalry or challenge to it inevitably a greater risk. All this underlies the notion that morality is an absolute quality, indivisible and unnegotiable, and its highest personification in office tolerates no competition. This rigid rule was to be tested more than once during the Tang.

＇ Impressed by Li Shimin's humanity, many modern readers are horrified by the account that this enlightened ruler had to murder an elder brother and a younger brother in order to reach his ascendancy. It happened that although he virtually created the dynasty by himself, Li Shimin was the second son. After the Tang was confirmed and secured, there was a great deal of tension between him and the heir apparent, his older brother, Li Jiancheng. The rivalry spread to the court circles and poisoned the retinues of both men. The future emperor's followers insisted that without acting first he would be eliminated. What actually happened was that in 626 Shimin ambushed Jiancheng, personally killing him with an arrow. A younger brother accompanying Jiancheng was cut down by a follower. After that Li Shimin also executed all ten sons of his two brothers. He demanded his father's retirement and took over the throne for himself.

This brilliant ruler tried to justify these merciless acts, but he never tried to whitewash them. They appear in the official Tang dynastic history along with Li Shimin's many splendid achievements, which historians have no grounds for suspecting were not genuine. For us to omit this story or even try to minimize it at this point would obscure the true nature of the traditional Chinese monarchy and along with it one of its great contradictions. It would destroy the continuity of history. For one thing, the deeds of Empress Wu, undoubtedly the next major milestone of our journey, could never be objectively explained. No doubt many readers of this book have already heard of Wu Zetian, the female ruler who preceded Catherine the Great of Russia by 1,100 years.

Empress Wu came from a wealthy family. Her father participated in the early stages of Li Shimin's empire building and later served as minister of public works in the new dynasty. In her early teens Wu Zetian was selected to be one of the "talented women" in the emperor's quarters. Technically, this means that as a chambermaid she had the status of an unranked concubine. Her great beauty, cited by some historians, cannot be established from the extant portrait. But there is no doubt that she was very gifted, very well-read, and above all very self-willed.

Upon Li Shimin's death in 649, Wu Zetian entered a Buddhist temple to become a nun. When the next emperor, Shimin's son Li Zhi, toured the place she caught his attention. In 654 she became a concubine of a lower rank. A year later Li Zhi discarded his empress to make room for her. By this time she was probably close to thirty. Subsequently she gave Li Zhi four sons and one daughter. Thus of the three early Tang emperors, two were  her husbands. Without exception, all seventeen remaining emperors that make up the imperial Tang geneology were her descendants.

The empress gained access to power because Li Zhi, who reigned for thirty-four years, was troubled by hypertension, which affected his vision. Wu Zetian was not only interested in state affairs but also, with her wide reading, well equipped to deal with them. By 674 she had already confirmed her position as co-sovereign. When Li Zhi died a decade later, she lost no time in making herself de facto ruler. Her first son had died earlier. Her second son, apparently uncooperative, was commanded to commit suicide. She removed her third son one month after his accession and put him under house arrest for the next fourteen years. Her fourth son was so intimidated by this sequence of events that he repeatedly petitioned to decline the vacant throne. Wu Zetian's daughter's first husband was also executed on her orders, although she continued to be fond of her daughter and considered the young woman to be in her own likeness.

For six years Wu Zetian ruled as empress dowager. But in 690 she replaced the Tang with a new Zhou dynasty. On this occasion she proclaimed herself "emperor," and the act was called a "revolution." Until shortly before her death in 705, perhaps at the age of eighty-one (some say that she was older), she had been sovereign for twenty-one years. During her reign numerous Tang princes tried to dethrone her. As she retaliated, dozens of those princes and hundreds of their followers were executed. The secret police were given wide power in dealing with political prisoners; the charge of treason cast its net further and further. In the end it was only when she was seriously ill and incapacitated that the movement to restore the Tang succeeded. The imperial throne went to her third son, who was later succeeded by her fourth son. She died a natural death, and the annals of her reign could never be expunged. Along the entire length of Chinese history there is no other story that even comes close to hers.

No authentic biography of Wu Zetian has ever been written. Obviously, merely to provide a convincing account one would have to engage in a great deal of speculation. The revenge of a female in a man's world cannot be discounted. Yet, the worship of male virility was also a part of her character. She told Ji Xu, a courtier, that with an iron bar, an iron whip, and a dagger she could handle any untamed horse. Then she boasted that she could handle men just as well as she handled horses. Until her declining years she spoke of Li Shimin in a tone of respect and affection. She was deferential toward Di Renjie, the governor and deputy censor-in-chief who risked the death penalty to argue over matters that he considered to have touched points of principle. Empress Wu was frequently visited by handsome younger men who dressed in fancy clothing and wore makeup. But upright officials dared to petition to Her Majesty not to allow characters who were "favored by means of hairpins and slippers" to ruin court discipline. One of her favorites, a Buddhist abbot, was slapped on the face by a prime minister. When the insulted mystic complained to the empress, she told him from then on to avoid the streets on which the fearless civil servant traveled.

We could and perhaps should have left these anecdotes to novelists and romantic writers, but without them the full dimension of the history of China in the late seventh century and the opening years of the eighth century could never be effectively presented. In other words, both the felicity and horror associated with Li Shimin and Wu Zetian are components of the institutional history of the Tang dynasty, and in certain circuitous ways they can be traced as leading up to An Lushan's rebellion.

The records of Empress Wu's reign show new disturbances by Tibetans, Turks, and a new group of Mongolian stock arising in Manchuria called the Qidans. All these were either repelled or pacified, however. Serious droughts occurred several times. One innovation was the palace examinations. Candidates for the civil service were ushered in before the imperial throne to be orally examined by the empress herself. The reign of terror, felt more by the top officials than by the general population, remained a mark of the era. Bronze chests were provided in public places for informers to turn in anonymous complaints. Some relief came in 697, when the chief of the secret police, Lai Junchen, was himself executed. But there were few policy and organizational measures that could qualify as innovative. In Wu Zetian's revolution the greatest innovations were feminine touches in her governmental offices. Gold, aqua, and white, being her favorite colors, appeared on banners and costumes to enliven the court. Following the *Rituals of the Zhou,* she renamed several ministries, for example, Offices of Spring, Summer, Autumn, and Winter. There was a Pheasant Cabinet and a Phoenix Pavilion.

But would this record justify the near wrecking of a major dynasty, or even the splitting up of the empress's own household? On what basis did history permit an old woman of such a dubious background to become, in name as well as in fact, the ruler of by then the most populous and most prestigious nation in the world for twenty-one years? Why, if Wu Zetian was so notorious by traditional standards, was she repeatedly praised by men of such divergent backgrounds as Lu Zhi, the discreet Tang prime minister of the late eighth century, Li Zhi, the nonconformist thinker of the Ming, and Zhao Yi, the versatile historian of the Qing?

These questions can only be answered by understanding that Confucian government of the traditional type, being a discipline no less than an institution, was loosely constructed. As in the case of the Tang, the equalization of land utilization had been made possible against the background of the calming of the waves of disturbance of several centuries. Once the program became solidified, the entire countryside was dotted with millions of self-cultivators, even though the distribution of manpower and tillable acreage rarely corresponded to the neat mathematical formula laid down by the government. These amorphous conditions excluded any possibility of a large-scale rearrangement. It was not merely a problem that the promotion of the economic interests of any special sector or in any particular geographical region could not be easily attempted, but also, there was no adequate provision for overseeing nongovernmental organizations engaging in such activities. The most crucial problems of the state, moreover, lacked institutional solutions, as the nomadic tribes could never be terminated, and droughts and famines could only be dealt with when they actually occurred, and then ineffectively. With the exceptions of water control and reclamation projects, there were no common efforts that profitably tied the governing and the governed together. The lack of substance of the government was felt even more in times of peace.

After consolidating the power of appointment, the Tang increased the volume of office activities. But as a rule the paperwork became a formality. Even under the Sui, the saying that "old office clerks died on desks with their files" was heard. In comparison to the conditions of the modern West, what was lacking was the representation of institutionalized private interests alongside the government offices who could challenge them, demand services from them, and pay for their costs. (But even in the West, this did not occur until at least a thousand years later.) Without parallel civil components that would provide the extra sinews, bureaucratic management of the Chinese type functioned on the strength of the code of honor of officialdom. Frequently at the lower level problems were real but diffused. At the top, on the other hand, the administrative apparatus tended to remain perfunctory and nominal. In order to keep the system operative at all, pressure had to be exerted from the very top all the way downward.

As Tang writers themselves suggested, the dynasty had no better ways to administer the empire than applying the penal code and using its power of appointment. Even in Wu Zetian's time, fraud and deceit among government officials must have been quite widespread, as the cases brought to her attention attest. In Hebei, the bureaucrats failed to protect the general population from a Qidan invasion. After the campaign, however, they proceeded to punish the civilians for giving aid and comfort to the enemy. These conditions required vigorous intervention by an alert center.

In sum, despotism did not come by choice. The tragedy of China was that the unification of an enormous empire was realized before local institutions and technological capacities had an opportunity to develop and mature. The lack of functional capability at the middle echelon deprived the government of an effective grip, for which despotic rulers had to compensate with their personal vigilance.

A combination of influences induced Wu Zetian to assume the role of despot. It seems that once she began to make state decisions for her sick husband she had already gone past the point of no return. In 675 her regency was proposed but was shouted down by the courtiers. The atrocities that she later committed revealed the extent of the risk she herself took. The basic Confucian tenets in public affairs being self-restraint and mutual deference, the power of final arbitration—that of the throne—nevertheless rested on the assertiveness of its occupant. Conflicting ground rules offered numerous ways for leading politicians to work out their game plans, and this fact became central to the political history of China. In this regard Empress Wu and Li Shimin had something in common. They each knew how to take the initiative and come out victorious. Historians might have gone too far in assuming that they had taken the elimination of their own kin as a part of the sacrifice in performing a greater good. But it is safe to say that both the imposing female ruler and the genuine dynastic founder held nothing back. They realized that in order to assume the supreme position they had to go all out, no holds barred.

Empress Wu's revolution may be less than a revolution from our present-day point of view, as, restricted by technical feasibility, it did not really alter the working of the the traditional Chinese state. Yet it remained a solid reform, substantial enough to be remembered by the

coming generations. Her purge of the Tang princes and veteran courtiers eliminated the aristocratic influence that was about to overshadow
the imperial court. If she did not change the structure of government,
she added vitality to it. By lining up sufficient numbers of young and
competent officials to service her new regime, she gave the bureaucracy new life. Some of the recruits, once mature, continued to distinguish
themselves during the later reigns. Until Wu Zetian died, her empire
was devoid of major disasters. For these reasons, her revolt qualifies as
a success.

When An Lushan marched his troops from today's Beijing area
toward Xi'an, the dynasty had come close to the middle point of its
tenure. Empress Wu Zetian had been dead for fifty years. Outwardly,
the registered population of the Tang had increased from some three
million households in the early seventh century to the 9,619,254 households of the mid-eighth century. But, while uncertain about the accura-
cy of those figures, we know that both Tang financial management and
government statistics had been deteriorating. The loss of ground could
not be blamed on corruption alone. Nor was the enlargement of private
and monastic estates the main obstacle to reform. By and large the land
allotment plan could not keep pace with population growth. Economic
growth and development, dynamic and varied in the provinces, ran
beyond the canvassing and investigating capacity of the state. In most
instances no such effort was even made. Only when the actual conditions deviated from the original schematic design were officials dispatched to the countryside to search for unregistered households, who
were offered opportunities to give themselves up in exchange for a
period of tax exemption and reduced taxes thereafter. New taxes outside the original package plan were institutionalized. A variety of commissioners were appointed to impose makeshift revisions on an unworkable order of things. In brief, a recurring paradox that troubled many
dynasties of China surfaced at the mid-point of the Tang. Having fostered rehabilitation and recovery of the empire from war-torn conditions, the dynasty found it difficult to live with the prosperity created
by its own power. This awkwardness was amplified under the Tang.
Since its rural population had been organized according to a neat formula, the structural simplicity at the beginning allowed the management
plenty of freedom of action. Once the complexities set in, the organizational discrepancy was more difficult to rectify at a time when bureaucratic management was increasingly stylized.

Traditional historians blamed the high living of the imperial court.
When An Lushan advanced to the south, the depots and warehouses
along the Xi'an-Loyang axis were full of goods. The ostentation at the

imperial capital in particular invited criticism. We read from the source materials that during the festivals in Xi'an, thousands of palace women contested at games such as tug-of-war. Even in the eighth century, those exquisite women adorned themselves with eye-shadow. Contemporary illustrations and sculptures further disclose that they dressed in printed silk, played polo, and performed chamber music. There is little doubt that they were a part of the city life. An idealist might argue that the expenses involved should have been diverted to national defense. But to us this sounds like a proposal to shut down the New York Philharmonic and the Metropolitan Opera for the benefit of winning the Vietnam War. Even if the suggestion should carry, there was no delivery system that could handle the switch.

The emperor in the tragic year of 755 was Li Longji, Empress Wu's grandson. Close to seventy-two, he had been on the throne for forty-three years. At the age of thirty-eight, Yang Guifei (p. 3), or Her Preciousness the Imperial Consort Yang, had been with the emperor for more than a decade. Both of them being musical and highly emotional, their life together is a story of fairy tale fantasy punctuated by occasional tempests. Their annual wintering at the Huaqing Hot Spring has added an element of glamor to that resort ever since. To make things more complicated, Li Longji had appointed Yang Guifei's cousin Yang Guochong to be prime minister, and his antagonism toward An Lushan had much to do with provoking the latter into open rebellion.

An Lushan was a general of mixed stock who grew up in today's Rehe region, then a Tang frontier. He worked as an interpreter in a market town before joining the imperial auxiliaries on the borderland, from which ranks he rose rapidly. An inspecting general brought his name to the attention of the emperor. In 743 An arrived in Xi'an for an interview. Thereafter he was commissioned as a general and quickly became military governor of three frontier districts concurrently. Some sources spare no word of condemnation on the foolish move of entrusting defense matters to such a character. But historical evidence points out that the true cause of the policy failure may have resided in a different area: The frontier management, which required incessant maneuvering on the spot, had outstretched what could have been adequately supervised by a bureaucratic center.

The rise of numerous warlike hordes on the steppeland in the eighth century may, in a modified way, suit Owen Lattimore's generalization that the nomadic cycle is a byproduct of the Chinese cycle. In the present case, when Tang China found prosperity and satisfaction in interior development, focusing on rice cultivation and water transportation, the northern frontier more or less swayed in favor of armed cattlemen. From Empress Wu to Li Longji, imperial policy toward the borderland had on the whole been passive. There were occasional bursts of Chinese energy and martial spirit. Victories were scored. Lost territories were recovered and trade routes secured. The rampaging Tibetans, Turks, and Qidans were temporarily put out of action. But there were also serious Chinese setbacks. In any case, marriage alliances and tributary relationships would follow each round of engagement. There were no annihilation campaigns, or punitive expeditions of substance, or permanent plans for settlement. Nor would such schemes have been practical.

During Li Longji's long reign the defense districts were reorganized. On paper, there was a total strength in the vicinity of half a million men, with 80,000 combat horses. The flow of supplies in grain and textile material was said to have been stepped up. But in view of the great discrepancies between the conditions of the forward posts and official correspondence that reached Xi'an, it is extremely doubtful that such figures bear out the actual conditions in the field. The more disturbing is that even if the manpower and supplies were deployed as prescribed, the defense strength, divided and sedentary, might still be inadequate in spots to cope with cavalry charges of the mobile tribesmen.

The northeast sector, where An Lushan appeared to be an issue, was in particular a crossroads for the Koreans, the proto-Mongol Qidans, and a Turkish people called the Xi (Tätäbi). The population was mixed and the conditions fluid. Economic growth and development was not even monitored by the state, much less under governmental control. The resourceful regional commanders provided themselves with what forces they could gather, not unlikely making deals of all kinds with the local tribesmen. Persons like An Lushan, multilingual and shrewd, had

the qualities that the imperial court had been seeking for its administration of the frontier districts. In fact, An was not the only "barbarian general" so commissioned. Furthermore, even after his rebellion the Tang government continued to retain foreign commanders of his type on its general officers' roster. With these facts in view, it would not be inaccurate to say that An Lushan, a self-made man of the frontier, traded his pledge of loyalty for an imperial commission. The bribes and flatteries that he delivered to Xi'an, including gifts to the emperor himself, confirm this point.

Of course this was not a gratifying situation when compared with the conditions of the early part of the dynasty, when the entire empire showed its rugged character and when the land allotment plan and the militia system were still working. So long as the imperial prestige remained high, the marching of the conscripted soldiers to the frontier posts alone was enough to cause the warlike tribes to think twice before taking up hostilities.

Now, in addition to a large military budget, the professionalism of the defense commanders arising with recruited soldiery worked against the normal functioning of the literary bureaucracy, which was still deeply entrenched behind the timeless doctrines of symmetry and balance, even though in reality its own members were also involved in bickerings and personality clashes of all sorts.

The rise of An Lushan could not help but stir up a controversy. It came in a spiral. Deemed competent, he was given more discretionary power; with it he was becoming more indispensible. As both his territory and jurisdiction grew, the emperor heaped honors and awards on him. A magnificent residence was constructed in Xi'an on his behalf. Li Longji went so far as to ask the Turkish-speaking general to call him father and Yang Guifei mother. Cousin Yang Guozhong, however, insisted that An Lushan would sooner or later betray the dynasty. Logically this was not unconvincing. But without providing any remedy, the opening warning itself was sufficient to touch off the explosion. When An took the step that Yang Guozhong had long expected he would, his initial justification was the elimination of the evil counsel to the throne.

As a result, many institutional weaknesses of the dynasty were exposed. With all the talk about inland commerce, the wares delivered to Xi'an by the southern provinces in the past had been consumer goods that fed into the capital to earn back a portion of the tax money for those provinces. The flow of goods had never gone both ways. The interruption of trade, therefore, would not cause such an agitation as to compel those whose livelihood was threatened to react in earnest and in wrath. The capital garrison was not much more than a palatial police force and an assembly of honor guards. A hasty recruitment program only rounded up large numbers of metropolitan hangers-on, who could not fight. The direction of the campaign against the rebels sacrificed strategic soundness for political considerations. The next summer Xi'an was threatened. The emperor, his favorite concubine, her cousin the prime minister, and an assortment of palace personnel fled in the direction of Sichuan. Less than 100 miles away from the capital the escorting soldiers rioted and first killed Yang Guochong; then they demanded the execution of Yang Guifei. The intimidated emperor was forced to consent, and she was strangled to death. The poignant account of the unhappy sovereign's sad journey to Sichuan exposes the flimsy institutional link between metropolitan Xi'an and rural China. His dialogue with the soldiers confirms our view that the Tang monarchy, in the form of absolutism, had so far rested on a broad base of Confucian discipline. When the latter vanished, the logic of the former became increasingly difficult to sustain.

An Lushan's rebellion was put down; so was the wave of subsequent uprisings by his son and followers. But the Tang never regained the central authority that it once commanded. In putting down the rebellion, the imperial court had to enlist the service of contingents of Chinese and non-Chinese armed bands on the borderland. Postponing the problem, it avoided a major disaster by compromising on numerous minor points. But neither did An Lushan nor the latter-day warlords have the capacity or even the organizational logic to replace the dynasty or even to integrate north China. The second half of the Tang existed on this uneasy balance.

The cornerstone of the dynasty's constitution, the paper scheme of land allotment, with the tax package and the militia service attached as riders, was never formally abandoned. But in fact it was allowed to fall into disuse. Its replacement came in 780, when a new tax plan was announced. Thereafter land taxes would be collected from the actual owners wherever they were found, instead of the fictitious land "grantees." National rates were never prescribed. The imperial government merely apportioned the tax quotas to the provinces and prefectures, which in turn decided on the internal procedures. In reality one third of the provinces, most of them in north China, never remitted anything to Xi'an. Revenue continued to arrive from the southern region as a form of tribute, more to ingratiate the governors with the imperial government than as the fulfillment of a state function.

Regional autonomy in various degrees prevailed over the next one and a half centuries. This, however, was not a repetition of the period of disunity prior to the founding of the Second Empire. Powerful clans played no part in this later era. In general, military men were in command. On the other hand, neither was this another period of incessant warfare. In this connection we see, as Edwin Reischauer has pointed out, that "Such matters are always relative." The magnificence and grandeur of the early part of the Tang might have been exaggerated; the attribution of gloom and doom to its latter part may also have been overdone. Decentralization can in fact be perceived from various angles. For example, Chengde District, covering four prefectures in today's southeast Hebei, remained in the hands of the same Wang family for over 100 years. This was not a sign of instability. General He Jintao was elected overlord by the army officers in 829 before being confirmed by the imperial court as military governor of Weibo District, in charge of seven prefectures between today's Henan and Hebei. According to official history he enjoyed popular support and was able to pass his post on to his son and grandson. These cases seem to substantiate a universal principle: Whoever had the taxation power controlled the territory. When regional variety was given preference over the general scheme abstractly designed for the empire, the shorter radius of the administration made it more effective.

But a weak center had its drawbacks. In 763 the Tibetans entered Xi'an and plundered the city. In 765 they joined forces with the Uighurs in the suburbs, preparing to sack the capital once more. General Guo Ziyi, then seventy, risked his life by dashing unarmed on his horse into the Uighur camp. Previously he had commanded nomadic legions of Tang auxiliaries. In this instance he succeeded in evoking the authority of the "heavenly khan" and induced the chieftains to renew their allegiance. When the Uighurs were won over, the Tibetans, feeling isolated, had to decamp and flee. Guo Ziyi's valor was much admired, but symbolically, this act of heroism was a far cry from the earlier practice of commanding the forces of one ethnic group to subdue another in order to push the imperial frontier thousands of miles away from the borderland. In fact, since An Lushan's rebellion all the empire's territory west of the upper Yellow River had been permanently lost to the Tibetans. Border clashes occurred repeatedly. In 787 when peace negotiations failed, the Tibetans captured 10,000 Chinese civilians and delivered them to other tribes as slaves. At a gorge the captors allowed the captives to wail toward the east as a farewell to their homeland. It was said that several hundred of the enslaved persons fainted as they wept and some jumped from cliffs. The Chinese pacified the Uighurs by marrying imperial princesses to their chieftains. The sorrowful stories of several of those young women who had to live the rest of their lives in degrading harems against a desolate landscape are still heart-rending to the modern reader.

In the ninth century large-scale internal rebellions arose, culminating in the case of Huang Chao. Much talked about, a great deal of Huang Chao's life story is still shrouded in mystery. His two biographies in authoritative dynastic histories contradict each other considerably. While both accounts indicate that he had been engaged in the salt trade, one version depicts him as a nobody, perhaps a peddler or a smuggler, but the other asserts that his family had been in the business for generations and was quite wealthy. Such discrepancies suggest that the exact details may never be known. It was sometime after 875 in response to the rise of another rebel leader that Huang took up arms and thenceforth gained notice. It seems that the disintegration of central leadership and the lack of coordination among the provincial authorities enabled him to maintain his drive even after several setbacks. From central China he turned toward the southeastern coast, gathering brigands followers along the way and converting government troops to his cause, which can be summarized as the termination of official inefficiency and corruption. In 879 he reached Guangzhou (Canton), by which time he already commanded close to a quarter of a million men. But he met with a series of setbacks. His demand for the military governorship of the province in charge of Guangzhou was rejected by the Tang court. Epidemics broke out at this point and the death rate among the ranks of his followers was high. An Arabic source says that in Guangzhou Huang's followers slew 120,000 Mohammedans, Jews, Christians, and Persians. This, however, is not corroborated by the Chinese writers.

Forced to turn back, Huang Chao reportedly had 600,000 men with him in late 880 when he entered Xi'an, which he held for more than two years. At first he still tried to win over the general population. But in the capital he fell into a trap of his own making. Lacking mobility, he was harassed by the converging columns loyal to the imperial Tang, now augmented by the troops of several Turkish generals. As supply became an acute problem, his relationship with the residents of the city worsened and his slaughter became more unrestrained. In the spring of 883 he abandoned Xi'an to head for the east. In the summer of 884 the rebel leader and several of his close followers were beheaded in today's Shandong Province to end the great disturbance—one of the most far-reaching in the entire length of Chinese history.

The Huang Chao affair exposes an enduring Chinese dilemma. While an efficient central authority is prohibitively expensive to maintain, the lack of it increases the potential for dire consequences. Superimposed on a map of the United States, Huang's expedition would amount to a march from the Midwest to the shores of Georgia, turning southwest to reach New Orleans, reversing the course north to go through Tennessee, once again transversing from the west to the east, covering parts of Virginia, Kentucky, and Maryland before completing the zigzag course to sweep over Illinois in order to take Des Moines, in other words, outperforming Sherman by many times. Huang crossed the Yangtze four times and the Yellow River twice. This greatest brigand of all time found enough seams and cleavages inside the empire to allow him to roam about, and the provincial officials were too preoccupied with local security to work out an effective strategy that could have cornered him. Nevertheless his feat cannot be dismissed as banditry on a colossal scale. It reveals that although imperial China still had plenty of organizational discipline, what it lacked was a workable organizational logic to put things in order. When Huang Chao raised his standard, 130 years had elapsed since the An Lushan Rebellion. The infrastructure of the Tang dynasty had far outgrown its original blueprint. It now required a different kind of overarching authority.

While Huang did not pull down the dynasty, it collapsed in the wake of his rebellion. With increasingly less revenue being delivered by the provinces the imperial court only hung on for another two decades. In 904 Zhu Quanchong, a former commander in Huang Chao's forces who had switched his allegiance to serve the dynasty, now ordered the hapless emperor to pack and go with him to Loyang, an area over which the warlord Zhu had firm control. This act was only one step removed from outright usurpation, and indeed Zhu did just that two years later when he formally terminated the dynasty of Li Yuan and Li Shimin.

Nor after 906 was Xi'an ever again to be the imperial capital. As China approached the present millennium, it became increasingly clear that the national capital had to be serviced closely by areas from which economic benefits were derived. The center of gravity had shifted to the east. The southeast was attractive for its fertile soil and excellent waterways. Even of the nomadic invaders beyond the pale there was also a preference for the tribes that had some agricultural experience. Natural selection thus made Manchuria a more favorable home base than the arid northwest—the breeding ground of the Tibetans and Turks. The future struggle between the Chinese and non-Chinese groups in the ensuing 400 years therefore was to take place on a north-south axis considerably away from Xi'an, the imperial city that had seen more than its share of ups and downs.

11

The Northern Song:
A Daring Experiment

With the rise of the Song in 960, China seemed to enter the modern era with a materialistic culture in evidence. The circulation of money became more widespread. The use of gunpowder, the flame thrower, compass navigation, the astronomical clock, the blast furnace, water power in spinning, and bulkheads and watertight compartments in shipbuilding emerged with the Song. During the first two centuries of the present millennium, the standard of living in prominent Chinese cities must have compared favorably with that of any other city in the world.

The founder of the Song dynasty, Zhao Kuangyin, was an army officer. He made no effort to redistribute agricultural land; nor did he design a universal conscription program. The Song was the only major dynasty in Chinese history to rely on recruited soldiers to fill out army ranks. Immediately after his accession, Zhao Kuangyin built an artificial lake in the southern suburbs of Kaifeng—the city that was to become the site of the imperial capital of the Song but that of no other major dynasty. Instead of giving lectures and attending Confucian seminars, the sovereign often visited the lake to watch naval and marine exercises and inspected the nearby dockyards, where warships were built. Aware of the fact that military sinew had to be backed up by economic strength, Zhao was determined to accumulate two million bolts of silk fabrics in his warehouses as financial reserves in dealing with the semi-Sinicized states on the northern frontier.

The shifting of administrative emphasis from orthodox abstractions to reality, from a preoccupation with agriculture to a new interest in commerce, and from a passive to a dynamic management, gave the Song a new image, which in many respects marked a breaking away from the doldrums of traditional China. This new trend was also confirmed by governmental organizations. To maintain outward continuity, the Song revived virtually all the departments and bureaus of the Tang. But it also created new agencies, which, with more functional flexibility, could bypass or work in tandem with the old agencies. Among them the most prominent were the Privy Council and the Financial Commission. Their institution made it clear that the new dynasty intended to govern with physical power instead of some ritualistic approximation of it. When the throne was at least partially freed from moral pretensions, it was able to become more humanistic. The dynastic founder made a vow never to apply the death penalty to those who disagreed with him. The written pledge was placed inside the imperial family temple and was handed down to his successors. To prevent the issue of succession from becoming a focus of contention, Zhao Kuangyin arranged beforehand that he would be succeeded by his younger brother Kuangyi, and in this way he distanced himself admirably from the example set by Li Shimin some 350 years earlier.

These efforts produced mixed results. In the area of the national economy, the Song witnessed the most spectacular expansion ever in Chinese history. Cities thrived. Inland waterways were filled with traffic. Ship construction progressed. Both domestic and foreign trade reached unprecedented heights. The use of metal coins expanded beyond any preceding period and was not to be surpassed by the succeeding dynasties. Owing to public interest, mining and smelting received a new impetus; so did the distillery and textile industries. In the area of the operation of the government, most obvious was that the atrocities that Zhao Kuangyin was determined to avoid were on the whole avoided; even palace intrigues were reduced in scale and intensity. After sustaining economic growth for more than 300 years, the Song could not go down in history as not having made an outstanding contribution to China's well-being. But within its duration factional quarrels among civil officials worsened. This time, however, the controversy did not follow the traditional pattern. Government policies were debated as matters of public concern, and genuine disagreements were the result. Only after the contention had reached a deadlock did opportunists rush in to reap personal benefits from the impasse, thus giving the disputation bad publicity and bringing worse consequences.

There were other ironies. While founder Zhao Kuangyin showed so little interest in ideology, during the Song new schools of thought, inevitably closely related to political philosophy, emerged stronger than ever. From the very beginning the dynasty's rulers and statesmen decided to take a more realistic approach to military affairs, foreign relations, and financial management. In the end it was in those areas that the Song fared the worst.

These paradoxes can only be fully understood with the benefit of modern hindsight. The case of the Song enables us to see what happens when a country that has strong bearings on the Asian continental land mass attempts to govern itself with techniques of monetary management before the society itself is ready for it.

In the previous chapter we noted that the Tang dynasty collapsed not because of moral decay, or entirely owing to a lack of discipline, but because the earlier structural arrangement of the empire had been overtaken by events while the stylized administration of the bureaucracy could not adjust to the change. Toward the end of the dynasty, decentralization ushered in warlordism. A military governor could carve out a territory as vast as a province and remain virtually autonomous. When he had to personally lead a campaign, he would appoint a deputy to oversee his government seat and thus keep the power base intact. In time his position became hereditary, as did those of his subordinates. Within his domain, army officers took over tax collection, imposing new levies and fixing rates on the old ones. When Zhu Quanchong seized the imperial throne in 907 it did not cause a stir because by then the dynasty of Li Yuan and Li Shimin, after being in existence for 288 years, had long since forfeited its *raison d'être*.

Yet, Zhu Quanchong couldn't pick up the pieces either. For fifty-four years from 906 to 960 (p. 89), China fell into a period that historians refer to as the "Five Dynasties and Ten Kingdoms." As if to reverse the order of the period of prolonged disunity preceding the Sui and Tang, this time five transient dynasties replaced one another in the north, while, with only one exception, ten simultaneous and overlapping kingdoms appeared in the south. In its simplest terms, while the dynasties tried one after another to establish a universal order but fell short of the goal, the military governors in the south took advantage of the situation to proclaim themselves independent.

The fact that the entire period of disunity lasted for only fifty-four years indicates that the remnants left by the Tang were not beyond salvaging. China remained basically a nation of small self-cultivators. But individual holdings varied; productivity in the several geographical regions, or sometimes even within one district, showed great disparity. New revenues could be derived from commercial crops, distilling and mining, and inland trade. Minting of money could prove profitable. This was no longer such a situation that public finance could be managed from the center by any conceptual scheme, or that local clans could extend their control over small areas to form pockets of autonomy. Warlordism was in fact history's answer for such a particular situation. As it developed, a regional lord could, with what legitimacy he claimed, impose universal conscription over his territory. In reality few soldiers were drafted from the population. Instead, mercenaries were recruited. The expenses, however, were borne by the public. In this way tax assessment was pushed to the highest point in many districts, as the local gazetteers attest. But the positive side was that when it was handled by hereditary lords who had a vested interest in the locales, more likely consideration was given to each individual's ability to pay, which a universal system imposed from the top would have ignored.

Another technique developed by these territorial lords during the interregnum was the constant transfer of the officers and men among the battle formations. The best personnel were absorbed by the center to form an elite corps, the subordinate contingents having to be content with inferior supplies and manpower. The senior commanders were taken by the lords as sworn brothers or adopted sons. With this arrangement, an interlink was established between the authority on the top and the governed below. As long as the territorial units remained competitive yet shunned devastating and protracted warfare, a balance was reached which kept the overall lineup intact. China during the period of Five Dynasties and Ten Kingdoms showed a certain semblance to medieval Japan.

Was this state of affairs undesirable? Traditional historians inevitably deplored the absence of a respectable authority during the period, when "criminals, bandits, and peddlers were crowned in assumed pomp," and men of character and fortitude had little chance. The high tax rates were often bemoaned. What those writers failed to recognize was that with the government's center of gravity shifting down to the provincial level, the governance was more responsive to the local situation. Financially, the omission of a two-tier government also provided considerable savings. The benefit was more likely to be felt by the whole area south of the Yangtze River, where a period of relative peace reigned. Marital ties were established between and among the houses of the territorial lords. Agreements for mutual aid in time of famine were reached. Efforts at promoting regional economy, such as by the Ma family in Hunan, who made the native tea available for export; the Qian family in Zhejiang, who organized large-scale irrigation projects; and the Wang family in Fujian, who encouraged foreign trade, could hardly be equaled by a centralized bureaucratic management whose attention was inevitably occupied by the least advanced sectors of the national economy in order to ease the internal tension.

Nevertheless, a divided China did make for a more vulnerable northern frontier. In 936, still within this period of division, an emperor of one of the five transient dynasties made a deal with the rising Qidans, a seminomadic people who had originated in Manchuria (p. 106). The aid that he sought from the warrior group did not leave an enduring imprint on Chinese history, but the price he paid did. The transfer to the Qidan of sixteen border prefectures within the Great Wall, including today's Beijing, left the gates of the frontier wide open, and this was to affect China's destiny for more than 400 years to come. The Chinese populace in the interior had yet to learn that the alien masters who took advantage of the agreement were by no means the same as the barbarians of the past. The new hordes were going to convert the border prefectures into a training ground. The semiagricultural peoples from farther north and northeast could now come in to learn how to manage the affairs of a large agrarian population within the pale, thus to sustain their southward drive.

The rise of the Song can be seen as a response to this challenge. It integrated the separate efforts of the *de facto* regional rulers who constantly upgraded the armed forces under their command and tightened the control of the local financial resources. While proclaiming a universal empire, the new dynasty assumed some characteristics of a national state. In rallying the south to face its rivals in the north, it took a competitive stance.

In the spring of 960, Zhao Kuangyin was the commanding general of the imperial forces of the last short-lived dynasty within the interim period, which was also confusingly designated as the Zhou. The army encamped at Chenqiaoyi, a small town barely a day's marching distance from Kaifeng, the Zhou capital. The next day before dawn Zhao was awakened by his officers and men, who put a yellow robe on his shoulders and made him emperor. Such coups had occurred before during the period of Five Dynasties and Ten Kingdoms. Similar cases of emperors being elected by soldiers can also be found in the history of Rome. Zhao Kuangyin, however, stands out in all the annals of history for his effort to consolidate an uncoordinated movement that had been worked out by provincial strongmen ever since the decline of the Tang. In the end he turned it into a centralized bureaucratic management. No other Chinese dynasty arose under similar circumstances.

When Zhao's army command returned to Kaifeng, the takeover from the Zhou was acted upon with ease. The original scheme to eliminate the alien groups in the north was shelved; the new dynastic founder realized that a divided China was in no position to challenge its northern adversaries. For the rest of his life, Zhao Kuangyin concentrated on annexing the southern states that still remained autonomous. The central Yangtze valley was taken in 963, Sichuan in 965, and Guangzhou in 971. At Zhao's death in 976, Fujian, Zhejiang, and the lower Yangtze valley remained beyond his reach. Their incorporation into the empire took place during the reign of his younger brother.

But in the areas which Zhao Kuangyin could lay his hands on, the policy of centralization was worked out with swiftness and firm resolve. The emperor's tact, moderation, and generosity in pecuniary matters facilitated his skillful maneuvering. Only a year and a half after his accession, Zhao personally negotiated an arrangement with several of the generals in command of his elite troops who had engineered the plot to enthrone him whereby they would voluntarily request retirement; the emperor promised them in return pensions and honorary posts. The potential danger of kingmakers around the throne was thereby removed.

The Song army was organized into three tiers. The "forbidden army" was superior to the "suburban army," which in turn was above the "country army." The units at the capital constantly took away the best personnel from the provincial units and sent their rejects to them. The annexed territories were thus deprived of the best trained soldiery. Walled cities previously maintained as impregnable bastions by the warlords were neutralized; they were transformed into interchangeable posts for the civil officials, who were rotated every three years.

Tax collection within the territories was likewise taken over by the bureaucrats. Ledgers and receipts were scrutinized with meticulous care. A 965 edict clearly affirmed the principle of centralized financing, with provincial and local governments, after deducting their own expenses, not allowed to retain any surplus. Warehouse and treasury deposits were regularly cleared for submission to the capital, in time making Kaifeng one of the most remarkable inland ports in the world. For the transferring of revenue, which always involved large quantities of moveable goods, the empire was divided into six fiscal districts; each was placed under the charge of a "transportation intendant" who took over matters of finance from the provincial governors and residential army commanders. During the reign of Zhao Kuangyi, which ran from 976 to 997, it was reported that owing to a lack of adequate care, the raincoats and tenting material in store at Kaifeng counting "several tens of thousand pieces" were ruined. The accumulation of material and supplies in the capital that this report hints at, a measurement of central finance, seemed to have exceeded that of any other place in the world at that time.

Yet, even with such preparations, the Song goes down in history as a weak dynasty. Its battle banners were never hoisted over the northern steppes, not to say Manchuria to the east or Central Asia to the west. It never gained a foothold in the south in Vietnam as the Han and the Tang had done. Indeed, at the risk of oversimplification one could say that the military history of the Song's 319 years is a record of retreat and defeat broken only by intervals of purchased peace. This situation is not so inexplicable if a number of factors usually omitted by traditional historians are brought into the discussion.

Tripartite Relations During the Northern Song

To the northeast of the Song was the Qidan state of the Liao. The Qidan, a people of Mongolian stock, had been active in that general area for over 300 years. Their Sinicized dynasty antedated the Song itself by fifty-three years. The Liao emperors were learned, the Qidan script having been in use since 920. They received tributary emissaries from the Koreans, Uighurs, Tibetans, and, before the founding of the Song, even the Qian family of Zhejiang. Not only was the annexed Chinese territory under Qidan control administered by native bureaucrats, but also, as a qualified observer witnessed, even deep in Liao territory most of the officials, literati, artisans, actors, sportsmen, monks, and nuns were men and women from China. The organizational capacity of such a mixed state was far more formidable than the quick-striking power of the nomads previously encountered by the Han and the Tang.

The Xixia was not a state of savages either. This ruling house of the Tibetans had in fact been prominent in that region ever since the early Tang. When it rose to challenge Song supremacy some 400 years later, a Sinicized government already existed. It used a Tibetan script, and the basic Confucian canon had been translated into the native language. By then a large number of Tibetans had taken up agriculture.

Thus by the tenth century when the minority groups in the peripheral areas had raised their cultural level, unquestionably with Chinese collaboration, the Song had to face its frontier problem in a manner not experienced by its predecessors. The nomadic peoples now possessed an agricultural base, they could take up walled defense, and the rugged terrain in the north worked to their advantage. Yet at the same time they retained a swiftness of mobilization and a high degree of mobility in field maneuvers, qualities cognate to their pastoral life. Although the Qidan and the Tibetans were sometimes at odds, in facing the Song they could give aid to each other. In 986 a Liao princess was married to the Xixia ruler, at that time still known as king rather than emperor.

The lack of unequivocal nationalist feelings among the Chinese was a serious handicap to the Song. Clearly enough, if the Chinese population under alien rule had been determined to cast away their foreign yoke, a war of liberation would have made the Song campaign easier. As it happened, the contest was largely carried out as a struggle between dynastic states.

The phenomenon can be traced to the growth of cosmopolitanism over a millennium. The Chinese themselves circulated the myth that all Asian peoples were the descendants of a legendary Yellow Emperor; only the separation by geography had made them different. Classical sources put every emphasis on culturalism rather than nationalism. Mencius, the Second Sage, especially made it clear that it was neither unscrupulous nor degrading to humble one's self in front of an alien ruler in order to advance the cause of public well-being. At one point he asserted that Shun, a sage-like king in China's legendary history, was "a barbarian from the east" and Xibai, the purported founder of the Zhou dynasty, was "a barbarian of the west." Those remarks were recited by practically every learned man in China and provided suffi-cient justification for collaboration. When the educated elite assumed such an attitude, the common people, who had no special interest in contesting the ethnic origin of the occupant of the throne, could not be very concerned with the issue of nationality. Additionally it should be noted here that the Qidan rulers were also perceptive enough not to give the Chinese populace under their administration a cause for griev-ance.

But what to date has not been adequately understood is that a great-er weakness existed in Song military logistics. Outwardly, this would seem unlikely. After all, the southern state was larger, richer, and more populous; it was more technically advanced and benefited more from the inland waterways. But a full realization of those advantages would have required a truly modern organization which was not available to China in the eleventh century and would remain unavailable many hundreds of years later.

While the supplies of the Song were more abundant, its supply lines were also much longer. The inclusion of numerous articles of equipment violated the military principles of simplicity and uniformity. There is no evidence that the data-processing capacity in those days could assure adequate coordination. Contemporaries pointed out that even vital fig-ures in the records of the Privy Council and the Financial Commission did not tally. The modern reader must realize that the Song experiment, to be fulfilled at all, would have required the submission of all governmental finances to commercial practice. Units and measurements must be clearly established; interchangeability must be affirmed and enforceable by an independent regulatory agency. The bureaucrats who managed the program must be technically oriented and not compromise their function with ideological and personal considerations. The scale of the operation, which was to service and supply an army growing to the mark of one million men, had made it mandatory to enlist civil support. A corollary is that numerous private business transactions lateral to and beneath the financial operation must also be organized on corporative principles, so that they could be held publicly accountable. In sum, everything had to be rendered mathematically manageable.

In practice, the Song activated an operation requiring service support that China even in the early twentieth century could not comfortably afford; the attempt was almost a thousand years ahead of its time. Aside from a sizable traffic on the rivers and canals, during the Song neither the governmental operation nor private business had come close to the modern standard of commercialism. The military affairs of the dynasty had to bear the consequence of this premature adventure. If the connection was not obvious enough, during the reign of the sixth emperor, Zhao Xu, the record of Wang Anshi's reforms brought it to the surface.

Song efforts to dislodge the Liao started early. But campaigns in both 979 and 986 failed. Emperor Zhao Guangyi barely escaped capture during the first campaign and reportedly sustained an arrow wound during the second as he personally directed the military operations. When the Qidan forces retaliated, they instigated incessant border clashes. A full-scale Qidan invasion was organized in 1004. Since Kaifeng was on a flatland and the threat was immediately felt, Zhao Heng, the third emperor, hastily authorized a peace settlement. Although the two sovereign states pledged to be fraternal equals, the Song was compelled to pay the Liao an annuity of 200,000 bolts of silk in addition to 100,000 ounces of silver.

In retrospect, the terms established in 1004 might not have been a bad arrangement. The annuities constituted only a small fraction of the Song state income; they could be handed over as a grant-in-aid to a less affluent neighbor to help with its trade deficit. The cost of the peace was indisputably cheaper than the cost of war. However, it would have required a complete detachment from contemporary affairs to thus accept the dictates of geopolitics. Lacking such foresight, it was most difficult for the Song court to accept the terms as a normal state of affairs. Historically, no universal empire of China worth its name had ever paid tribute to a peripheral state that it considered to be a cultural inferior. On the other side the Qidan, counting the annual payment as a form of war indemnity, could not believe that they were under any moral obligation to show gratitude to the giver either. When they demanded an increase in 1042, it was backed up by force.

The Chinese had yielded to the Tibetans a less prominent place. Theoretically the Xixia occupied the territory, a part of it in the Chinese heartland, under Song suzerainty. When in 1038 the ruler of the Xixia proclaimed himself emperor, the imperial court at Kaifeng immediately declared him an outlaw and suspended all trade relationships with his domain, until then an autonomous kingdom. But subsequent Chinese suppression campaigns failed ignominiously. When more Chinese forces were committed, more forts were lost and casualties mounted. After a fruitless struggle lasting several years, a peace settlement was reached in 1044. The best the Chinese negotiators could do was to induce the Tibetan ruler to call himself "son emperor" when sending greetings to "the father emperor of the Great Song." In return the Chinese were to pick up the tab again, this time to the tune of an annuity of 255,000 units, payable in silk, silver, and tea.

This background set the stage for Zhao Xu's accession in 1067. At eighteen, this sovereign had already established a reputation for his diligence and devotion to state affairs. His driving ambition was to wipe out the humiliations that the dynasty had suffered from the two peripheral states in the north, aiming at nothing less than the recovery of the territories that were considered to be a part of China. Like dynastic founder Zhao Kuanyin, Zhao Xu believed that the empire's financial resources could be mobilized to attain this goal. Inside the palace compound he constructed a number of warehouses, on which he posted poems he had composed as reminders that as a filial pious son he must use earthly goods to fulfill the wish cherished by his ancestors. When he and Wang Anshi, a literati-official who had achieved a reputation for being talented but unorthodox, met to settle the issue of the first priority, their shared purpose drew them together.

The package of Wang Anshi's reform programs was referred to as the "New Policies." One of his innovations was the Green Crop Money, by which the government loaned money to the peasants in the planting season. The return of the loan after the autumn harvest carried a 20 percent interest, a rate not considered exorbitant by the standards of the day. Another program had to do with the commutation of service. The Song local government enlisted the service of a number of office attendants, including runners, scribes, jailers, etc. Hitherto those positions were unpaid; people were drafted from the general population, which shared the expenses. Wang ordered that a new tax be collected to pay for these jobs. Goods stored in government warehouses, sitting idle, were unproductive. Under Wang's direction they were made available to merchants on credit; interest was charged when the account was settled. In the interim, precious metals and real estate could be used as collateral. In a similar manner the transportation intendants who carried native merchandise to the capital as tax proceeds could dispose of the cargo en route to make a profit, replacing it with other commodities that had more resale value at Kaifeng. To restructure the land taxes, Wang Anshi planned to conduct a sweeping land survey in which taxable land was to be gridded into squares of 5,000 feet on each side. Within each unit soil productivity was classified into five grades, on which differentiated tax rates were assessed accordingly. For the supply of military manpower, Wang decided to revive the militia.

From the very beginning the New Policies met strong bureaucratic opposition. Disputes of various kinds were heard. None of Wang's programs produced tangible results. They only divided the court. The reformer himself was dismissed, recalled, and dismissed again. In the end he was sent to Nanjing, given insignificant positions, and then retired with the honorific title of duke.

This sequence of events made Emperor Zhao Xu an unhappy man. The New Policies were supposed to strengthen the empire's fiscal sinews so that he could wage wars with impunity. This goal was nowhere fulfilled. One outspoken courtier told him bluntly that His Majesty would do well to sit peacefully on the throne for twenty years before engaging in warlike talks. During Zhao Xu's reign more territory had to be ceded to the Qidan. In the west the Song army did score a victory against the Tibetans. But the win came after many setbacks. Whenever news of adversity at the front reached the palace in the middle of the night, the troubled sovereign paced around his bed. The 1081 campaign was said to have committed 320,000 men. After sustaining an unusually large number of casualties, only four fortified towns were captured. When Zhao Xu died in the autumn of 1085 at the age of thirty-six, the pacifist courtiers in Kaifeng decided to return the four towns to Xixia to avert a protracted war which they concluded the Song had no chance to win.

Zhao Xu was succeeded by his son Zhao Xi, who was at that time not yet ten years old. During the minority of the young sovereign his grandmother served as regent. Under her direction all the New Policies were suspended, and Wang Anshi's followers were dismissed to make room for his opponents. The great historian Sima Guang acted as prime minister. In 1093 the empress dowager died. Zhao Xi, now seventeen, made another reversal. He revived the New Policies and banished the anti-reform group. The purge extended to many statesmen who had been dead for a number of years. The format of the civil service examination was revised; even the annals of the departed emperor were rewritten to assure historical justification for the policy change. However, a proposal to posthumously deprive the empress dowager of her title failed to carry.

It wasn't over yet. When Zhao Xi died in early 1100 at the age of twenty-three, he was childless. The throne went to his half brother Zhao Ji, the eighth emperor and a famous painter. During his tragic reign, Zhao Ji took two different positions with regard to the New Policies. For two years he sided with the anti-reformers. Thereafter he went over to the pro-reformers. The reputation of Wang Anshi, by then dead for close to two decades, rose and fell with the policy fluctuations. His reputation reached its zenith in 1104: an imperial decree made him the Third Sage, allowing him a place inferior only to Confucius and Mencius in the Confucian temple. Meanwhile, the names of 309 of his opponents were inscribed on stone tablets to establish that they were evil men. Their infamy was expected to pass on to posterity.

The story of Wang Anshi is one of the great issues in Chinese history. Sides have been taken throughout the centuries. In modern times, it has also become a subject of international interest. Books and articles in different languages have been published about the deeds and career of this controversial figure. Most of the studies, however, are too scholarly and specialized to be of much interest to the general reader.

When the Wang Anshi episode is considered in the late twentieth century, we are amazed by the fact that some 900 years before our time, China had already made the first attempt to institutionalize the monetary management of state affairs, in a scope and degree unheard of anywhere else in the world. When Wang Anshi told Emperor Zhao Xu that state income could be widened without tax increases, he apparently understood that the advance of capital could stimulate production, and the greater productivity would in turn generate more public revenue. This expansionist view differed from the traditional economic perspective, which saw everything as a fixed quantity. In this sense, Wang Anshi has more appeal to modern readers than he did to his contemporaries.

But one factor never occurred to the Song reformer and rarely to his admirers many centuries later: Modern monetary management is all encompassing. Its jurisdiction must be inclusive and exclusive. Clearly enough, the respect of property rights and the division of labor according to its exchange value would be ineffective if they were considered valid in some areas but not in others. Having two sets of laws and customs would open loopholes and incite disputes. In order to make the system work, matters of money and credit must attain universal interchangeability, like liquid in a pipeline under general pressure. In world history, no such system has been installed without painful struggle. The old institutions and the vested interests associated with them must be destroyed before the universal interchangeability of services and goods could be established. Wang Anshi's reform did not touch off a clash on such a scale because the constitution of the Song had not evolved social components substantial enough to call for a showdown. It was a political impulse rather than an economic movement. The fight was thus confined to the court and to the civil bureaucracy.

With hindsight we can nevertheless see that in order to commercialize the fiscal operation of the empire, monetary management would have to be in place and ready. Laws affecting bills of exchange and lading, charter parties' insurance policies, rules of average loss, bottomry and respondentia bonds, partnership, salvage claims, and so forth would have had to appear in statute books and remain enforceable. Even more essential, legal proceedings affecting inheritance, bankruptcy, foreclosure, and fraud and deceit would have had to be compatible with the volatile conditions of a society where money reigned. There was no evidence that the inland trade during the Song had ever advanced to such a degree.

More inadequacy existed in the infrastructure of Chinese society. Wang's reform affected the entire agrarian population, and its ultimate aim was to deliver the benefit to the battleground in north China. It would be difficult to see how a commercial organization supporting the program could by itself function without the grass-roots support of the rural areas. But in Song China as well as in previous dynasties, the parcelization of land in the villages, a legacy of many centuries preceding, remained typical. The abscondence of peasants from land was constant. The inability to accumulate capital within the agricultural sector of the national economy, aside from a few exceptional cases, was not fundamentally different from the situation of very recent times. When those conditions prevailed, neither could the service sector of the economy gain a foothold to make a start. Turnpikes were never built. A regular mail service was missing. Court expenses alone would have prohibited the growth and development of civil law. The bureaucrats serving as magistrates found the peasants maneuverable only by blocks. The universality of the empire therefore continued to remain centered on the social discipline developed from cultural cohesion rather than on the interchangeability that had yet to go hand in hand with the power of money.

More short-comings of the Song

Lacking our understanding, the Song civil servants argued over the issue largely on moral grounds. But the polemics brought out a number of technical observations that reflected the conditions of contemporary society. The Green Crop Money, for instance, was never handled in a legally acceptable manner by any modern standard. There were no adequate provisions for applying for a loan, for investigating the need, for putting up collateral, or for seizure of the same in case of arrears. The county magistrates simply parceled out funds to the village leaders and held them collectively responsible for the principal and interest, regardless of the wishes of the villagers and their obligations to one another. The money to be loaned out came from the granary reserves earmarked for famine relief, of which not every county had maintained its quota. There were some cases where no loans were made, but the demand for a share of the interest compelled the magistrates to assess a surtax on the population to make up for it. The distribution of government properties on credit attracted only a few merchants; most were apprehensive about getting involved. The buying and selling of commodities by officials drove wholesale dealers out of existence. At times the officials had to fix the prices themselves. On one occasion it involved some of them in peddling fruits and ice on the street, and that brought criticism from the emperor. The commutation of service in reality forcibly demanded the circulation of money in the rural areas, while the government should have concentrated on strengthening the banking business and wholesale trade and organizing an insurance business in the cities.

The militia system contradicted the other measures in Wang's package. The conscription would have been effective if the Song had adopted the equalization of land utilization program of previous dynasties. In that case, compulsory military service could ride along with lightened and uniform taxation. Since the Song had already increased taxes and promoted the use of money, the additional levy on manpower was inevitably burdensome on the poor. The land survey also involved more technical difficulties than its schematic design suggested. In 1082, for example, the prefect of Kaifeng reported that the survey covered only two counties each year. It would take ten years to complete the process over the prefecture's nineteen counties. When those remarks were made, a decade had already elapsed since the scheme was first announced in 1072.

Since the New Policies ran into such insurmountable difficulties, one must ask what the rationale for their enactment was. Why were they revived after they failed, not only once but again and again? When considering this question, the reader must realize that while the Song bureaucrats did not have our perception that monetary management is contingent on a number of prerequisites, which would have put them far ahead of their time, the lack of such an historical understanding saved them from taking our fatalist view that the experiment was bound to fail. It was their experiment and their struggle.

If it had not been pushed through on a national scale, but developed *in situ* and ad hoc by some local officials and certain specialized functionaries, Wang's reforms would not have been completely unworkable. Although free from its fixed target the piecemeal approach would not qualify as the monetary management of state affairs, without the uniform demand from the top, government operations in selected areas and on a reduced scale could sometimes have cut into private trade. To cite one example, during the Tang dynasty a statesman of some business acumen by the name of Liu Yan had traded government properties in his custody with profit and succeeded. Before launching his empire-wide program, Wang Anshi had served as the magistrate of Yinxian, the site of modern Ningbo and since Tang times an important seaport. In that capacity he had the personal experience of lending public funds to peasants at interest, to the satisfaction of both sides. Similar cases must have deluded Emperor Zhao Xu and his sons into thinking that the anti-reformers were all obstructionists. Compounding the problem was that the program, congenial to the situation or not, was difficult to revoke once it became sanctioned by law. The undesirable consequences of suspension could cause the administrators to have doubts about the safety of a retreat. In sum, the Wang Anshi affair, disturbing the court of the Northern Song for no less than a half century, involved miscast emperors and their evil counsels. But given the character and strength of the principal figures who were also entangled in the controversy, we may consider it as representing the dilemma of an era. China's political unity advanced too far ahead of the nation's economic organization. In the end both suffered.

12

West Lake
and the Southern Song

Hangzhou first gained national prominence during the short-lived Sui dynasty. When the Grand Canal was constructed in that era, the city became its southern terminus. Unlike Kaifeng, the Northern Song capital, which remained more or less a consumers' market, with government functionaries and their associates providing most of the purchasing power, Hangzhou, the capital of the Southern Song, became a major manufacturing center. Shipbuilding, silk production, and porcelain- and paper-making increased dramatically in this city during the Southern Song.

For the modern tourist, West Lake, within walking distance of the city, is a major attraction. Originally a shallow bay surrounded by mountains, it remained so as late as the early seventh century. But when its outlet to the mouth of the Qiantang River silted up a lake was formed, and the trapped water in time became desalinated.

The lake is only slightly smaller than the city itself. Two causeways shorten the distance from points on the curved northwest and west shores. The Bai Causeway, named after Bai Juyi (p. 4), leads to the island of Solitary Hill. The Su Causeway is named in memory of Su Dongpo, the poet, painter, and prose-writer who in the eleventh century vigorously opposed Wang Anshi's reforms. Although they lived almost 300 years apart, both Bai and Su became governor in the Hangzhou area and both ordered the dredging of the lake. The causeways are left from their works. The governments of traditional China had a point, although it may have been fortuitous, in their effort to recruit functionaries from among men of aesthetic tastes. They generally took better care of ecology and the environment than ordinary bureaucrats.

A Chinese opera that is becoming well-known in the United States nowadays, *The White Snake*, owes its origin to the West Lake setting. The curtain rises on its shores. The spirits of two snakes, one white and the other black, turn into two beautiful maidens called Bai Suzhen and Xiao Qing. They meet a handsome young man on an arched stone bridge on the Bai Causeway. Suzhen falls in love with him. They get married and have a son. Xiao Qing serves as a housemaid. Having discovered the supernatural origin of the bride, however, the abbot of the Jinshan Temple captures her with a magic bowl, on top of which he builds the Leifeng Pagoda. As the legend goes, she was to be sealed under tons of bricks as long as the tower stood. But Xiao Qing, having escaped from bad fortune, returns a number of years later with an army of fighting shrimps and crabs. The grown son of the couple also participates, and eventually they rescue Suzhen from captivity. What happens thereafter no one knows. But there was a Leifeng Pagoda on the shore of West Lake. It collapsed in 1924, and today only its foundation is visible.

Even in folklore the Chinese seem compelled to regard a nuptial tie following a romantic encounter as something unpropitious. Instead of a snake who misleads the woman, the woman is the snake itself. Yet in this case at least, ultimately the spirits of exuberant life triumph over an authority that cannot do better than sacrificing human value to protect a convention. The audience is invited to see that while the traditional high-brow culture fortifies itself with intellectual snobbishness, the little tradition (p. 72) has a tendency to identify itself with the peasants and fishermen. When that is not enough, it marshals shrimps and crabs to establish the association.

Not too far away from the Xiling Bridge, which leads to the Su Causeway, is the tomb of Yue Fei, a junior officer who arose from the ranks of recruits to become the most outstanding general of the entire Song period. He died in confinement in 1141 on a charge of insubordination framed by Prime Minister Qin Gui. Circumstances further suggest that Qin engineered his murder in the death cell. At that time Qin was working closely with Emperor Zhao Gou to reach a peace settlement with the invading Jürched, who had built up a Sinicized state called the Jin (this is a different Chinese character from that of the Jin dynasty mentioned in Chapter 7) and pushed the Song south. Yue Fei's sin was that during the period of chaos he had disciplined his troops, won support from the populace, successfully suppressed the rising bandits, and defeated the Jürched cavalry with infantry tactics. By then thirty-nine, his survival would not only have jeopardized the impending peace that had been negotiated with difficulty and was still tenuous at best, but also threatened a shaky regime that wanted so much to find breathing space.

Twenty years after his death, Yue Fei was posthumously rehabilitated by the Southern Song court. The tribute that the Chinese habitually pay to fallen heroes has since then elevated him to a position second only to Guan Yü (p. 70). Yet, unlike Guan, Yue Fei was not a soldier without polish. He combined the traditional virtues of loyalty and filial piety with his schooling. Today a temple next to his tomb encases his statue, fourteen feet high and in full military gear. Above the statue are four characters, supposed to have been reproduced from his own calligraphy. The banner may be literally translated as "Return Our Mountains and Rivers"; better still: "Recover Our Lost Territory." In fact, Yue Fei was an inspiration to the rising nationalism in modern China. Before his tomb are four cast iron statues in a kneeling position. They are Prime Minister Qin Gui, his wife, and two accomplices in Yue's murder. In the 1930s the local police had difficulty in preventing visitors from urinating on these figures. The use of hard objects, including rifle butts, on the face of Qin Gui was common. Only Wang Jingwei, who himself later defected to and collaborated with the Japanese during World War II, dared to say that Yue Fei was an uncontrollable warlord.

Yue Fei was not a warlord; and he was in fact quite controllable. Otherwise he would not have, upon his victory over the Jürched in central China, obeyed the summons of Qin Gui in the name of the emperor to suspend his operations and meet his machinated death. But the fluctuation between war and peace was a major Song characteristic, and it can be traced back to the Northern Song when the capital was Kaifeng. The inability of the dynasty to pursue either policy successfully for any length of time was more adverse to its destiny than any evil deeds of a treacherous prime minister and his instigating wife.

The story begins with Zhao Ji (p. 118), the eighth emperor of the dynasty. He could have led a much happier life as a book illustrator and art connoisseur than as an occupant of the imperial throne. During his reign there was not only the Wang Anshi controversy, but also the Jürched, a Tungusic people from whom the Manchus later descended, arose in the upper Sungari region in Manchuria. In 1113 they rebelled against the Liao, and a year later they established the Jin dynasty. By this time the Northern Song had been paying tribute to the Liao for over 110 years. In 1118, dazzled by the success of the Jin, Zhao Ji authorized an alliance with the new state against the Liao in the hope that the joint military operation would enable the Song to recover the sixteen border prefectures which had been lost to the Liao and thus fulfill a dynastic obsession. Surprisingly, the Jürched Jin dismantled the Liao Empire of the Qidan with great ease. In 1125 the job was finished without Song assistance, and the next year the warriors from the northeast were ready to take on the Song as well. At the last moment Zhao Ji abdicated in favor of his eldest son, but when the Jürched entered Kaifeng, they captured both the new emperor and the retired emperor. Subsequently the father and son were sent to Manchuria, never to return. The Northern Song ended in 1126.

Zhao Ji's ninth son, Zhao Gou, lord-sovereign of Yue Fei and Qin Gui, proclaimed himself emperor to continue the dynasty as the Southern Song. But as soon as the accession ceremony was performed, he had to run for his life. For the next four years he was hunted by the Jürched from central China to the south of the Yangtze, from Hangzhou to Ningbo. Once, to avoid capture he had to take refuge on a seafaring junk hugging the coast. Only in 1132 after the Jin retreated did Zhao Gou return to Hangzhou, then known as Linan. Only in 1138 was the city made the capital. Yet, still called *Xingzai*, or "visiting headquarters," the new capital was not meant to replace Kaifeng, where the imperial tombs were located.

The peace of 1141, for which Yue Fei was sacrificed, allowed Zhao Gou's mother, who was also captured during the fall of Kaifeng fifteen years earlier, to return to the south. The Huai River was the boundary between the Southern Song and the Jin, and the former acknowledged itself to be a vassal of the latter. When the investiture ceremony was performed, the regalia for Zhao Gou to wear were given to him by the Jürched Jin, whose capital was on the site of modern Beijing. As a vassal state, the Southern Song paid to the Jin an annual tribute of 500,000 units, half in silk and half in silver.

The empire of the Jürched, which had already assumed overlordship over the Koreans, the Uighurs, and the Tibetans of Xixia, was now able to proclaim a universal rule of the Chinese type. Before the Song emissary arrived with tribute, a bureaucratic system was announced, and a civil service examination was held. The ruler began to wear the Chinese-style imperial garb. A forty-ninth generation descendant of Confucius was made a duke, and the sacrifice to Confucius was attended by the Jin emperor himself.

In retrospect, the most effective argument in the Song court against the settlement was the issue of vassalage. Yet the greatest objection of the southerners to a peaceful settlement was that it would deny the reunion of the sovereign, now in charge of a government in exile, with his own mother. Few historians have noted that before the settlement the central Yangtze valley was infested with bandits. The Jin was trying to create a buffer state in this middle belt of land. It also commissioned a handful of collaborators to infiltrate the frontier provinces of the Song. Worse yet, under renewed assaults by the Jin, the fiscal administration of the Southern Song was in disarray, and the procurement of military

Tripartite Relations During the Southern Song

manpower was difficult. And although battle formations were hastily organized, the exile government in Linan had little confidence in its own chances for survival.

In 1161, the same year Yue Fei was rehabilitated, the Jin made another attempt to take the Southern Song. Although the outcome was inconclusive, war and negotiations dragged on for four years. Only in 1165 was a compromise reached. After much haggling, the Jin allowed the Song to drop the outright vassal status, and the annuity was reduced by 100,000 units.

Before the close of the twelfth century, Han Tuozhou, a powerful figure in the court at Hangzhou, attempted once more to undo the settlement. Han's father was Emperor Zhao Gou's brother-in-law; Han himself was married to the empress' niece. As the empress continued to dominate the court of the Southern Song, Han had the influence of a king-maker. Taking over the premiership concurrently as the president of the Privy Council and with the title of Grand Preceptor, he had the power to formulate a war policy and carry it out. In his private life arrogant and a man of many wants, Han Tuozhou alienated himself from many within the Song government. So when he launched an offensive in 1206 and it backfired, few were sympathetic with him. We might note that in this same year when the Song forces were being beaten back by the Jürched, farther north the Mongol Timüjin was proclaiming himself "Genghis Khan," that is, a Mongolian Son of Heaven. Meanwhile, the Jin, capitalizing on its victory, demanded Han Tuozhou's head and got it. In 1207 the unpopular man's body was desecrated to satisfy Beijing. Some historians, however, assert that many stories about Han's misdeeds are untrue and that, unworthy as he was, he forfeited his life for a cause. The new settlement increased the Song annual tribute to 600,000 units, and the sovereign of the southern state had to call himself "nephew emperor" in addressing the "uncle emperor" of the Great Jin. A few years later the situation changed drastically. In 1214, the Song took advantage of the fact that the Jürched Empire was pinned down by the Mongols to terminate the tribute. In 1233 it had an opportunity to inflict revenge on its adversary of many generations. That year the Mongols proposed to the Hangzhou court a joint military operation against the Jin. While many Song courtiers still remembered that 114 years ago at Kaifeng Emperor Zhao Ji had committed the dynasty to a similar course, in that instance allying with the Jin against the Liao, at this time the enmity toward the Jürched was so intense and so deep-seated that the clamor for war drowned out the voices for prudence, the historical lesson notwithstanding. The alliance was entered, and as the Jin had done to the Liao before, the Mongols finished off the Jin in two years without Song help. Having already terminated the Xixia in 1227, the descendants of Genghis Khan could now turn their full attention to the remaining state in China. In one aspect the Southern Song did better than the Jin in the North: It survived for another forty-five years.

In the wider frame of macrohistory, the dispute over war and peace during the Southern Song and the factional quarrel over Wang Anshi's reforms in the Northern Song were related. The inability of the dynasty to achieve an economic breakthrough predetermined its later military impotency.

Zhao Kuangyin arose in 960 when a central authority, with taxation in the hands of army personnel in the field, maintained an interlink between the superstructure of the state and its infrastructure. The concentration of power in the capital of Kaifeng gradually modified this and caused the interlink to vanish. The financial resources, while enormously large, could not be adequately organized and serviced. This institutional flaw, which was fundamental, outweighed the many blunders and moments of indecision in the 319-year duration of the dynasty.

The theory of a "commercial revolution" and even a "renaissance" arising during the Song, at first advanced by a few Japanese scholars and later picked up by Chinese and Western students of Chinese history, deserves a closer look. When we say a revolution, we mean a social upheaval that goes beyond the point of no return. In the Western experience, a commercial revolution causes many state institutions, and certainly the legal system, to follow mercantile practice. The history of China's early modern era does not display a state of change that is so metamorphic.

The Song nevertheless impresses the latter-day reader with the

dazzling splendor of its visual arts and with its impressive statistics. Among the former is Zhang Zeduan's *Spring Festival on the Bian River*, a scroll about eighteen feet long. It depicts the city of Kaifeng at the height of its glory, perhaps only a few years prior to the Jin invasion in 1126. The painting presents a panorama over a period of time. On the right, there are villagers driving donkeys loaded with farm produce down a country road toward the city. The morning mist is still hanging in the treetops. On the left, evening is approaching. The pedestrians are tired. They fold their umbrellas and carry their wares, walking languidly, ready to leave the city. In between, the scroll shows cross-streets, back alleys, the waterfront, and an arched bridge near the city center. More than 500 persons, about an inch tall, are depicted. More than twenty ships and boats are in view, some of them with comfortable cabins with awnings to suggest private pleasure excursions. On the streets peddlers sell pastries and cutlery. Food is being served in various quarters, ranging from roadside booths to the private rooms on the upper level of a three-story building. All wine shops fly a flag with three vertical stripes, giving the impression of a trademark of some sort, possibly because the distillery industry was licensed by the state. The crates, sacks, and barrels on ships, mules, camels, carts, and buffalo-pulled carriages speak clearly to the large volume of commerce in the imperial capital. The signs on the stores seem to have been reproduced from the real thing. The structures of ships and buildings are authentic. The designs and mechanisms of the illustrated objects are corroborated by independent literary sources.

As an historical document the *Spring Festival* is unique. Perhaps the closest thing to it in the West is the Bayeux Tapestry. In terms of materialistic life there is little doubt that in the early twelfth century China was showing the way to the world. Zhang Zeduan's masterpiece unquestionably verifies contemporary narratives about *Xingzai*, or the so-called visiting headquarters of the Song. Since business activities on such a scale existed in a metropolis that by itself was not a center of manufacture, no doubt the prosperity of the southern capital one and a half centuries later, better situated and better endowed, was at least equal to that of Kaifeng and indeed probably surpassed it by a wide margin. The painter, with his inexhaustible patience for detail, also substantiates the journals of Marco Polo, habitually prone to hyperbole though that writer was.

But it falls to the historian to point out that this urban life was there to service a large literary bureaucracy. Unlike what happened later in modern Europe, commerce in Song China failed to establish a universal interchangeability that would have set a new tone of governance. Notable by their absence in the aforementioned painting are money and credit institutions, insurance brokerages, and offices of attorneys-at-law—none of which existed in the artist's time. Instead, he paints a residence marked as belonging to an "esquire," a physician noted for the governmental appointments that he holds, and men of distinction dressed up in the styles of the civil service are given prominent positions in the composition. This indicates that in Song times the advanced sector of the national economy could not have been a guiding force in the daily life of the citizenry. Its richness kept a sprawling administrative overhead comfortable by the standards of the day. As an appendage rather than a coordinator, it could not function as an interlink between the superstructure and the infrastructure.

Often cited in the current literature about the Song is that in the year 1021 the state income reached 150 million units, each unit being equivalent to 1,000 copper cash. The original source of this information does not disclose the nature of the statistics, but according to the contemporary conversion ratio, this sum would have had a value of 15 to 18 million ounces of gold. Restated in current value, this would be about $6 or $7 billion. Nowhere else in the world was wealth circulated in such a prodigious sum.

While there is no hard evidence that casts doubt on these numbers, there was an element of false reporting mingled with genuine price inflations. In any case, circumstances lead us to believe that by then the Song administrators were facing a mathematically unmanageable situation. The causes of confusion and dislocation were many. There were times when deposits in some warehouses were literally overflowing while shortages were being reported in other places. In Song fiscal accounts, grain by the hundred-weight, copper cash by the string, and silk fabrics by the bolt were supposed to be interchangeable. Yet the commodity prices fluctuated widely between different places and also in time. The official history of the dynasty acknowledges that the actual conversion ratio was pretty much decided by the tax collectors. "The taxpayer has no resort for appeal." When tax farmers and official collectors worked against one another, it was difficult to say whether the proceeds should follow a fixed quota or go by the adjustable amounts. Some of the fiscal officers even acted as tax collectors and disbursers. There were cases where the receivables were mixed with items that had already been checked in. The losses were rarely written off. Before double-entry bookkeeping was invented, these things also occurred in Europe, but on a smaller scale.

Under pressure from the top, overreporting was a general tendency. Some of the army units likewise inflated their strength to increase their pay and supplies, knowing beforehand that the allowances would never be handed down in full. Soon rival commanders followed suit, or else they alone would suffer reduced appropriations. In the opening years of the present millennium the paper strength of the Song standing army exceeded one-million men. Frequently, the court dispatched commissioners to various parts of the empire to check "superfluous personnel," without notable success.

The selective standard for the recruiting of the Song army was maintained until 1035; in that year a soldier's pay was still differentiated according to his height. Thereafter, induction became indiscriminate, and the early standard could no longer be maintained. The in-depth organization of the army units into a three-tier arrangement became a matter of the past, even though some of the designations lingered on in name only. Sometimes bounties were offered for recruits. Refugees, beggars, and criminals were recruited. While the payroll became increasingly more burdensome, the number of combat soldiers decreased. On the eve of the Jin invasion in 1126, Song soldiers had to be tattooed on the right arm to prevent desertion.

The condition of a nation's armed forces reflects the state of its fiscal management, which in turn should reflect as closely as possible the livelihood of the population as a whole. Not necessarily by choice, Song management violated this fundamental organizational principle. Its major problem was to diminish the distance between the peasant taxpayers, whom it governed, and the peasant soldiers, whom it recruited. Its revenue derived from "commercial sources"—basically salt, tea, incense, potash, yeast, wine, and vinegar (silk was collected as a part of the land tax and was a substitute for currency)—was dominantly represented by farm produce and scattered cottage industries. The centralized tax administration, while bringing about a mathematically unmanageable situation, did nothing to shorten this distance. Indeed it lengthened it and exacerbated the situation with bureaucratic abuses.

It is generally understood that the adversaries of the Song, because of their seminomadic background, had the unsurpassed advantage of the cattleman over the farmer. Less often mentioned is the fact that once having north China in their control, they extended universal conscription to the Chinese population as well. The Liao attached a large number of Chinese households to every tribe. Each battle formation, including the elite corps of the imperial command, was assigned a Chinese manpower quota along with that contributed by the Qidan. The Jin sent the Jürched hereditary military families to live with the indigenous Chinese. Some fifty to 300 native households were grouped into a *"mouke"*; eight to ten *mouke* formed a *"mengan."* (In many cases, however, the numbers varied.) In principle, the chiefs of these units, holding offices by inheritance, were restricted to the Jürched. Thus taxation and conscription, under the close scrutiny of the warrior group, achieved a degree of organizational effectiveness unmatched by the cumbersome management of the Song. The flexibility at mobilization provided the northern states an extra advantage over their southern rival, which was compelled to maintain a large standing army. These advantages are an additional reason for the military supremacy of the alien dynasties.

The control of horse-breeding grounds also had a decisive influence on the relative strength of the contestants. The dynastic history of the Liao admits that in its trading with Song China, horses and sheep were on the embargo list. It further acknowledges that in its showdown with the Jin, the loss of its supply of horses had been fatal. In Zhang Zeduan's *Spring Festival on the Bian River*, the use of oxen and water buffalo in place of horses deserves special attention in the context of the embargo. Horses could be bred in central China, but owing to the particular kind of farm economy there, breeding would have been prohibitively expensive. Moreover, the horses raised in areas of intensive farming were usually inferior.

Thus, as we move into the history of the early modern era, instead of "key economic areas" (p. 67), we now become aware that China is divided more by latitude into several major sections. There is a belt of pastoral land in the far north. Contiguous with it in north China is an agricultural zone noted for its relatively simplicity. In contrast, the south, the region of rice and tea and water transport, was an area of complexities even before the industrial era. These characteristics can be readily observed by the tourist. In the context of this chapter, those geographical divisions accounted for the prolonged struggle between the agricultural Chinese and the seminomadic Mongolian and Tungusic peoples. Yet a long-term observation in the cosmopolitan spirit may point out that the contest for the middle belt of land has, over the centuries, caused the several national minorities to blend with the Han Chinese. Evidently, as an anthropological designation the latter is becoming increasingly more cultural than physical in connotation.

As for the Song, the retreat to the south gave it at least some temporary respite. The land of lakes, rivers, and canals made the northern warriors less effective. The Jin invasion of the south of the Yangtze in 1129–30 was nearly a disaster, with the Song forces able to block its retreat with war junks. The freedom of action by the military commanders during the confusion also facilitated their operations. Yue Fei's command, for instance, was largely comprised of peasant rebels, surrendered bandits, and conscripted Jürched natives. He could select his personnel and enlarge his battle formation.

But the political centralization of the Song, worked toward by Emperor Zhao Gou and Prime Minister Qin Gui, eliminated the tendency of military autonomy. After losing Kaifeng, the southern court was pressed by the problem of army logistics. If by this time Hangzhou had any commercial institution of substance, the exile government would undoubtedly have harnessed it to service the army. In actuality, the emergency was met with tax increases and with improvisation. These devices surfaced in short order. *Jinzhi qian* can be rendered into English as "superintendent's money." *Yuezhuang qian*, likewise, can be called the "monthly forced savings." *Banzhang qian* is a "special general account." "Superintendent" is the Song designation for the transportation intendant (p. 112), a regional fiscal officer. There was no great difference between and among these accounts. In practice, a universal surcharge was added to every item of revenue, and quotas were assigned to regional offices. Administrative income, including fines, charges for legal services, and license fees, increased. When those were not enough, paper currency was used to make up the differences.

The last item, a novelty to Marco Polo, had come into use in Tang times. Called "flying money," it was originally authorized by the government as a draft that permitted merchants who sold commodities in Sichuan to receive payments elsewhere, thus to save them the burden of carrying the native currency of iron cash. During the Northern Song, the negotiable notes were printed in quantity for the first time in 1024. After extensive circulation, the paper currency was printed intermittently. Like government bonds, each issue had a maturity date, usually three years, at which time it was retired. The Southern Song pledged the proceeds from its inland customs houses against its issue. In 1247, money was issued for permanent circulation, not to be redeemed. Without adequate security in its backing, its value dropped precipitously. The inflationary influence distressed the public and made the government's own position more difficult. It must be considered as a contributing factor to the dynasty's decline and fall.

Yet, once the alien dynasties had consolidated their hold over north China, they imitated the centralized finance of the Song and practiced monetary management after a fashion; in doing so they lost their agrarian simplicity and ran into technical difficulties. It was worst for the Jin which, while a bitter enemy, was at heart an admirer of the Song. From astronomy and calendar-making to court music, it copied many Song institutions. When it printed paper money, it established an inflation record that still stands in Chinese history: 60 million-fold.

The Song dynasty was a period of technological innovation. Movable type in printing was first mentioned in the records in 1086. The astronomical clock at Kaifeng was installed between 1088 and 1092. The use of the compass for navigation was mentioned in a book with a preface dated 1119. Song oceangoing junks carried four to six masts and had as many as twelve sails and four decks. As for armaments, a flame-thrower operated by a pump came into existence before 1044. The first paddle-wheel warships with rams were commissioned by a brigand leader by the name of Yang Tai, who used them against Yue Fei in 1135. General Yue in turn used rotten wood and wild grass to jam the vessels' mechanisms. Catapults launching explosive grenades appeared in 1161.

The inability of the Song national economy to lead the way to social reconstruction cannot be discounted as a major reason for the lack of systematic follow-up. In the experience of Western Europe, such a breakthrough came at a moment when the influence of commerce outweighed that of agricultural production by some margin. China in the early modern era did not come close to this jumping-off point. Commerce, even though large in volume by world standards, was spread thin over the mass of peasants. Military operations, moving inward from the peripheral areas, became a contest for control over agricultural land and agrarian populations, which put a premium on quantity over quality, on homogeneity over diversity, on endurance over ephemeral flashes of brilliance. These conditions worked against further efforts to widen the uses of inventions.

The large number of small self-cultivators continued to keep China bound to its traditional character—a fact that was clearly revealed during the debate over Wang Anshi's reforms. The small-scale production kept farm wages at a very low level. The incessant warfare, which created large numbers of displaced persons, some of whom became indentured laborers, did not help the situation. The abundant cheap labor is even evident on Zhang Zeduan's painted scroll. For this reason, while the people of the Song showed ingenuity at solving technological problems, they as a rule remained uninterested in seeking labor-saving devices.

Instead, their intellectual energy was channeled in a different direction. Philosophical rendition became the most prominent specialty of

Song scholars. They established a general trend of building Confucian ethics on Taoist and Buddhist metaphysics, an approach that came to be known as neo-Confucianism. Breaking away from the Han aesthetic approach, the Song learning emphasized self-cultivation. They saw the universe as an organic being and man's inclination to do good as a manifestation of Natural Law. This indulgence in discourse on disposition and destiny produced a special kind of socio-psychology. It enabled these thinkers to exercise spiritual self-assertion yet still remain comfortable with the traditional communal living. Of course, the state affairs of the Song had an influence on the formation of this particular type of thought. While all the leading thinkers had, within their intellectual genealogy, drawn inspiration from a mystic by the name of Chen Tuan, they themselves were involved in contemporary politics. During the Northern Song, Cheng Hao, Cheng Yi, and Zhou Dunyi were either actively opposed to Wang Anshi or associated with the anti-reformers. During the Southern Song, while Zhu Xi was at first held back because he spoke against the peace settlement with the Jürched, he later reversed himself and antagonized Han Tuozhou, the war leader. Lu Xiangsan was censured for an outspoken memorial to the throne. Thus without exception they all suffered persecution of some kind for their political opinions. As a result, their emphasis on the individual's moral strength could not help but reveal the noble intention of the "Opposition," who silently supported a cause of some kind without being openly politically active.

Comparative studies of these thinkers, already produced rather extensively by Chinese, Japanese, and Western scholars, belong to the arena of philosophy. The historian cannot deny that these scholars endowed later-generation Chinese with Confucian rectitude and vigor. As broad in scope and varied in approach as they strove to be, however, they were trapped in a world dominated by a large and undifferentiated peasantry governed by a large and undifferentiated bureaucracy. With this restriction their devotion to quietness and veneration differed from the free expression of the Renaissance men, whose creative energy was synchronized with the rise of commercialism. Dante left a household of the decaying nobility to enter plutocratic circles. Chaucer was employed as a comptroller of customs in London. From Michelangelo to Rembrandt, the patronage ranged from the papacy to burgomasters. In contrast, all five Chinese philosophers named above, along with their numerous friends and associates, wore mandarins' robes. They were teachers of the bureaucrats.

Yet, the omission of a commercial revolution and a Renaissance from China's early modern history was more geographically and technically than ideologically determined. The 319-year struggle of the Song established that China's south, with its richness but inability to attain the needed organizational integrity, was no match for a northern state structured with simplicity and ruggedness.

The later final assault on the Song by the Mongols was based on a strategy of a grand detour. First a southward drive cutting across Sichuan went as deep as Vietnam. The second phase of penetration took the twin city of Xiangyang-Fancheng as an intermediate objective, the siege of which lasted more than four years, from the autumn of 1268 to early 1273. Once that fortress was taken, the forces of the Yuan, as the new dynasty of Khubilai Khan was called, followed the Yangtze downstream with little resistance.

The last important prime minister of the Southern Song was Jia Sidao, a man of cool composure and, obviously, abundant ingenuity. Too feeble to wage war yet with too little on hand to bargain for peace, he took a business-as-usual approach to calm the public. In the last years of the dynasty the supply problem worsened, as both currency inflation and tax increases reached their limits. Jia's last resort was the government purchase of private land, one-third the amount in excess of 200 or 300 *mu* within each household. The order was put into effect in six prefectures in the Yangtze Delta, where the concentration of ownership was exceptional for the empire, and where the Hangzhou government still maintained effective control. The purchase, paid with miscellaneous notes along with some cash, was perhaps little more than commandeering. Despite public agitation, the scheme, with the emphatic backing of the throne, was carried out. It seems that the income from the land shored up the dynasty for at least a dozen years. Jia pleaded for peace from Khubilai without success. In 1275 he went to the Yangtze River front to direct the fighting himself. When the situation became untenable he was cashiered and soon afterward murdered. The next year the Mongols entered Hangzhou. Three more years elapsed before the Yuan naval forces annihilated a Song fleet in the South China Sea, drowning the boy emperor of the Chinese throne. Thus the year 1279 marks the extinction of the dynasty that started in 960 with an elected emperor near Kaifeng.

Contemporaries, unaware of the technical complexities of the situation, spared no condemnation of Jia Sidao, as if his treachery and mismanagement were responsible for the dynasty's downfall. Indeed, Jia made at least one serious mistake. In 1259, when Khubilai's brother the Great Khan Möngke died, the Mongol forces suspended the expeditions against the Song. With everything at stake, Khubilai himself returned to the north for the election of the next Khan. At this point Jia Sidao dressed up the suspension of action as a Song victory. Traditional historians seized this error and many other purported misdeeds of the prime minister to make him appear as a man of greater wickedness. Among the numerous malfeasances was the fact that decades before, as a fun-loving young man, Jia had organized many evening parties at West Lake. Once, watching from the palace, the emperor noted the lights shining brightly on the water and remarked that Jia Sidao must be having a good time. Indeed he must have been, at least until he was elevated to the highest office of China's richest dynasty.

13

The Mongolian
Interlude

Marco Polo was a tourist *par excellence* before tourism had even appeared as an organized institution. He went to China without the conventional desire to trade goods for profit or the religious zeal to save
souls. His wide-eyed curiosity enabled him to furnish pre-Renaissance
Europe with a series of most unusual observations which seemed, by
the standard of those days, to have touched all the far corners of the
world. Credulous or exaggerated, his accounts speak with the experience of an eyewitness that could arouse the interest of other potential
visitors. As he repeatedly and tantalizingly put it, "you have to see it to
believe it"; he was inviting the listener to stretch his imagination to
appreciate all the uniqueness and variety inherent in distant lands.

The towering figure in his narratives is undoubtedly Khubilai, grandson of Genghis Khan. The young Marco was in Khubilai's court when
the Yuan forces closed in to wipe out the last contingent of the Song
navy in 1279, which made the Great Khan the unchallenged ruler of all
China, a position so far not attained by any alien prince. The emperor
and the visitor from Venice treated each other with respect and affection. Marco ran errands for the great master, held high office in his
government, and wrote interesting reports for him.

For Marco Polo, China was Cathay, the southern Chinese the *Manzi*,
and Beijing Cambaluc or, as the Mongols called it, "Khan-baliq," or the
city of the Khan. Hangzhou, which the Song Chinese called *Xingzai* (p.
128), was slightly modified to *Quinsay*.

Paper currency was a great novelty to the European visitor. Asbestos was a substance taken from mountains, crushed, divided "as it were

137

into fibers of wool," and "made into napkins." Coal was "a kind of stone that burns like wood"; it was also dug out of the mountains and then lighted to give out great heat.

From Marco Polo's account we have gained an extra angle to observe Khubilai Khan the man. He was apparently a leader of great intelligence with an alert mind. Obsessed with conquering, he nevertheless maintained a genuine desire to see the basic wants of all men and women under his reign satisfied. He regarded religion more or less as a utility: faith could provide the cohesive power to consolidate his empire or the subversive influence to wreck it. Consequently, his tolerance toward different creeds varied in accordance with the ways in which they fit his political schemes. Marco spoke fondly of Khubilai Khan's benevolent despotism; but he never held back on criticism. At one point he noted: "There were many disloyal and seditious persons, at all times disposed to break out in rebellion." At another he observed: "All the Cathaians detested the Great Khan's rule because he set over them governors who were Tartars, or still more frequently Saracens, and these they could not endure, for they were treated by them just like slaves. You see the Great Khan had not succeeded to the dominion of Cathay by hereditary right, but held it by conquest; and thus, having no confidence in the natives, he put all authority into the hands of Tartars, Saracens, or Christians, who were attached to his household and devoted to his service, and were foreigners in Cathay."

The seizing of a dominant role in world affairs by the Mongols is unique in history. With a population of something like a million, they stretched their conquest over the span of the Eurasian continent with not much room to spare at either end. Clannish cohesion and the rugged character of cattlemen provided their fighting forces with excellent soldiery. Cavalry tactics for large battle formations had been worked out by the Qidan Liao and the Jürched Jin, but Genghis Khan and his followers added new elements to the war machine that made it irresistible. The troops moved with lightning speed and with discipline. War plans were drawn up ahead of time and adhered to in every detail. Individual soldiers could live on the milk of their mares for days or even weeks. Psychological warfare was broadly employed, from rumors disseminated by refugees who ran ahead of the advancing columns to atrocities and the wanton destruction inflicted on the cities that dared resist the invaders. Military and technical talent among the subjected was utilized to the utmost. A Chinese general saw action in the extermination campaign against the caliphate of Baghdad in 1258, and a thousand Chinese engineers were enlisted to man the catapults that launched flammable substances. A decade later, at the siege of the twin city of Xiangyang-Fancheng (p. 135), Khubilai sent for two Persian engineers who designed heavy catapults that shot stones weighing up to 150 pounds.

Genghis Khan died in 1227 while attacking Xixia, and his empire was divided into four parts. The Golden Horde controlled most of Russia, including Moscow and Kiev. The khannate of Persia embraced the territory from the frontier of Afganistan to Iraq. Another khannate incorporated the inner Asian frontier of today's Soviet Union bordering the People's Republic of China. But the Great Khan had the power to oversee the above three. His domain stretched from the Mongolian desert to the South China Sea, a vision that was brought to realization more than fifty years later after the death of the greatest conqueror on earth.

Khubilai was not elected Great Khan as called for by the Genghis law. Instead, he assumed the title himself in 1260 and in so doing had to overpower his own brother Arik-buga. After that, he had to deal with the federation of Mongols arising in Central Asia, headed by his cousin Kaidu, who insisted on living up to the standard of Genghis. The struggle persisted until Khubilai's death in 1294. In this way, curiously, he actually shielded China from the nomadic rampage, even though he himself also played the role of the conqueror of Song China. Under the circumstances, his suzerainty over the other three khannates was less than nominal, and he made no special effort to assert that right. His interest was in China, from which he intended to dominate the rest of East Asia. In 1271 on the advice of his Chinese counsellors he proclaimed the Yuan dynasty. But as already noted, it was not until eight years later, in 1279, at the final elimination of the Song that he was confirmed as Son of Heaven with no more contention.

To some students of history, Khubilai is remembered as the unsuccessful invader of Japan; from the disasters of his campaigns the *kamikaze* legend emerged. There were actually two invasions. The 1274 attempt, launched before the collapse of the Southern Song, used Korea as a springboard. The combined fleet involved some 800 large and small vessels, and about 25,000 Mongols and Koreans participated. After seizing several outlying islands, the invading force landed at Hakata Bay on Kyushu on November 20. The Japanese had already dug in, awaiting the arrival of reinforcements. The fighting was indecisive. That night a typhoon swept over the invading fleet. When the Mongols decided to withdraw, there was total chaos, and subsequently, according to Korean sources, no less than 13,000 men were drowned during the unplanned disengagement.

The 1281 attempt, after the fall of the Song, enlarged the scale of the

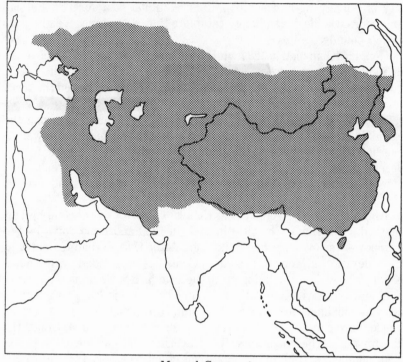

Mongol Conquest

operation by several times and involved two invasion forces. Some 40,000 Mongol and Korean soldiers on 900 ships took the northern route as in the first campaign, to be reinforced by 100,000 Chinese under Fan Wenhu, the Song general who had surrendered to the Yuan only several years earlier. The southern armada involved 3,500 ships of assorted sizes, sailing from Zhoushan Island off Zhejiang. This overseas invasion force was the largest in world history until recent times.

Again, the outlying islands were seized with ease. Again, the invaders landed at Hakata Bay, this time, however, to discover that during the intervening years the Japanese had constructed a continuous series of stone walls on the beaches, which effectively impeded the Mongol cavalry. The invasion bogged down. Fighting continued throughout June and July, with no prospect of a breakthrough in sight. In August another typhoon descended on the invading fleet, and ships capsized by the hundreds. The admirals and generals, including Fan Wenhu, escaped with the capital ships. An unspecified number of men lost their lives at sea. Others, stranded on the beaches, were rounded up by the Japanese and executed en masse. Today a "Mongolian burial ground" on one of the beaches bears witness to the punishment of the *kamikaze*,

Mongolian invasion as seen by the Japanese

or the divine wind. The Koreans counted their losses at slightly over half the men who participated. There is not even an estimate of the Mongol and Chinese losses. Japanese studies emphasize the ineffectiveness of the Mongol light cavalry in such campaigns as well as the low morale and poor equipment of the Chinese forces.

The Japanese infuriated Khubilai twice by beheading his envoys and humiliated him twice by turning his invasions into ignominious routs. It seems that in order to demonstrate his will to win his place as the Son of Heaven in Cambaluc he had no alternative but to mount yet another invasion. Accordingly, preparations for a third attempt went forward. Ship construction was given a high priority on the east China coast, on the Pohai gulf, in Manchuria, and on the Korean peninsula. Commercial vessels were commandeered. Supplies were stored. Experienced sailors were recruited. Combat troops were assigned, surrendered pirates commissioned, and sentences of prisoners commuted so they could take part in the pending expedition. In late 1285, one million hundredweight of grain was dispatched from the lower Yangtze to Korea, giving the impression that an invasion was imminent. But most unexpectedly, in early 1286 an imperial edict cancelled all preparations. An instruction from Khubilai himself explained that the Japanese were no more than "island barbarians in the remote region"; it was therefore not justified to "overburden the imperial subjects with another expedition." Although the announcement made sense, it admitted past errors and exposed present weaknesses. Khubilai could not have made the acknowledgment without moral courage.

In the wider frame of history the Mongolian setbacks demonstrate that prior to the rise of modern technology, it was most difficult for a land power to become a sea power. The costs of maintaining a fleet and sustaining its losses were prohibitively high, the more so when the seafaring adventure worked against the normal pursuits of the populace at large. In those years when preparations for the third attempt against Japan were being made, Khubilai was already having difficulties pacifying Vietnam and chastising Burma. In early 1293 he was to conduct an overseas offensive against Java to no fruitful end. The invading party landed, but was pushed back with heavy losses. This sequence of events indicates that toward the end of Khubilai's reign, the greatest land power in world history had reached its limits of expansion.

The Chinese used to say that the Mongols, after conquering the world on horseback, intended also to rule it on horseback. There is a certain truth in this criticism. It would be misleading, however, to assume that the descendants of Genghis Khan ignored the problem of administration altogether. Khubilai, for instance, spent a good portion of his life pondering how to manage his sprawling empire. He was not only restricted by the forces of geopolitics but also handicapped by his times. The remnants of previous dynasties could not be assembled as the congenial components of a new order. Yet the problems at hand gave him no respite to work out any system of enduring influence.

Despite the poor racial relationship described by Marco Polo, Khubilai was tutored to respect Chinese culture. Unlike his grandfather Genghis, who was known to have been influenced by a Qidan versed in Chinese affairs by the name of Yelüchucai, Khubilai was surrounded by a large number of Chinese advisers, many of whom served him for decades. Yao Shu and Liu Binzhen were with him when he was still a young prince; later they accompanied him on the southern expedition to Yunnan. He considered Xu Heng to be a trusted confidant. Shi Tianze, after contributing substantially to his military campaigns, became a vice premier. Even Fan Wenhu, the surrendered Song general, was retained by Khubilai to take charge of the Privy Council many years after the ill-fated second invasion of Japan.

But it is also true that in his later years Khubilai Khan drifted away from his Chinese counsel. Several reasons help account for this. After the fall of the Song, Chinese loyalists would not give up. Now and then rumors were circulated that a restoration movement was in the offing. The Mongols were bickering among themselves. The khan had to explain to his close followers that he was making vital decisions on his own and was at no time under undue Chinese influence. Beyond all this, one must realize that the Mongol conquest was indeed a conquest. Behind it there was a fundamental geopolitical problem that defied military solution.

The Mongols, few in number and culturally inferior to their Chinese subjects, had no chance to maintain their identity unless they retained their martial spirit and organization; their rough riding was inseparable from their unmannerly living habits. They remained an elite corps in the Yuan army and were expected to deliver the main thrust in most field campaigns. At the same time, a legion of non-Mongol tribesmen was organized under the name *tanmachi* to provide second-echelon striking power. North China, which by then had been under Qidan and Jürched control for several centuries, featured a mixed population. Although unable to withstand the Mongol cavalry charges, they proved sturdier than the Song southerners. Under the Yuan they were drafted into military service and saw action in the conquest of the Song. Contemporaries referred to them as the "Han" people, although they included Koreans and many other ethnic groups. Finally, after the fall of the Song, the capitulating divisions of the relinquished empire were not disbanded but maintained as separate units. The Yuan dynasty further decreed that all households under military registration were to remain so permanently. The ethnic components of the army therefore sanctioned something like a caste system, and this affected the social status of the several segments of the population as well.

There is no evidence that Khubilai was inherently a racist. He was striving to provide a universal rule, as cosmopolitan as possible without prejudicing the position of his outnumbered countrymen. Yet, throughout his reign no attempt was made to create a Chinese-style literary bureaucracy. He never held a civil service examination. In his school system the Mongolian script took a position at least equal to that of Chinese characters. As a rule, top officials in charge of all governmental departments were Mongols.

The sovereign harbored strong misgivings toward Confucian scholars who indulged in abstract polemics. His instructions that officials must familiarize themselves with clerical work underlined his emphasis on paying attention to technical details, a demand that he made on himself as well. This new direction not only characterized Khubilai's reign but was also carried forward by his successors. At a glance, this seems to be a major improvement from the practice of previous dynasties. Also, it was fitting that it was the Mongols that made the change, since their armed conquest had amounted to an undisguised show of force with little attempt at moral justification.

But in doing so they failed to take into account the hidden rationale of the Confucian type of government. Indeed, bureaucratic management of the Chinese tradition was cumbersome and wasteful, and sometimes perfunctory and hypocritical. But the arrangement provided low-cost government to the millions of poor peasants who were taxpayers. The lecture on self-restraint and mutual deference silenced many contentions beforehand. A social order based on kinship relations, when sanctioned by law, omitted much jurisprudential sophistication involving personal rights and property rights. Empowering the clans to discipline their own members, the government offices lightened their own work load. The bureaucrats, philosophically and poetically eloquent, were assured that precision was not expected of them and that the administering of justice was only a relative matter. Since they did not take regional particularities into serious consideration, they could always accept the lowest common denominator as the national standard. In this way practically all the posts within the civil service were interchangeable and the empire could be managed abstractly and doctrinally. It was the general tone of government that counted, not particular issues. The inadequacy of such a system was there for all to see. Yet, a thorough departure from it, running up against the formidableness of China's size and internal complexity atop the current level of technical support, proved less practicable than it first seemed.

China under Mongol rule made further technological advances. Shipbuilding reached its zenith, only to decline in the late fifteenth century under the Ming. Many stone bridges, especially south of the Yangtze, bear inscriptions testifying that they were constructed during the Yuan period. Yuan hydraulic engineers performed the feat of executing the modern Grand Canal, which, connecting Beijing with the region south of the Yangtze, was an artificial waterway running over a summit. Both Marco Polo and Japanese observers were impressed by the fire bombs and projectile grenades used by the Yuan army. Guo Shoujing, astronomer, mathematician, and hydraulic engineer, whom many writers still consider to be the world's foremost scientist of his day, served Khubilai. The alien dynastic founder also authorized the compilation of the *Basic Elements of Agriculture and Sericulture*, which was to appear in many editions. The 1315 edition alone was printed in 10,000 copies. Most of the farm implements in that book look identical to those observed in China during the early part of the present century, over 600 years later. It may be added here that it was during the Yuan that two important plants—cotton and sorghum—were introduced to China, to affect the clothing and nutrition of the country's millions for ages to come.

But Khubilai and his followers failed to create a social atmosphere to sustain this progress. Unwilling to surrender to Confucian supremacy, which from his point of view would inevitably lead to Chinese supremacy, Khubilai Khan was searching for a common spiritual denominator for the people under his rule, who varied not only in racial stock but also in life-style. Before he became the overlord of the whole of China, he asked Niccolo and Maffeo Polo, Marco's father and uncle, to bring him "some hundred wise men learned in the law of Christ," even though it is still uncertain whether a universal conversion to Christianity had entered into his thinking or not. His embracing of Lamaism, on the other hand, showed a clear political motive. In addition to commissioning the Tibetan monk Phags-pa to be "Imperial Mentor," Khubilai also ordered that the surviving boy Song emperor, who had surrendered with his mother at Hangzhou, be taken to Tibet to study Lamaism. Although the result is not mentioned in the records, this episode nevertheless excites the curiosity of the historian. What an ingenious maneuver it would have been if the youthful ruler, who after the dethronement still commanded the adoration of Song loyalists, could have been made a spiritual leader, to serve the new Son of Heaven from the other land, and to confirm the latter's authority!

As it was, Phags-pa and Lamaism had no more influence on the Chinese than Confucianism had on the Mongols and Tibetans. The casual observer would think that the doctrine of *karma* entwined with reincarnation, which transformed spiritual worth into secular power, together with the rituals of shamanism, should have had a strong appeal to the illiterate Chinese peasants. But to serve a political purpose it implied theocracy, which would have to do away with the middle-echelon intellectuals altogether. History proves that such a system functions better in a primitive economy, in which both the division of labor and social mobility are severely restrained. These were not the conditions of China in the thirteenth century.

To neutralize and dilute the overwhelming Chinese influence, Khubilai sought talent from many quarters. Persians, Uighurs, Kipchaks, and many others—lumped together by the contemporaries as the *Semu*, which means "various kinds"—served in his government. On balance, however, their influence was not great. Several of them, being Khubilai's favorites, met violent deaths. When Prime Minister Ahmed Benaketi was assassinated by a Chinese army officer, Khubilai had the assassin executed. Yet later, to placate the public, he had to reverse himself by ordering the opening of Ahmed's coffin and the desecration of his corpse. Sangha, vice premier in charge of finance, was put to death by imperial order under strong public pressure. From the historian's point of view the accusations of personal evil-doing against the two ministers of foreign birth should never be allowed to confuse the main issue behind them: There was an intense antagonism toward the two men and their fiscal policies, which aimed at opening up tax sources for a greater state revenue. The alleged abuses by the field representatives of the accused could very well be true, given the untenable situation created by the multi-nationality power structure. Yet circumstances speak loudly to the possibility that the tragic fate of these two men could have been caused in part by a lack of understanding. We ourselves need to study many similar cases to understand that bureaucratic management of the Chinese type necessitated tolerance toward inefficiency at least to a point in order to accommodate the benevolent tone of governance. Because of the ineffective control in those days, if the platform of magnanimity was abandoned on the top, the excessiveness of the functionaries at the lower level could be appalling. Neither Sangha nor Ahmed seemed to have grasped the subtlety. Very likely in their effort to achieve a higher level of efficiency, they had gone beyond the tolerable limit. Their foes could then turn their technical errors into moral offenses to claim their lives.

After a series of failures, public finances under the Yuan dynasty were never settled. Taxation in north China differed from that in south China. In the north the concept of a tax package (p. 88) took hold; it accepted the household as the tax unit, and insofar as possible, uniform payments were collected from all households, even though in practice there were variations. This was a legacy of the Qidan and the Jürched, who needed the simplified taxation system to accompany their military conscription. In the south, however, the Yuan assessed land taxes on acreage, very much in line with the practice of the Song. Also, Khubilai Khan and his predecessors had awarded a number of households whose tax payments were supposed to form annual stipends for the grantees to more than 150 princes, princesses, and army officers and civil servants who had achieved outstanding merit. The titleholders posted their agents with the local government, yet they were not supposed to take over the land as manors or the population as serfs. Ranging from more than 100,000 households to only a few, those estates sowed a great deal of confusion.

On paper, tax assessments during the Mongol period remained lower than they were under previous dynasties, especially for the southern provinces. In his campaign to annihilate the Song, Khubilai declared the abolition of all the surtaxes imposed by the contested dynasty, only the basic assessment remaining in force. In practice, he could not fulfill the intent of this act. His oversea expeditions, for instance, were financed with off-schedule impositions of many kinds. But when those levies were discontinued and the effort to widen revenue got nowhere, the statutory level of collection remained low. Khubilai himself has been showered with compliments by historians for his kindness. In reality, his failure to either institutionalize a system or make sweeping changes handicapped his successors. When they were unable to meet expenditures with regular income, they were compelled to print more paper currency—the easiest way to live off the future.

In macrohistory, the Mongol period appears as a transition between

China's Second Empire and Third Empire. The
Yuan carried on the mood of growth and expansion established by the Tang and Song, and it
continued the technological advances. Yet it supplied no additional fuel to sustain the drive. When
it achieved no breakthrough in governmental finance and, statutorily, set taxation at a lower level, and with its "agricultural first" policy, it virtually ushered in the general trend of retrenchment
of the Third Empire, which only needed to assert
its introverted and noncompetitive position to
complete the change, which indeed is what happened in the Ming dynasty.

The Third Empire

Yuan — 1271 / 1368

Ming

1644

Qing

1911

Dynastic founders in Chinese history were
law-givers. They alone in situations of fluidity
and instability could apply military power to enforce their will and make adjustments on a grand
scale. This general observation appeared to be more valid during the
Mongol period, the dynasty's conquest being so overwhelmingly decisive. In many ways, the history of the Yuan dynasty is dominated by
Khubilai's life. His descendants could apply few modifications to his
works, which were continued. Yet, in retrospect, we can see how much
of all this had been predetermined by geography. Nature had offered
the hard-riding Mongols an opportunity to subdue the millions of agricultural Chinese working on small plots. But it was beyond their skills
and power to organize the conquered populace for mutual progress
without sacrificing the conquerors' own cultural identity.

Khubilai was troubled by gout in his later years. He never felt
comfortable in the intense heat of the south. Before his enthronement,
his annual visits to Shangdu (Coleridge's Xanadu), or the "upper capital," from the late spring to the early autumn were interrupted only on a
few occasions. This seasonal schedule was also used by all succeeding
Yuan emperors. Their prolonged absence from the throne hall of imperial China didn't serve to promote confidence in that particular type of
monarchy where personal touches meant so much. Succession caused
an additional problem. When Khubilai died in early 1294, he was succeeded by his grandson Timur, who reigned for thirteen years. Thereafter there were eight emperors in twenty-six years. As if the descendants were obligated to imitate the proceedings of their eminent
ancestor, few of the successions did not involve coups and plots, giving
the impression of great instability. They were followed by the last
emperor, whose reign lasted for thirty-five years before he himself was
expelled from China.

Perhaps the only major decision of Khubilai's successors independent of the dynastic founder's empire-building was the resumption of the civil service examination in 1315. Thenceforth thirteen metropolitan examinations were held. Yet, the purpose was not to create a literary bureaucracy of the Chinese type. During the examinations the Mongols and the Semu were treated as separate classes, and the successful candidates, most of them Chinese, were given minor positions within insignificant offices. Many frustrated literati, finding no adequate outlet for their talent, became playwrights. Eventually Yuan drama, mixing literary expression with colloquialism and stage jargon, opened up a new vista in Chinese literature and ushered in a golden age of Chinese theater.

With the Mongol period the need for macrohistory is even more compellingly evident. There are cases in human history where long-term rationality cannot be assessed from brief visions. The judgment of individuals may require a view of interlinks that run beyond their lifespans. Perhaps that is why Marco Polo wrote about Khubilai with some ambivalence. It may also explain why Zhu Yuanzhang, who terminated the Mongol dynasty in 1368 and spoke strongly of Chinese nationalism, continued to pay public homage to Khubilai's name tablets, as well as to those of the founders of the Han, Tang, and Song dynasties.

14

The Ming: An Introverted and Noncompetitive State

Of all the dynastic founders in Chinese history, Zhu Yuanzhang came from the humblest origins. When drought and famine afflicted his home locale in 1344, his parents and an elder brother perished within weeks. Unable to afford coffins, Zhu and another brother buried them hastily with their own hands. Thereafter they went their separate ways. The future emperor of the Ming dynasty, then not yet sixteen, turned up as a novice in a Buddhist monastery performing menial work. Not long after, he became a mendicant, begging for food while wandering around the Huai River region. In this way he got in touch with the peasant rebels and secret societies that were to be instruments of dynastic reconstruction. In the last decades of the Mongol period, famine relief was not properly undertaken, public works gathered large numbers of laborers who were poorly treated, and Yuan generals were bickering among themselves—ripe conditions for insurgents to entertain imperial aspirations. Self-taught and a skillful manipulator, Zhu Yuanzhang was able to use his organizational talents to pick up the pieces. With a combination of hard fighting and clever finesse, it took him a dozen years to consolidate the territories of a host of self-made men like himself. Once that was done, his position became unchallengeable. In 1368 his holdings in the Yangtze River region were secure enough for him to proclaim the Ming dynasty. The Mongols were dislodged with surprising ease. At the fall of the Yuan dynasty the last Mongol emperor also did something unusual: He escaped death and ritualistic surrender by fleeing to the steppes where his ancestors had come from. Zhu Yuanzhang situated his imperial capital at Nanjing. Previously called Jiankang or Jinling (p. 64), this is an "unlucky" national capital. No dynasty that took it as the seat of government managed to remain in existence for long—a jinx that in modern times was not broken by the Taiping rebels or by Chiang Kai-shek. Sun Yat-sen, however, called Nanjing "a place where a high mountain and deep water converge next to a large plain"; it had the appeal of majesty to gratify his vision. Fittingly, today the magnificent granite and marble mausoleum that encases Dr. Sun's remains, visible at a great distance, is located on Purple Mountain, which overlooks Nanjing.

Having risen from the gutter to become the ruler of fourteenth century China, Zhu Yuanzhang too had to do things on a grand scale. His imperial capital was surrounded by a city wall close to thirty miles long. Today the massive brick structure is still there, making Nanjing the largest walled city in the modern world. Airplanes land and take off within its bounds. Located inside the wall's circumference are ponds, bamboo groves, and acres of vegetable gardens. Nanjing needs no suburbs. The city itself is suburban.

In a manner no less dramatic, Zhu Yuanzhang also left a permanent imprint on Chinese political, economic, and social history whose effect can still be felt nowadays. Centralization of power was the most striking feature of his style of management. If this system were ever activated in the United States, Washington would not only be empowered to appoint the governors of California and Texas, but also the mayor of Sacramento and the sheriff of Austin, and beyond that to regulate their salaries and scrutinize their office budgets. We cannot think of another case in world history where such tight control over such a large country was ever exercised by the center.

This stringency derived its justification from the failures of previous dynasties. When the Mongols were expelled, the alien dynasty was of course discredited. The laxity of the Song was also under criticism. It was argued that China would never have been subjected to the domination of foreign minorities if discipline and solidarity had been maintained by the bureaucracy and by the population. Despotism always has its way of finding moral sanction. In the case of the Ming, Zhu Yuanzhang was his own spokesman. Several pamphlets authored by the dynastic founder spoke of his own cruel and tyrannical rule as his solemn duty under heaven.

Certainly, it required more than just discipline to realize his type of centralization. In fact, a reign of terror accomplished most of it. During the thirty years when he was emperor, Zhu Yuanzhang is known to have conducted four waves of political purges, running from 1376 to

1393. The victims were high officials, ranking army officers, ordinary bureaucrats, government students, local landowners, and clan leaders. The proceedings established a pattern. At first the principal offenders were charged with treason and corruption. Justified or not, the investigation extended the scope of the case until accomplices and suspects were rounded up en masse. Affiliation with the accused was proof of guilt. A general moral charge could send the defendant to death. Specialists have estimated that no less than 100,000 persons lost their lives in these trials, and when the dust settled, the emperor also found sufficient charges to send the presiding judges to their deaths.

State and society after the bloody inquisition appeared unusual even by Chinese standards. The position of the prime minister was abolished, not to be revived for the duration of the dynasty. The emperor himself dealt with a large number of officials on matters both significant and trivial. The censorial branch of the government was empowered to speak up to challenge policy inadequacies and bureaucratic irregularities and, as circumstances warranted, to remonstrate against the emperor himself. For the censors, even deliberate silence was a serious offense, for it implied neglect of duty. Yet, neither were they granted immunity in carrying out their functions. Throughout the Ming period, many censors suffered the vengeance of the throne and died ignominiously for their outspokenness.

Similar to the Bismarckian concept that Germany toward the end of the nineteenth century was "saturated," Zhu Yuanzhang was determined to hold the center core of China intact without involving it in external liabilities. He left a permanent injunction to his descendants against sending expeditions to fifteen states, starting the list with Korea, Japan, and Vietnam and ending it with several South Seas countries. When Japanese pirates infested the China coast, he moved some of the local population inland. Imperial subjects of the Ming were not allowed to take to the sea. But contact with foreign nations, including limited volumes of trade, was maintained through the tributary relationship and was closely supervised. On the northern frontier the construction of walled barriers was a serious undertaking. Most sections of the Great Wall being visited by tourists these days were built by Zhu Yuanzhang's general Xu Da, with the watchtowers added in the sixteenth century by another Ming general, Qi Jiguang. For the Mongols and Semu people remaining inside China, the founder of the Ming had a special ruling: They were forbidden from marrying within their own ethnic groups; in other words, they had to take Chinese wives and husbands. Anyone who violated this law was liable for eighty lashes from the whipping club before condemnation to slavery.

The military establishment followed the Yuan pattern. But instead of setting up a caste system based on ethnic division, the Ming divided the population into military and civil registrations. In principle, the households under military registration paid fewer taxes or no taxes at all and, where possible, were granted small parcels of public land. They were, however, obligated in perpetuity to provide manpower to the armed forces. Regimental and battalion headquarters were established on the frontiers and in the inland provinces. Each of those had a designated pool of hereditary military households to supply its personnel. Battle formations of divisions and above were organized as the situation required. At the high point of Zhu Yuanzhang's reign, some 1.7 to 2 million households were placed under military registration. As long as the system worked, it simplified the problem of personnel procurement. More important, it prevented military mobilization from constantly disturbing the agrarian population at large.

Still more far-reaching in effect were Zhu Yuanzhang's tax plan and his fiscal management. After his purges, it was confirmed that the entire country was packed with small self-cultivators. Minimum rates of taxation were assessed, even though regional differences were wide. The collection, wherever possible, was in grain and textile materials. But while the basic assessment was low, taxpayers, under the direction of appointed community and village leaders, were obligated to deliver the consignments to designated warehouses and depots, some of them in far-off regions. Moreover, numerous kinds of service support essential to the routine operation of the government were not made organic to the offices themselves, but requisitioned from the taxpayers item by item. Office attendants, including messengers and jail keepers, were unpaid; local communities furnished them. Stationery and supplies, even office furniture and building maintenance, were likewise requisitioned from the taxpayers piecemeal. Official travel was controlled by the government, with the Ministry of War issuing passes. But travel services were provided by the general population. A chain of public hostels dotted the empire, each supported by a local community, which provided free food, lodging, and transportation to the next station when the traveler produced his pass.

Every county had a ledger of the authorized requisitions; the entire population was organized into platoons and companies to answer calls for service. The obligation was rotated. When the system was put into effect by the dynastic founder in the fourteenth century, each household within the general population was liable to service calls for only one year over a ten-year period. But some of the service obligations incurred fiscal responsibilities. A warehouse receiving man was held accountable for every bushel of grain and every candlestick checked in. A community leader taking charge of the distant delivery of supplies had to make up any shortages from his own purse. And the liability could be unlimited. The hostels were obligated to satisfy all travelers. The more passes issued by the government, the heavier the financial burden to the local manager for providing food and drink, horses and sedan chairs. In principle, those obligations were separately assessed on the more affluent households. In 1397, the Ministry of Revenue reported that there were still 14,341 households across the empire that possessed 700 *mu* of land (about 120 acres) or more. A list of the landowners was kept by Zhu Yuanzhang himself. Apparently, while under imperial scrutiny, those households were expected to undertake a substantial portion of the load of governmental maintenance in their communities, thus effecting progressive taxation of a sort.

When the system is studied close to 600 years later, we are not so much impressed with its procedural details as we are amazed that such a general scheme could have been put into effect at all. Clearly enough, the dynastic Ming built up by Zhu Yuanzhang had certain utopian features. It seemed more like a huge village community rather than a nation. Centralization was feasible because structurally the organization had been simplified. When a country of millions of square miles was rendered into a compact and homogeneous whole, certain administrative controls could substitute for the complex division of labor and interchangeability of services and goods that normally would have been worked out by the national economy.

Mere praise or condemnation of Zhu Yuanzhang the man does not even begin to answer the most crucial question here: How could such a grotesque management system be introduced and proved workable, regardless of whether its implementer was the vilest conspirator or the sanest inventive genius? Circumstances suggest in this regard that the bewildering legacy of the Mongol conquest must have been more disturbing than is generally realized. The need for retrenchment and integration also marked a reaction to the policies of the Song, which had attempted to use the criteria of the advanced sector of the national economy to integrate the empire's fiscal resources, which only led to disastrous consequences. At the founding of the Ming, the only major dynasty in Chinese history that owed its origin to peasant rebellions, the adaptation of a primitive economic base as the national standard and the do-it-yourself type of service procedures met the requirements of the time. Zhu Yuanzhang was by no means unlettered, being an author of several books on a wide range of subjects. He was also advised by a host of learned men. Intellectually unattractive, his schemes were nevertheless effective at least for the short term. Sacrificing quality for quantity, he united a nation of peasant masses.

But the long-term effect of his creation was depressive. It virtually announced to the nation that China, as a large conglomeration of village communities, could be content and happy without the complications of commerce. Not interested in developing service facilities of its own, the dynasty also remained thoroughly apathetic toward diversifying the nation's economy. There was even less concern for providing a legal apparatus to facilitate diversification.

Bureaucratism under the Ming thus appeared to be the most rigid of its kind. The reliance on social values as the basis of governance deepened. That man was superior to woman, the aged superior to the young, the educated elite superior to the illiterate was more than ever held as self-evident as a part of the Natural Law. Since these principles carried neither the weight of economy nor the variance between and among the several geographical sections, their universality strengthened the empire's solidarity. But the reliance on cultural cohesion made the Ming empire static. Its timeless and changeless outlook forbade development in any new direction. Toward the end of the dynasty, genuine clashes of interest could not be stated in explicit terms. Power struggles, even arising from disputes that were technical in nature, had to be disguised as moral issues. On several occasions the private life of the imperial family was seized by the silk-robed officials as a focal point for their polemics.

For some time in the early fifteenth century, all the work of Zhu Yuanzhang seemed to have been undone by Zhu Di, his fourth son. When the dynastic founder died in 1398, the throne in Nanjing, following the principle of primogeniture, went to Zhu Yunwen, the surviving grandson of the first born. Within a year Zhu Di rebelled. The fighting went on for three years, and in 1402 the uncle emerged victorious. The nephew probably perished when the palace caught fire.

Having seized the throne, Zhu Di did several things to reopen the settlement of his father, the dynastic founder. Against the latter's injunction, he dispatched an invasion force to Vietnam. The initial success of the expedition was so quick and sweeping that the elated emperor lost no time incorporating north Vietnam into his domain as a Chinese province. But when the Vietnamese took up guerrilla warfare the expeditionary force bogged down. Communication was difficult. Supply became a serious problem. The dilemma dragged on and remained unsolved when Zhu Di himself died in 1424.

Unconvinced of the concept of limited liability, Zhu Di personally led five successful expeditions against the Mongols beyond the steppes. Twice he reached or crossed the Kerulen River, deep in the territory of today's Mongolian People's Republic. Before him no Chinese emperor had ventured so far with such a personal command, often close to a quarter of a million men. It was while he was returning from his fifth expedition that Zhu Di succumbed to illness and died near Dolonor.

The construction of Beijing by his orders proceeded for fourteen years. It engaged 100,000 artisans and a million workmen. The city wall, forty feet high, ran to a circum-

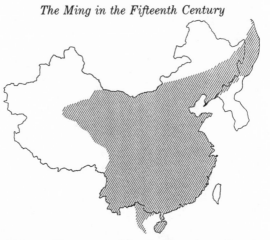

The Ming in the Fifteenth Century

ference of fourteen miles. The wall was razed in the decade ending in 1962 to facilitate traffic flow. Today only the Qianmen (Front Gate) and Dianmen (Gate of Earthly Peace), castle-like structures with multistory towers above them, remain to testify to China's historical vitality that had withstood wars and rebellions from the fifteenth century onward until our time. On the other side, at present the Imperial City halls and the residential quarters of the Forbidden City are well preserved. The palace compound had more than 9,000 rooms. The entire ensemble, initiated by Zhu Di and with additions during later reigns and with major reconstruction by the succeeding Qing dynasty, is the largest extant exhibit of traditional Chinese architecture. With this work the third emperor of the Ming dynasty also modified the imperial scheme of the first emperor. In 1421 he made Beijing the national capital. Nanjing was demoted to "rear echelon capital." Zhu Di had already reconstructed the Grand Canal, built by the Mongols, widening and deepening the channel and adding watergates to it.

While all this was taking place, Zheng He, a eunuch commissioned as an admiral, was repeatedly sailing to the South Seas. The first voyage began in 1405. Sixty-two large ships and 225 small ones participated, with 27,800 men onboard. The largest ships were 440 feet long and 186 feet wide. The middle-sized ones were 370 feet long and 150 feet wide. None of these has survived, but in 1957 near the site of the dockyard a huge wooden rudder post was discovered. It is believed to have been fitted with a rudder blade measuring over twenty feet in both dimensions.

Altogether Zheng He led seven such maritime expeditions. The last, in 1432–33, was after Zhu Di's time; authorization was given by his grandson and the fifth Ming emperor, Zhu Zhanji. On the average, each

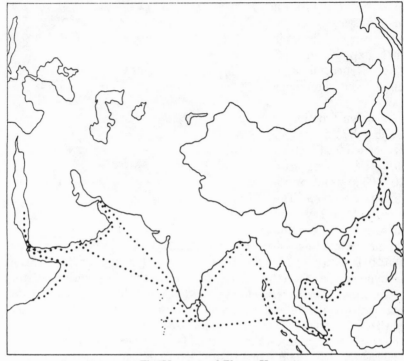

The Voyages of Zheng He

voyage lasted about twenty months. The fleets engaged Chinese pirates in the Malacca strait, intervened in the local politics of Java and set up one contestant as the legitimate king, captured the king of Ceylon (who had attempted to seize the ships) and brought him back to Nanjing, and induced dozens of states to pay tribute to the Chinese emperor. Some of the kings of these states arrived at the Chinese court in person. The armadas visited the Indian Ocean, dispatched smaller fleets to far-off areas, arrived at Hormuz on the Persian Gulf, Zanzibar on the African coast, and Aden near the entrance of the Red Sea. Seven Chinese visited Mecca.

After Zheng He, never again were the expeditions resumed. The personnel were dispersed, the ships laid waste, and the navigation charts burned by a minister of war by the name of Liu Daxia. Modern Chinese scholars are often puzzled and angered by the failure of Zheng He's contemporaries to follow up his efforts after such a brilliant and promising start. It seems absurdly frustrating that not much longer than a hundred years after the voluntary suspension of the seafaring enterprise China had to suffer the presence of Japanese pirates on the eastern coast and see Macao taken over by Portugal; at best the nation was not to have any navy worth the name until the late nineteenth century, and even then the purchased ironclads were sunk and towed away by the Japanese in short order.

There is the unanswered question. The events in Zhu Di's life involved some strange timing. Tamerlane, on the eve of his planned invasion of China, died in 1405, thus saving the fortunate monarch of the Chinese from a clash with one of history's great captains. And the maritime powers in Europe did not rise until Zhu Di's armada had had an opportunity to cruise the South Seas unopposed. The grave consequences of his headlong adventures did not flare up in his lifetime, but they were to encumber his descendants. The timing of those circumstances we cannot explain. But as for the paradox of what happened, it is not so inexplicable. Zhu Di had overextended himself. His empire had been overtaxed nearly to the breaking point, and his successors had to make a drastic retreat in order to save the dynasty.

It must be remembered that Zhu Di's extraordinary expenses had to be met with extractions from the village economy restored by his father, and this economy had neither interprovincial nor interservice links within it. The demand for additional revenue, therefore, could only have been met by several direct and counterproductive means: withdrawal of the forced savings of his frugal father the dynastic founder, paper currency inflation, and horizontally applied downward pressure to demand extra contributions and unpaid services from all quarters. Being a shrewd man with a certain charisma, Zhu Di gathered around himself a large company of literati who skillfully graced his annals and polished his formal pronouncements for publication. But the traces of his misrule were so widespread they could not be covered up. Local gazetteers complained that when the capital was moved to the north, surcharges on tax payments suddenly jumped prodigiously to cover the transportation costs for the 800-mile journey. The Ministry of Works reported that the workers drafted for construction in Beijing were retained for years; by statute they were liable to an annual service of only thirty days. A prefect who protested against the extra requisitions was put into a cage and wheeled to the capital to be personally questioned by the emperor. For merely trying to persuade the emperor to cancel his desert campaign, Xia Yuanji, Zhu Di's minister of revenue for twenty years, was imprisoned for close to three years, not to regain freedom before the emperor's death.

Extant sources indicate that in preparation for his missions, Zheng He was authorized to make direct requisitions from the local governments in the coastal region. The voyages were exposed to criticism because economically they were utterly unproductive, although apparently some merchants took part in them. Zheng He's large ships were constructed with four decks, comprising cabins and public rooms.

Some of the cabins were fitted with closets, and the occupants held keys to their units. There were women and children aboard. But those civilians traveled as favorites and insiders of official circles; there is no evidence that they conducted business independently. The lack of staple goods was a major weakness of the operation. The junks carried out silk fabrics, copper cash, porcelain, and camphor. They returned with incense, gems and jewelry, cutlery, ointment, botanic medicine, and tropical birds and animals. Gratifying to the palace, none of those goods was appropriate for a mass market. Even pepper and sapanwood, two major imports that were handed out by the government to the officials as a part of their salary, were not of a commercial value to justify the maintenance and operation of such a mammoth oceangoing fleet. Despite Zheng He's victories on land and sea, after many engagements his casualties ran to several thousand men. The Longjiang Dockyard at Nanjing had to launch seafaring vessels by the thousands. All material and labor were requisitioned.

A maritime nation becomes a sea power by natural instinct. The enterprise is commercially profitable, and the savings from the exchange of goods lowers production costs. The mutual benefit of trade allows specialization in manufacture on both sides, which in turn brings up real wages and stimulates technological inventions. The cost of maintaining a navy is therefore more than compensated for by a general higher standard of living, as the revenue is recycled through the national economy. In contrast, the benefit of the Ming voyages was largely one of prestige and ceremony; materially, it only fed into palace consumption. Thus the splendors of Zheng He's voyages were a drain on the nation, so the discontinuation of the expeditions cannot be blamed entirely on the blindness to future prospects of the orthodox Confucian bureaucrats. The conditions after Zhu Di's death justified it.

When Zhu Di died in 1424, he was succeeded by his son Zhu Gaozhi. In less than a year the succeeding emperor followed his father to his grave. The throne went to Zhu Zhanji, the fifth emperor, then a young man of twenty-six. Well advised and well tutored, the new sovereign demonstrated powers of deliberation, a rare quality among the Ming emperors. His artistic accomplishment is comparable if not superior to that of the Song Emperor Zhao Ji (pp. 118-124). Today Zhanji's paintings are on exhibit at, among other places, the Fogg Museum of Art in Cambridge, Massachusetts, the Nelson Gallery of Art in Kansas City, and the Metropolitan Museum of Art in New York. But Zhu Zhanji was by no means the weakling that the Song emperor was. When the situation required it, he could be very stern and very resolute.

Immediately after he came to the throne, the threat on the northern frontier eased a bit, as the Mongols, fighting among themselves, had split into eastern and western groups. A more pressing problem came from the south. The invasion of Vietnam had been going on for close to twenty years, with no prospect of successful pacification in sight. It seemed that China's manpower and supplies were being poured into a bottomless pit. Zhu Zhanji's enthronement was greeted with a rout of the Chinese expeditionary force by the indigenous guerrillas. The new emperor sent one of his trusted generals to take command and fresh troops were rushed in. But the situation turned worse. The best this new commander could do was to negotiate with the Vietnamese leader for safe conduct to pull out the Chinese civil officials and the remaining troops. Upon returning to China in 1427 he was sentenced to death.

On the home front, internal upheavals had not yet flared up; but the danger was clear and present. The Yangtze Delta, the richest region of the empire, was the source of the most imminent danger. A controversy had arisen from certain legal ambiguities traceable to the Southern Song, which had attempted to forcibly purchase cultivated land from private owners in that area (p. 135). Until the fall of the Song the promised installments of the purchase price had not been paid off. The Yuan continued to hold the properties as government land and extended its acreage. When the dynastic founder of the Ming took over the territory by military force, he too circumvented the legal problem. Zhu Yuanzhang simply declared that because the populace in the general area had supported a rival contender for the throne, he was justified in taking over their properties. Yet, no agency was ever established to administer the estates in question. The rents on them simply merged with the regular land taxes. After parcelization of the acreages for sale among the cultivators on the one hand, and topographical changes over the decades on the other, who the lawful owners of the land were became less of a pressing issue; the problem was that the payments in some counties and prefectures were exorbitantly high as compared with the tax rates elsewhere, sometimes beyond the means of the small cultivators. Zhu Di's extra imposition worsened the situation.

In the last years of his reign, some counties in the delta area began to accumulate large arrearages. Tax delinquency in China was always contagious. When a considerable number of taxpayers were behind in their payments, others would follow suit, knowing that the government had no alternative but to write off at least the excessive portion of what was overdue. In 1430, Suzhou Prefecture alone had an accumulated arrearage of some eight million hundredweight of grain, amounting to the district's quota for three years. Suffice it to say that Zhu Zhanji did not inherit a throne that could be sat on with ease and comfort.

Forced with the twin problems of the war in Vietnam and unrest in the Yangtze Delta, the young sovereign had to make some courageous decisions. His proposal to disengage from Vietnam divided his court. Because the territory had been annexed for twenty years, of course imperial honor and prestige were at stake. That is why Zhu Zhanji had to use his own influence to silence the war faction. When the decision to withdraw was carried, he also pardoned the general who had retreated without authorization. To the Yangtze Delta the emperor sent as governor Zhou Sheng, a diligent and unpresumptuous man who was to remain in that position for the next two decades, much beyond the end of Zhu Zhanji's own reign. Under Zhou's management, tax reduction took effect quietly without giving the impression that the government was yielding to the pressure of a resistance movement. Governor Zhou also visited the villages, interviewed a large segment of the population, investigated tax procedures, studied the causes of arrearages, put an end to the loopholes, and made remedies. For the currency problem, the emperor accepted the suggestion of his minister of revenue, none other than the previously interned Xia Yuanji, to introduce a number of commercial taxes collected only in paper notes to produce some deflationary effect. Zhu Zhanji did not stop Zheng He's voyages altogether, but he reduced their frequency. In his ten-year reign he authorized the expedition only once. On his orders, numerous construction projects were postponed.

These were reactive policies that in no way enhanced imperial power and influence. It would be difficult to guess what would have happened if these corrective measures had not been taken. But in view of the conditions under which the retreat was made, a conservative observer could say that with some slight modifications in the circumstances, a less lucky Zhu Di could have come down in history with a reputation as bad as that of the second Sui emperor, Yang Guang (p. 90).

When Zhu Zhanji died in 1435, the Ming empire had passed the point where it could be manipulated from the top. Major Chinese dynasties were not made and unmade to serve ephemeral goals. The power structure rested on a large social if not economic base, the revamping of which could not avoid some degree of violence. When Zhu Yuanzhang was in control, the society was plastic enough for him to institutionalize his austerity program. The principles of rural organization, however, were basically village autonomy and noninterference, and an atmosphere of simplicity and frugality prevailed. The entire civil bureaucracy had fewer than 8,000 positions. Their salary was set at the lowest level even by the Chinese standard because, according to the peasant emperor's theory of governance, a civil servant had literally to be a servant. Likewise, the clerical workers were organized into a subbureaucracy. Many of them were drafted into service and not paid, and for those who were paid, the salary amounted to no more than food rations for their families.

Under imperial direction, each village drew up its own charter patterned after the model set up by the central government. In every community two pavilions were erected, one to commend the good deeds of the residents and the other to reprove evil-doers. In these pavilions the village elders arbitrated disputes over inheritance, marriage, property holdings, and cases of assault and battery. The good and bad deeds of the villagers were also posted here.

Twice a year, in the first and tenth lunar months, every community held its local banquet, with attendance by all households compulsory. Before food and drink were served, there were chants, lectures, the reading of imperial laws, and the reprimanding of individuals who had committed misdeeds in the village. A person who had committed an offense yet chose to absent himself from the public denunciation was declared an "incorrigible subject," whom the village community must then recommend to the civil government for a sentence of exile to the frontier. The routine functions of the local government were so thoroughly carried out at the suburban level that the civil officials could remain within their respective city walls. Their venturing into the rural areas without special authorization was a capital offense.

After close to seventy years, most of these bylaws and procedures had slipped into disuse. The membership of the civil service had been grossly expanded, on its way to double and triple the original size. Officials in fact lived comfortably, deriving quasi-legal income by a variety of means. The 14,341 households whose landholdings warranted the personal attention of the throne were no longer mentioned. They had been replaced by a "gartered and sashed" class, usually referred to by Western scholars as the "gentry." By definition the gentry included members of the civil service and their immediate families and associate degree holders, who were also authorized to wear a special kind of cap and belt. Far more numerous than the names on the dynastic founder's roster of the rural affluent, they did not seem at any time during the dynasty to have exceeded two percent of the population, and this uncharacteristic high was probably reached only toward the end of the dynasty, when both the concentration of landownership and government-authorized purchases of rank had accelerated. Precise figures are hard to come by, but after scanning through a large body of personal and family data, biographies, official accounts, and local gazetteers, we can estimate that those families, perhaps less than a quarter of a million of them, owned anything from less than 200 *mu* of land (about thirty acres) upward to 2,500 *mu* (slightly more than 400 acres), with those on the lower level significantly outnumbering those on the upper level. Those owning more land than within this range were exceedingly rare.

Maintaining close ties with the civil service or even as members of it themselves, those medium and large landowners served as functionaries of the dynasty yet commanded local influence in their home districts. Serving as an interlink between the empire's superstructure and infrastructure, they were noted for their political consensus in recognizing that good government hinged on the upholding of traditional social values. The membership of this gentry group was moreover periodically renewed by the power of social mobility. The rise and fall of families, usually in parallel with success and failure in the civil service examinations, added new names to the roster and weeded out some old ones. In the Ming and Qing dynasties, this setup undoubtedly provided a great deal of the stability of traditional Chinese society for a remarkable length of time. But its lingering effects also presented a substantial obstacle to China's social reconstruction in the twentieth century.

Since the bureaucrats were preoccupied with the concept of governance through cultural cohesion and maintained a fixed vision of a multitude of self-cultivators engaged in intensive farming, they could hardly appreciate the mechanics of modern economics, which works on imbalance and thrives on particularity. They managed to make all districts appear artificially identical. Against the trend of the world, they turned inward and acted in a way opposite to the Song reformers.

The taxation system was a handicap. It could be said that the first emperor of the Ming had created a fiscal framework that was too crude and simple for its time. After being overburdened by the third emperor to serve purposes for which it had not been designed, this system was rescued by the fifth emperor of the dynasty from a total collapse. But by then any possibility for a restructuring had already slipped away. A more integrated system would have required the introduction of new accounting methods, which would have called for a reorientation and reorganization of the bureaucracy, not to mention the creation of banking and other service facilities. In the event, the court in Beijing did not even have the monetary means to maintain the old system in a generally satisfactory manner. The paper currency, despite Zhu Zhanji and Xia Yuanji's effort to give it a new lease on life, fell into disuse. Past irresponsibility in over-issuing the notes had pushed them beyond the point of no return. Moreover, relying on paper money as the legal tender, the foregoing Yuan dynasty had neglected to mint bronze coins, the traditional medium of exchange. With the inflow of silver from overseas the unminted metal was embraced by the population; its circulation was spontaneous and widespread. In the end the Ming dynasty had not only to ignore its own order prohibiting its use in private transactions, but also to accept it as a standard in public finance. By then the lack of control by the government was complete: it had no knowledge of the amount of money in circulation; much less did it have the ability to manipulate it.

Its separation from the natural power of the national economy was a characteristic of the Ming administration. As the government had little functional maneuverability, its reliance on Confucian ideology intensified, and its exercise of political power became excessive. In many respects it turned into a negative influence. This applied even to the prerogatives of the throne. The emperor could punish any official or group of officials; but he would have great difficulty promoting a favorite or putting him in a responsible position. He could authorize exceptions to existing laws; but he had no such power when it came to introducing a piece of legislation that could invoke a sweeping change over his empire. If there was a general proclamation, it was either a ritualistic gesture or an official acknowledgment of something that had already taken place without imperial auspice.

This does not mean, however, that the history of the Ming dynasty was uninteresting. On the contrary, this stalemate led to many intriguing and unusual kinds of maneuvering and rationalization, except that without some basic background knowledge, the reader may feel lost in the labyrinth of subterfuge, not knowing what is significant and what is not, or able to distinguish eccentric pretensions from true strength and character. The reader is reminded that during the Cultural Revolution in the 1960s the history of the Ming dynasty was used as a weapon, to be thrown back and forth by the propagandists.

15
The Late Ming

The Ming dynasty had sixteen emperors. The first emperor was buried near Nanjing. The remains of the second emperor were never found (p. 154). For reasons to be discussed later, the seventh emperor, Zhu Qiyu, alone was buried west of Beijing. All remaining thirteen emperors found their resting place about twenty-five miles north of the capital city, in thirteen mausoleums over a belt of land that looks on a map like a huge horseshoe around a reservoir. Few visitors to Beijing fail to go out to the "Ming tombs." One of these, that of Zhu Yijun, the thirteenth emperor and generally known to Chinese and Western readers by his regal name "Wanli," was opened up by archaeologists in 1958. Millions of visitors have since then been inside his burial chamber.

When we look at the historical records, we find something quite unusual about these emperors. After Zhu Zhanji, few of them were seriously involved in the decision-making process that affected the destiny of their empire as a whole. Only the last emperor, Zhu Youjian, was an outstanding exception; but by then it was all too late. For most of them, there was little difficulty in reaching agreements with the bureaucrats on issues of peace and war. But their private lives were constant public issues. The bickering among the civil officials went up to and included the sovereign's personal and family matters, as if the most important issues in the world always happened inside his ancestral temple or inside his living quarters.

The sixth emperor, Zhu Qizhen, ascended the throne when he was not yet eight years old. From childhood he was under the influence of eunuchs. In 1449, then close to twenty-two, he was persuaded by one of these to make a personal inspection of the northern frontier. During the journey he was surprised and captured by Esen, chieftain of the Oirat Mongols. The imperial court, after consultation with the empress dowager, decided to enthrone Qizhen's half brother Zhu Qiyu so that Esen would not have the advantage of negotiating with a reigning emperor in his custody. The strategy worked. A year later Esen returned the sovereign to Beijing unharmed. Now "retired emperor," Zhu Qizhen was assigned to live in a residential hall outside the imperial palace, and in fact remained a prisoner. Six and a half years later, in 1457, Zhu Qiyu became ill. The former emperor's close followers seized the opportunity to carry out a "restoration," which succeeded. When Zhu Qiyu died, he was denied the title and honor due an emperor, including the dynastic burial site. Modern historians agree that the 1449 incident symbolizes a turning point for Ming military power, the beginning of a long decline. Beyond that it is difficult to assess the significance of Zhu Qizhen's split reign. Nor does it seem to be justified to emphasize so much the 1457 coup, which was basically a feud between brothers.

The ninth emperor, Zhu Youtang, was born of a woman belonging to a certain minority group in Guangxi. Captured during a local uprising, she was brought to the palace to become the maid in charge of a storeroom. Her intimacy with the eighth emperor was kept a secret. Until Zhu Youtang was five years old, his imperial birth went unnoticed. But in 1475, as soon as his mother died, he was recognized, and in 1487, at the age of seventeen, ascended the throne. Traditional historians lavished kind words on him, praising him as an enlightened and thoughtful ruler. Reviewing the same records, we see only a timid and insecure youth who through freakish happenstance was called to preside over an integrated bureaucracy for eighteen uneventful years. The only significant turbulence in his reign occurred in 1494, when the Yellow River changed its course. That was effectively dealt with by Liu Daxia, the same minister of war who had burned Zheng He's navigation charts in order to preserve the empire's manpower and resources.

In terms of personality, the tenth emperor, Zhu Houzhao, was by far the most colorful if not the most appealing of the Ming monarchs. By an unusual combination of circumstances, he received very little parental guidance before ascending the throne in 1505 when he was not yet fourteen. Not long after, he moved out of the palace quarters to take up residence in a cluster of buildings that he had constructed for himself called the "Leopard House." Eunuchs and army officers were his company most of the time; sometimes he was also entertained by women of dubious reputation. Lamaist monks and magicians from other lands made up the rest of his retinue. There was no limit to his fun-making and adventurousness. One time he barely escaped injury while trying to tame a tiger.

Zhu Houzhao introduced the practice of meeting his court in the evening. He transferred his tutors to remote posts when those Confucian scholars and regular members of the civil service tried to steer him away from his unconventionality. In 1517, when Batu Mengke raided Ming outposts north of the Great Wall, the young emperor accepted the challenge; he put the frontier forces under his personal command and went out to meet the Mongol leader head-on. Contact was established and the enemy was repulsed. But the civil officials, excluded by him from the tour, insisted that the casualties of the Ming forces far exceeded the damage that they had done to the Mongols.

The emperor went out in search of the Mongols again in 1518, this time reaching the edges of the Ordos desert without encountering the enemy. When the bureaucrats argued that the Son of Heaven should never take such risks, Zhu Houzhao responded by making himself a full general in the army. Next he made himself a duke as well, with an annual stipend. Later he even conferred on himself the title of Grand Preceptor, the senior member of the civil service who outranked all court officials from the bureaucracy.

In the spring of 1519, when word spread that the emperor was to tour the southern provinces as Grand Preceptor, duke, and generalissimo, 146 officials knelt in front of the palace wailing, beseeching the sovereign to call off the journey. The implied impropriety of the imperial decision finally annoyed the emperor. He ordered that those who refused to leave the palace ground be punished with thirty strokes of the whipping club. Eleven of them eventually died of their injuries.

The emperor delayed his tour until autumn and then stayed in the south until the end of 1520. During a fishing trip the boat he was manning capsized. Though he was rescued, it is said that he never fully recovered from the accident. Early the next year he died in the Leopard House without an heir. After the courtiers held a secret meeting with the empress dowager, cousin Zhu Houcong, a teenager who lived in a southern province, was called in to be the eleventh emperor.

The general understanding was that the young prince would consider himself not only the successor to the throne but also the direct descendant of the continuous imperial line, so he was to conduct himself at sacrificial services as the adopted son of his uncle, the ninth emperor. This Zhu Houcong absolutely refused to do. Once enthroned he continued to honor his own parents and announced that he would grant his father the posthumous title of emperor and his mother the status of dowager empress. The court was divided by the proposals, and the controversy lasted for years. In 1524 a large group of officials protested the imperial decision by wailing in front of the palace gate. Enraged, the emperor imprisoned 134 of them; sixteen died of flogging. To make things worse, Zhu Houcong's reign lasted for forty-four years.

The record of the thirteenth emperor was even more disturbing. Zhu Yijun, or the Wanli Emperor, whose tomb is at present open to the public, reigned for forty-eight years. He is known to have been indolent and extravagant. And his greatest moral failing, according to classical historians, was to allow his private life to impede on the proper functioning of his government. A few years after the birth of his first son, Changluo, he became infatuated with the mother of his third son, Changxun. When his intention of letting the younger son replace the elder son as heir became known, the entire court was agitated. Unconvincingly, the emperor denied that what was said had ever come into his mind; yet repeatedly he vetoed the proposals to have Changluo formally installed as heir apparent according to the dictates of dynastic tradition, producing many excuses that hardly enhanced his credibility. This recurred when Changluo was four and when he was seven, and again when he was in his earlier and later teens. In 1601, under public pressure, the emperor finally gave in and declared his eldest son to be the imperial heir. But the controversy did not end there. Palace intrigues and attempted murders, assumed or real, continued to shake the court. Statesmen were forced to resign and officials were divided into factions as this single issue ignited many other clashes. Zhu Yijun died in 1620, and Zhu Changluo, at the advanced age of thirty-eight, eventually succeeded as the fourteenth emperor. A month later he was also dead, with faulty prescription of medication by a physician as the suspected cause. Tracing the responsibility, the court was once again embroiled in polemics, which never fully ceased during the remainder of the dynasty, for twenty-four years.

Stories like these always pose a dilemma for speakers and writers who attempt to introduce the essence of Chinese history to a Western audience. One cannot ignore these episodes, and of course, history is always woven with stories of human interest. Why should we avoid Anne Boleyn in discussing the Tudor Reformation, and the murder of Peter III when narrating the reign of Catherine the Great? Moreover, as capricious and irrelevant as some of the events might seem to us, so long as contemporaries took them seriously, the historical value of those deeds was already elevated by the power of belief. What is embarrassing about working through the records of the Ming dynasty, however, is that the trifling detours are endless. Sometimes the account of a whole decade consists of nothing but fribbles.

On reflection, we sense that there was something never explicitly brought up by the contemporaries: Once the Ming dynasty had become settled, the mainstay of the government was the bureaucracy, not the monarchy. The civil service selected its own members through open examinations, and it evaluated and disciplined them according to established procedures. Even though the office of the prime minister was abolished by the dynastic founder and never revived, "grand secretaries" came to fill the void. Originally scholars who had been appointed to draft the emperor's edicts and proclamations, the grand secretaries gradually attained rank and influence as coordinators and spokesmen for the entire civil service. They nevertheless needed the emperor's authority to finalize decisions and policies.

Indeed, this was a rather unusual and paradoxical arrangement. In a country that was not mathematically manageable, a constitutional monarchy would be out of the question. Yet, absolutism also had its limitations. Insofar as the court in Beijing conceived itself as to be holding a conglomeration of village communities together in a delicate balance, it could not encourage the emperor to exercise his personal power, theoretically totally unlimited in every case. The solution was to temper divine monarchy with humanism, or to compulsorily institutionalize benevolent despotism. Before enthronement as emperor, the heir apparent was tutored by the literary-educational branch of the bureaucracy to be familiar with the principles of self-restraint and mutual deference. In the milieu of the late fifteenth century and onward, perhaps the emperors realized that their only effective authority resided within the power of punishments, which could only be used sparingly. On the other hand, ritualistic exercises were repeatedly and relentlessly conducted in the court to promote the mystique of the throne, until an atmosphere of make-believe prevailed. Thus when problems in state affairs came up to which no rational solutions were at hand, with the aforementioned preparations the emperor's arbitration from the throne would be sufficient. When the sovereign was uninvolved and disinterested, his rule carried the weight of the will of the Son of Heaven. Obedience was expected. Where rationality ended, discipline was supposed to take over.

Now we can see why the mischievous Zhu Houzhao tried to separate himself as a person from the monarchy as an institution when he conferred on himself ranks and titles. The bureaucrats, however, did not take his frivolity lightly. Unable to revolt openly, they resorted to passive resistance. Then there was the case of the other extreme: A cloistered Zhu Youtang, bland and colorless, suited the role of the Ming monarchy well. In a sense, his lack of talent was a virtue.

Other cases indicate that the bureaucrats were intensely concerned with the inheritance of the throne. They defended the principle of primogeniture almost religiously. The matter became sensitive because the security of the civil officials themselves was at issue; if emperors could be made and unmade, or manipulated on all matters, the mystique of the throne would be punctured, the power of belief among the civil officials would begin to waver, and no one could predict the consequences. With this understanding we no longer see the anecdotage involving the several emperors as merely fribbles or personal affairs. So many learned men risked their lives in the controversies—they were struggling by clumsy means over what they considered to be constitutional issues during an awkward age.

The Ming empire became mathematically unmanageable for two principal reasons: Its hereditary military system declined quickly, and its taxation system, aligned too closely with the village economy, could not be overhauled.

The military decline is easily explained: Not all those who were placed under the military registration in the early years of the dynasty had been enrolled voluntarily; many had been pressed into service. If these households were assigned public land to support them at all, the acreages were not kept contiguous in one area, but scattered among private holdings. The users sold and mortgaged the parcels of property at will. By the time several generations had passed, death and desertion had thinned the army ranks; there was great attrition against few replacements on the roster. The frontier units, military colonies of a sort, fared somewhat better. In the opening years of the sixteenth century they still retained about forty percent of their prescribed strength. That of the interior regiments and battalions, however, was rarely at ten percent of their original authorizations.

Taxes, of course, had been increased from the low level set up by Zhu Yuanzhang. Yet the increases were not made in any systematic fashion. The basic land tax assessment, in hundredweights of grain, was subject to only minor adjustments throughout the dynasty's duration of 276 years. But numerous increases were made in the guise of surcharges, readjusted conversion rates, transportation costs, etc. They usually took effect piecemeal by order of the local government responding to demands from the top. The early practice of assessing service obligations on the rich was abandoned. The burden was at first split among the middle-level landowners and then apportioned to the entire pool of taxpayers. The unpaid services, with certain exceptions, were gradually converted to monetary payments. The service cycle (p. 152) that burdened all taxpaying households once every ten years was halved to two five-year cycles, and then converted to an annual basis. All these steps had the tendency to settle to a single annual payment in silver to

cover both the land and the poll tax of the household. Detailed procedures might vary from one district to another depending on the degree
of economic development in the locale, but the trend was ubiquitous. In
the late sixteenth century, it was referred to as the "single-whip
method."

In practice, however, no county ever achieved the ideal goal of a total
merger of all payments and a complete conversion. The practice of
assigning fiscal responsibility to the taxpayers could never be completely shaken off. Lacking service facilities, the central government merely
paired off the revenue agencies with the disbursing agencies and directed them to make lateral transactions; then as far as the Ministry of
Revenue was concerned, the incomes and expenditures had cancelled
each other out item by item. When taxes were collected in kind the
empire was covered with short, crisscrossing supply lines; after commutation the silver payment was still handled in the same fashion. An
army post might receive supplies from a dozen counties; at the same
time a prefecture could make deliveries to a score of warehouses and
depots. With few modifications, this method was also used by the succeeding Qing dynasty. The government's lack of logistical capabilities
at the middle echelon was a striking feature of the Third Empire.

From a modern point of view, even after the increases the tax rate
remained low, although the exact amount differed from one county to
another. Because it was horizontally assessed on all self-cultivators
including the marginal taxpayers who possessed three to five mu of
land, the collection easily reached the saturation point in terms of the
taxpaying population's ability to deliver. Exemption for the destitute
or progressive taxation on the affluent was not contemplated. As it was,
the taxpaying households were already too numerous and their holdings too minute for the local government to manage them with comfort.
Further technical complications would surely cause the system to collapse. Not yet sufficiently recognized, this single factor accounted for
most of China's awkwardness in the modern era. The empire's financial
resources could not be fully mobilized, and the quality of the government could not be upgraded. The untaxed surplus of the affluent was
rarely reinvested in constructive ways; it either turned to usury or
vanished in consumption. Since the financial administration of the government itself hovered only just above the villages, there was little
chance that it could give cottage industry and local commerce any
assistance to allow them to develop and operate at a higher level.

Worse yet, since there was no mandatory tool to tighten the fiscal
administration, its data, bad as they were, could not maintain even a
degree of uniformity. Thus loopholes existed everywhere and irregularities had to be tolerated. Despite the rigid control exercised by the

center, the pressure from the top was lessened by the technical incapacity at the operational level. The unhappy combination persisted.

In the mid-sixteenth century, the serenity was broken by the invasion of the *wokou*, appearing in Western works as "Japanese pirates," who created waves of turmoil along China's eastern seaboard. In reality, their leaders were Chinese, and mixed bands of Chinese took part in their campaigns. But within the fighting element, the role played by the natives could not be more than auxiliary. The invasion was based in Japan, and the Japanese furnished all the military skill and equipment. Not pirates in the strictest sense, they never operated on the high seas but landed on the coast in numbers, besieging and taking cities.

Because of its particular constitution, the Ming empire had to remain insulated. The piracy problem was linked with contraband trade, which had been involving international adventurers in the coastal region for some time. Governmental officials got involved, and the local gentry too went along. In the absence of a maritime court, certain powerful ship captains carried out *ad hoc* contractual enforcement and armed arbitration, and these men eventually emerged as pirate leaders.

It was when these strongmen began to openly repair their ships ashore and serve "subpoenas" to summon the villagers to their "courts" that the government became alarmed. Such a maritime usurpation of local authority, even in its inceptive stage, had to be dealt with sternly as it challenged the agrarian dynasty in theory as well as in practice. Yet as the problem grew more serious, the government thoroughly exposed its own weaknesses. Most regiments and battalions could not be mobilized. The hastily gathered recruits either would not or did not know how to fight. And there were no ready funds to meet emergency expenses. Starting from 1553 the *wokou* infected the southern seaboard for no less than twenty years.

At long last, however, the pirates were successfully suppressed by the resourceful Qi Jiguang, a general who virtually recruited, organized, trained, and equipped an entire army corps from scratch. His officers, hand picked by him, formed a fraternal bond around him, and his soldiers were recruited exclusively from the inland farm districts. Steadiness rather than nimbleness was openly stressed. He drilled them relentlessly; he demanded teamwork from them and threatened them with the death penalty for noncompliance. The minimum pay for the foot soldiers was only slightly higher than farm wages, and their equipment was locally produced. Politically, therefore, his organization bore no traces of an elite corps and was completely in line with the dynasty's rural constitution. The expenses were met by a universal surtax that rode on practically all existing taxes. Collected almost entirely from the area where the pirate problem was felt, the small extra amount did not cause much hardship. But in some districts, because many taxpayers were already so close to the poverty line, future tax potential may have been exhausted.

In the north, the Mongol leader Altan Khan had since the 1540s been building up a large confederation stretching from Manchuria to Kokonor, with the capability of deploying perhaps 100,000 mounted warriors in battle. In the 1550s he made annual raids into China every autumn, sometimes getting close to the outskirts of Beijing itself. Fortunately, Altan had no substantial agricultural bases, and his Chinese advisers were few. In 1570, China's frontier commanders were able to seize the opportunity of Altan's grandson's defection to its side to negotiate a peace settlement with him, awarding him with the rank of prince and granting him trading privileges and annual subsidies. Throughout the rest of the Ming period never again did the Mongols reappear as a major threat to the dynasty. In other words, neither the *wokou* nor Altan mounted a challenge serious enough to force a major reorganization of the empire.

While the era seems stagnant and uninspiring to us, this may not have been the feeling of those who lived through it. Especially for the members of the gentry-official class who were content with the status quo, the social tranquility and atmosphere of changelessness were not unrewarding. Once he had reached prominence through the civil service examinations, a member of the social elite was rather secure, with the income of a middle-level landowner or above. Real estate changed hands frequently, in part reflecting the regular degree of social mobility connected with the rise and fall of families caused by one's success and failure in the exams. On the other hand, honesty in pecuniary matters in office-holding was only relative. In the absence of an economic pulsation to compel everybody to better himself ceaselessly as we modernists are subjected to, one could fulfill several years' public service and then retire early to live in comfort if not in extravagance.

These conditions created a world of introspection, a mood revealed in the prose, poetry, painting, and philosophical discourses of the period. With few exceptions, Ming artists and men of letters belonged to the gartered and sashed class. These gentlemen of leisure, freed from mundane struggles, tended to see the outside world from flashes of their own intellect. Novel-writing was a great accomplishment in Ming times. It branched out into historical and social themes, and into erotism and fantasy. Yet each of the great novels of this age portrayed a world complete unto itself. The authors were confident in dealing with the characters and events in a gigantic structure, usually symmetrically

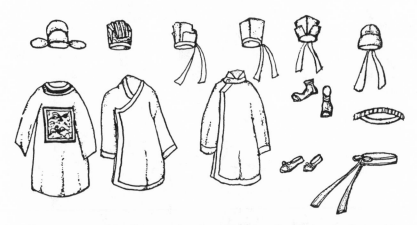

The costume of the "gartered and sashed class" suggests its link with officialdom yet association with leisure in private life.

arrived at and running through a full cycle. Even elements of realism had to be subsumed in the preconceived universal schemes. When that was not enough, the fiction writers laced their stories with rhymed lines to demonstrate their wisdom larger than life. In this sense, the craft of these novelists was similar to that of the Japanese who designed rock gardens.

The greatest philosopher in Ming times was Wang Yangming. He applied the Buddhist doctrine of instant enlightenment to his Confucian studies, even though toward the end of the Ming period, Wang's emphasis on natural instinct led to a wide spectrum of schools of thought that bore little semblance to the disciplined mind of the master himself.

For the gentry-official class, being cultured came before being rich. Scholarship and taste and manners were stressed. That was why the Italian Jesuit Matteo Ricci, who went to China in 1583, marveled that the nation was governed entirely by a large number of "philosophers." But ostentation was impossible to avoid, especially for the upstarts. A prosperous gentry family might erect several flag poles in front of its house to proclaim the number of sons who had passed the examinations or through contributions to state coffers had secured associate degrees. Some of the local elite traveled in sedan chairs surrounded by platoons of attendants. Gardening and furniture-making, which enriched the living quarters of the well-to-do, gained prominence in the late Ming. Art connoisseurship became popular; antiques were valued. Sometimes a writing ink slab could fetch thirty or forty ounces of silver, sufficient for a peasant family to live on for a year.

But there is little substance to the theory that a capitalist class was rising during this age. Although some salt merchants became enor-

mously rich, they were extremely few. Commercial farming was limited to a handful of scattered cases; and there is no evidence that the pioneering work was ever followed up. Cotton-cloth manufacture remained a cottage industry, the wages of the women workers spinning the yarn supplementing the income of the tenant farmers. Although akin to the putting-out system in contemporary Europe, it by itself was insufficient to fuel a social change. Above all, a fundamental weakness in the theory of a potential economic breakthrough during the late Ming has to do with the conditions of the service sector of the national economy. There were no credit and banking institutions, and insurance was unheard of. In their place, pawn shops appeared by the thousands. Nor were there civil laws or court proceedings that might encourage the growth and development of capital. Indeed, legal practices essential to modern commercial operations, anchored in property rights, would have contradicted the teaching of Mencius and challenged the theoretical foundation of the bureaucratic management. As mentioned earlier, since the mid-fifteenth century the Ming government had not been in a position to formulate any meaningful fiscal and monetary policies. How could commerce come of age when so many key ingredients of modern commercial organizations were missing?

Technological advances, after reaching a high point during the Song, did not show signs of a vigorous continuation under the Ming. It seems that from silk looms to porcelain kilns, special devices and mechanisms

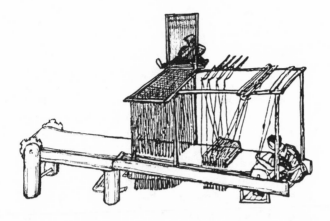

were being invented from the craftsman's approach to problems. Because of the benefits they brought, hydraulic engineering and pharmacology were two areas in which the Ming people did well. But a lack of interest in creating labor-saving devices and knowledge for its own sake may have prevented further explorations that could have led to the use of more refined mathematical tools to measure the mysteries of the universe.

In agriculture, the major events were the introduction of tobacco, maize, the sweet potato, and the peanut into China from the New World. The last two food plants were of particular value, since they could grow on hilly land that previously had been uncultivated. But no significant progress was made in agricultural methods and techniques. That the general farming implements illustrated in the handbook on agriculture commissioned by Khubilai Khan (p. 144) remained unchanged over centuries may indicate that within the limits of the traditional farm economy, agricultural technology had already reached its limits for some time.

Nevertheless, more than any other dynasty, the Ming rendered the core of China homogeneous and uniform. After the middle period, the population in north China no longer showed noticeable traces of alien components. Inter-province migration took place in south China, dispersing the population more widely over many regions and bringing more pressure to bear on the minority groups in the southwest. Estimating the population in traditional China is always a risky undertaking, but there is a consensus among scholars that around 1600 the total figure might have reached 150 million—an all-time high. Chinese nationals were still forbidden by law to take to the sea, but emigration to the southeast Asian countries did not seem to have been halted at any time. In 1567 the court in Beijing authorized limited maritime trade at Yuegang near modern Amoy. The shifting of active trade from Macao to Guangzhou may have started in 1578.

Matteo Ricci, who arrived in Nanjing in 1595 and Beijing in 1598, left an interesting account of the late Ming. Reading it with the benefit of hindsight, we can see that China in the late sixteenth century was like a jade ornament: aesthetically self-contained but structurally fragile. Within the limits of its laws and institutions, the potential for internal development was almost exhausted. Naturally such a state, difficult to mobilize, had little strength to withstand external pressure.

Actually, before Ricci traveled on the Grand Canal to the capital, the Ming Empire had already made its last attempt to regenerate itself. This effort came from the single-mindedness of Grand Secretary Zhang Juzheng, the Wanli Emperor's tutor. When the emperor was enthroned in 1572 at the age of nine, Zhang, with the trust of the empress dowager, acted as the young emperor's guardian. Maintaining an understanding with the chief eunuch inside the palace, the grand secretary wielded sufficient power to function as prime minister all but in name. He put his protégés in key positions, extended his influence to both the censorial-supervising branch and literary-educational branches of the government, as well as exercising control over the ministries. A tireless man, Zhang wrote numerous personal letters to governors and governors-general, discussing a wide range of problems. Thus policies and operational procedures had already been decided upon, privately and informally, before those officials submitted their reports and petitions to the throne, and the grand secretary drafted rescripts in the name of the child emperor. Career advancement, something that Zhang had the power to manipulate, provided the incentive for his followers. In this subtle way Grand Secretary Zhang Juzheng controlled state affairs for ten years, until his untimely death in 1582 at the age of fifty-seven.

A great difficulty confronted by this resourceful, intriguing, energetic, and persistent man rested in the fact that the empire created by Zhu Yuanzhang was not intended to be restructured. It had spread out more like an encasement of culture than a nation. The hereditary military system could not be replaced in some areas, and financial resources throughout the country were diffused.

Zhang's campaign was neither a major nor a minor reform. It was limited to austerity and the restoration of discipline. Under his direction, all unnecessary expenditures were postponed, and budgetary cuts were extended to numerous areas. Accounts were audited with vigor, and forced savings at the local government level were pressed for without respite. Officials at all levels were required to see their tax quotas fulfilled. Those who failed to do so could not be promoted or transferred, and those who had already retired could be called back to answer questions. The effort, simultaneous with the conclusion of the *wokou* campaign and the peace settlement with Altan, enabled the empire to lay away 12.5 million ounces of silver in the state treasury within a decade. Later twice, in 1592 and 1597, Ming forces had to be sent to Korea to meet the invading Japanese army dispatched by Toyotomi Hideyoshi. The fighting was inconclusive, and both sides blundered. But the Chinese expeditionary force managed to hang on until Hideyoshi's death in 1598, thus fulfilling its war aim without a clear-cut victory. A major factor contributing to the success was the availability of the treasury deposits accumulated during the Zhang Juzheng era.

But Zhang took no steps to reorganize the government or restructure the bureaucracy. Aside from tightening frontier defense, his only move toward a major reform was the national land survey ordered in 1580. Unfortunately, before the returns could be processed the grand secretary himself died. The data received scant attention from his successors.

Yet even Zhang's limited campaign made the life of the bureaucrats difficult. Once the organizer of the austerity passed away, his opponents and those who were banished by him staged a comeback; their alliance with those who honestly believed that the grand secretary had abused his authority was effective enough to launch a counterpurge, to eliminate his cohorts and suspend his programs.

The Wanli Emperor, now gaining maturity, endorsed the charge that his tutor had deceived the throne. He ordered that Zhang Juzheng be posthumously stripped of his honors and titles. What the young sovereign did not realize was that the bureaucrats, already divided and split because of numerous nexus and conflicts of interest that could never be openly parleyed, seized the opportunities of the purges and counterpurges to form factions. And Wanli's own clumsiness in handling the succession question (p. 167) made the situation worse. The two cases were not connected, but both involved the empire's constitution and both were wrapped with moral values as the contemporaries perceived them. Those issues added fuel to the partisan polemics. Starting in about 1587, the critics gradually moved to remonstrate against the emperor himself, charging him with extravagance, indolence, and being partial to the mother of his third son.

At first Wanli was enraged. But when he realized that his punishment only made offenders popular among other protesters, he too adopted the method of passive resistance. He left petitions unrescripted and important positions vacant, and then he himself withdrew from public view.

The monarch could not have done the civil service a greater harm than denying it the binding arbitrating authority at the top that the officials themselves could not provide. Later the malcontents shifted their criticisms to the grand secretaries, making no competent man feel comfortable at remaining in that position. When state affairs continued to deteriorate, a group of young officials, motivated by their zeal to reverse the situation, started a moral rearmament movement within their ranks. Because several leaders of this group were associated with the Donglin Academy in Wuxi, their campaign is known to historians as the Donglin Movement. But if saving the dynasty was their goal, they could not have chosen a worse approach. As we see it, the Ming bureaucracy was top heavy with moral precepts. Being abstract, polemics on the ideological constituents only distracted them from a hard fact that required their attention: Many technical problems of their time had gone beyond their capacity to handle them, including the "constitutional crises" outlined above. As the Donglin people indulged in making character assessments from their own narrow perspectives, their opponents followed their example, calling themselves good elements and all others bad elements, with the emperor remaining detached and aloof.

Still later, during the reign of Wanli's grandson Zhu Youjiao, or the fifteenth emperor of the Ming (who followed the reign of Wanli almost immediately, as the son, the fourteenth emperor, had lasted for only a month, see above, p. 167), a "eunuch dictator" came to power. He harassed the civil officials with the secret police, a turn of events that made the public angry. Yet when the modern researcher looks at the records closely, he has to recognize that by then the bureaucracy was a completely ungovernable body, and the civil officials, quarrelling without a clearly defined aim, were by no means completely free from blame.

More things happened during the long reign of Wanli than it is generally realized. The circulation of silver, for instance, benefitted the southeast more than the northwest. Provinces in the latter region needed the annuities delivered by Beijing to the frontier army posts to maintain their balance. Furthermore the total amount of unminted metal in circulation was rather small; for example, when Zhang Juzheng began to accumulate it as treasury reserves, a deflationary effect immediately set in, causing the prices of major commodities to drop. When the Ming empire had to fight the Manchus in the northeast, the redeployment of the nation's financial resources must have prejudiced the interests of the northwest. We cannot discount that factor as one of the contributing causes of the widespread banditry that eventually arose in that region to topple the dynasty. Also, during the years when the court in Beijing was paralyzed by discord, there was a steady decline of the quality of local government nationwide.

Those latent factors must be considered along with the more obvious reasons for the dynasty's fall, such as Wanli's indolence and extravagance. Yet, above all, the most depressing factor was the lack of any sign of positive influence coming from any direction. Zhang Juzheng's posthumous disgrace served notice that the dynasty could no longer be reformed.

The cynic Wanli was not to escape the consequences. In April 1619, not long before his death, his army of 100,000 men was routed by Nurhaci in Manchuria, a campaign in which the latter could not have had more than 60,000 mounts. He in fact dared to use cavalry charges against Ming forces equipped with firearms. Extant documents show that the founder of the future Manchu dynasty had the vision to see through to every weakness of his rival, whose mandate of heaven he challenged.

Nurhaci was to die in battle on another occasion. Zhu Yijun, or the Wanli Emperor, had a little over a year to live. Then his throne was to pass to the son whom he had tried so hard to disqualify. A month later it went to one of Wanli's grandsons, who occupied it for seven years. Another grandson survived for seventeen more years before he ended his own life at the fall of the dynasty. But with the fate of the dynasty sealed, it was a distressing quarter of a century. The vicissitudes on the battlefront could not change the fundamental reality: The Ming Empire had to fight a protracted two-front war, against the peasant guerrillas in the northwest and the Manchu cavalrymen in the northeast, while its financial resources, favorably located in the south, could not be methodically and efficiently mobilized to sustain the war effort. The impetuous temperament and uncompromising character of the last emperor only enabled him to demonstrate to the world that within his tragic role, he had given everything he had.

16
The Role
of the Manchus

There is no easy way to explain how the Manchus, with a population of about one million, could by 1644 seize the throne of China. They had devised a writing system for their spoken language only in 1599. Their "banner system," which gave their tribal organization a bureaucratic touch by regulating the mobilization procedure and its agricultural support, came into existence no earlier than 1601. In 1635 they began to call themselves Manchus. Another year lapsed before the Qing dynasty was formally proclaimed. It took less than a half century for this loosely constructed confederation of tribes to elevate itself to be the governing body of an enormous empire with a profound cultural heritage.

The Qing conquest of China differed from the experience of previous alien dynasties. Earlier invaders took advantage of China's disunity to become one of the contenders. They gained a foothold inside the Great Wall and governed a mixed population before moving south. The Manchus took China from the outside in one sweep.

In early 1644, peasant leader Li Zicheng entered Beijing through its back door. He occupied the high points along the Great Wall and took the area of the imperial tombs before descending to the capital. Hours before Li broke through the defenses of the inner city, Emperor Zhu Youjian hanged himself. His last testimony declared: "Bandits, I invite you to quarter my body, but I forbid you to do harm to my subjects, anyone of them!" Today the spot of his death scene, a hillock on the north side of the palace compound, remains an emotion-evoking place to visitors.

In the spring of 1644, the only imperial troops available that could have averted the disaster were those under Wu Sangui, guarding the fortresses toward Manchuria. As Beijing was threatened, Wu's command was instructed to abandon the forward posts facing the Manchus so that his troops could be used to relieve the siege of the capital. But the dynasty fell faster than the plan could be fully implemented. Wu Sangui now opened the gates for the Manchus. He needed their help because the Beijing garrison had surrendered to the rebels. Under these conditions the rebellion of Li Zicheng was crushed. A legend persisted that General Wu was least concerned with the dynasty or the emperor. He was about to surrender to Li Zicheng, but upon hearing that his favorite concubine, Chen Yuanyuan, had been seized by Li, he reversed his decision, and in so doing triggered an act that was to affect the destiny of millions of Chinese for centuries to come. The story began to gain currency and even historical respect when a contemporary man of letters wrote a poem about it. That man, Wu Meicun, was in fact a Ming official who rose later to serve as chancellor of the Imperial University under the Qing.

This episode, even if it were true, hardly addresses the basic question. Like other legends passed on in those days, it reflects the national psychology of the Ming. As the dynasty was set up, the organizational principles were few; but the complexities under the umbrella of this simple state structure were many. Often, contentions arising from the latter could not be dissolved by the crude mechanism of the former. The doctrine of self-restraint and mutual deference in fact inhibited open debate on practical issues; it allowed no one to speak up in a self-interested voice. We have already observed that during the late Ming problems of military manpower and governmental finance were pressing. The scope of those problems was wide. Persons who shared responsibility for them were numerous. Yet, lacking technical means to tackle those "hard" problems, the bureaucrats busied themselves with polemics on "soft" issues, such as moral standards and imperial succession. The story of the dynasty's downfall was handled in a similar fashion, with a certain intellectual subtlety involved. Whether a distorted vision was preventing them from seeing what was really going on, or a conscious effort at rationalization was helping them to put aside their own guilt and discomfiture, contemporaries came up with specious explanations for the events occurring rapidly in a grossly confusing short period under influences that, in retrospect, could not be considered healthy or even normal.

April 25, 1644, the day Beijing fell into rebel hands, was a tragic date for Ming loyalists. On that day Minister of Revenue Ni Yuanlu hanged himself in his residence, and twelve members of his household followed him. Others who committed suicide included the minister of works, the censor in chief, a vice minister of justice, and the chief justice of the Grand Court of Revision. Officials of middle grades and junior ranks who chose to die rather than survive the dynasty were countless. Some 200 women drowned themselves in a creek that flowed through the palace compound.

Apparently, the dynasty had not completely lost the devotion of its loyal subjects. Then how could Li Zicheng, who had started out by declaring his new dynasty only two and a half months before at Xi'an, manage to cross the Yellow River, march across the entire length of Shanxi Province, seize the fortress on the Great Wall, and overpower the capital garrison with such ease?

Immediately after the Qing takeover, local resistance to the alien regime, at first flaring up in scattered locations on the Yangtze Delta, and then continuing in southern Huguang and Guangxi, gave a strong indication that the communities in the south were quite willing to make sacrifices to stand up to the Manchus if properly led. Why had those local communities been so short-sighted as not to have contributed their manpower and resources earlier, so that the enemy could have been checked hundreds of miles away, instead of being allowed to press in on them at such close range?

There are no simple answers to these questions.

The magnitude of the tragedy compels us to reexamine some of the fundamental issues involved. There is a consensus among historians that the Ming dynasty collapsed owing to financial failure. Until 1644, pay in arrears due the recruited soldiers had accumulated to several million ounces of silver. Most of the troops had not been paid for months if not years. Behind this deplorable situation there was the feeling that the nation had been overtaxed. But in reality this was not a simple matter of the supplementary taxes having exceeded the nation's ability to pay. But rather, the existing structure of financial management broke down under the unprecedented strain of mobilization.

The administration failed on several counts. First, when the empire had to fight a two-front war, the cost should have been assessed on the districts that were better able to pay. But lacking adequate data and enforceable authority, the Ministry of Revenue could only take the easy way out by horizontally apportioning the burden to all districts according to the recorded acreages of tilled land, which was inaccurate and outdated. It inflicted unbearable burdens on the poorly situated districts. As early as 1632, tax arrears of over 50 percent were already being reported in more than a quarter of the counties of the empire. Subsequently, 134 counties delivered no payment whatsoever to the central government. Second, within each district the burden was also horizontally assessed on all taxpayers. In the past the sale of rank had enabled many well-to-do households to obtain gentry status by making lump-sum contributions so that their tax liability was reduced or written off. Toward the end of the dynasty some counties had more than 1,000 of these households. Thus the tax burden was progressively shifted to the marginal landowners, who were least able to pay. Third, military remittances, with few exceptions, were made in silver, with major portions coming from south of the Yangtze River. The annual remittance was targeted at twenty million ounces, out of a possible 250 million ounces that was estimated by a contemporary writer to be in the hands of the entire population. The take was simply too large in proportion to the total amount of money in circulation. And fourth, this flow of precious metal, if realized as anticipated at all, was not backed by the private sector of the economy. Under the ordinary conditions of the late sixteenth century, some five million ounces of silver were delivered annually by the southern provinces to Beijing and the frontier army posts, where the recipient districts used the money to purchase cotton, cotton goods, and other necessities that originated in the south. The two-way traffic kept the bullion in circulation. When military expenditures suddenly boosted the northward flow of cash, no arrangements were made to ensure its prompt return. The unloading of silver often caused price inflation in an economically undeveloped area. As early as 1619, Supreme Commander Xiong Tingbi observed at Mukden that even with such abundant cash he would not have been able to find suppliers to furnish the clothing and equipment he needed. His soldiers put on armor over their naked bodies, without any undergarments whatsoever. Subsequently, censorial officials revealed that parcels of the precious metal, unspent on the front, were shipped back to the interior by the army officers who had intercepted them.

Neither the Manchus nor the insurgents, who lived off the country and stayed away from the money economy altogether, had such problems.

For the Manchus, the seizure of Beijing on June 6, 1644, marked only the beginning of the dynastic change. In order to confirm that the Qing was here to stay, they had to anchor their power in the population, and a sequence of arrangements during the organizational phase accomplished this. These measures also demonstrated that with the assistance of their Chinese collaborators, the Manchus knew how to rejuvenate a decadent empire. It was not without reason that they had risen to take over the Ming.

Once a foothold was secured, they transplanted their banner system to north China. A "banner" was not a combat formation but an administrative umbrella over a number of military colonies that furnished manpower quotas to the army when needed. In 1646 and 1647, large areas in several northern provinces were designated for the maintenance of this setup. Landowners within the cordoned-off areas were relocated, so that the vacated farms could provide support to the new hereditary military households, most of them having recently arrived from Manchuria. The problems of military manpower and army logistics that had troubled the previous dynasty so much were thus eased, especially when the bannermen, formerly raiders of China's frontier, were now transformed into its protectors.

In the south, reorganized Chinese troops spearheaded Manchu units to put down the resistance, including the campaigns of three Ming princes who vainly claimed succession to the vanquished dynasty. When that was accomplished, the Manchus occupied the intermediate provinces, concentrating their troops in the major cities. Fujian, Guangdong, Guangxi, Sichuan, Guizhou, and Yunnan were left in the hands of three defector Chinese generals, including Wu Sangui, of course.

The occupation was therefore characterized by in-depth deployment. The homeland in Manchuria remained intact. North China was reinforced with combat-support manpower, and occupation forces were stationed at key spots south of the Yangtze. Only the far south where the Ming loyalist influence lingered on was dealt with by collaborators. In this way the Manchu strength was not overextended or overexposed. State revenues in silver, maintained at the Ming level of twenty million ounces annually, was by and large spent in the south. This arrangement remained in effect until 1681, the year when the "three feudatories" were finally eradicated, following which Taiwan was taken from the Ming loyalists in 1683. Only then was the entire country occupied.

In governmental finance, one of the reasons why the Qing succeeded where the Ming had failed was that the direction of expenditures was reversed. Instead of extending the influence of silver into peripheral areas, the new dynasty compressed the circulation of the precious metal within its own familiar ground. Furthermore, the disentitlement of Ming rank-holders cleared a major obstacle to local tax administration, at the same time opening the door for new forced contributions and the fresh sale of ranks. The latter practice would eventually become a serious handicap for the Qing, no less so than for the previous dynasty, but it would be a long time before its effects were felt. In the meantime, as alien conquerors the Manchus had the power and influence to enforce the tax laws. In 1661 the prosecution of tax delinquency in the Yangtze Delta area listed 13,517 offenders, meaning that virtually all gentry households were affected. Some of the offenders were accused of owing back taxes of such preposterously infinitesimal amounts as several thousandths of an ounce of silver. This action was effectively intimidating, which was perhaps its original purpose. Minting bronze coins, a state function that the Ming had persistently neglected, was taken up by the Qing in earnest. During the first decade of the new dynasty China produced more of those coins that the previous dynasty had in its entire 276 years. Thus cheap money was made available to the populace.

Nationalism in China during this era was a complicated matter. Instinctively, no natives would voluntarily embrace the idea of venerating an alien group as their masters, not to mention that the Manchus, only a decade before their takeover, had encircled Inner Mongolia, breached the Great Wall, and come down onto the north China plain to sack cities and loot the population. Most of the Chinese advisers who went over to the Manchus prior to 1644 had been captured and forced to give service. In an age when the code of war held that captives could either die or change allegiance, and the reprisals for desertion were not only severe but also extended to one's kin, individuals who fell into enemy hands and became prisoners-of-war had little choice.

On the other hand, the Manchus, physically hardly distinguishable from the northern Chinese, had an immense drive and aptitude for Sinicization. Aside from enforcing the outward and ritualistic obedience that was required for the protection of the nascent dynasty, they avoided doing things that would exacerbate the feelings arising from ethnic differences. Intermarriage was forbidden, but there were no provisions for distinguishing the two racial groups before the law. The Manchus formed a military caste of a sort; yet special banners were organized for the Mongols and the Chinese. When the Manchus took Beijing in 1644, they ordered all Ming officials to remain in office. The civil service examination was resumed the next year, in 1645. It was the Manchus who made the effort to speak and write in Chinese, rather than the other way around. The Qing emperors, on the whole, lived much closer to the expectation of the Chinese tradition than did numerous indigenous rulers of preceding dynasties.

From the historian's point of view, the Manchus succeeded because they broke a constitutional deadlock. They effectively provided the arbitrating power required of China's monarchy that in the mid-seventeenth century the Chinese were unable to supply themselves. The Zhu ruling house had been thoroughly discredited. Li Zicheng, before taking Beijing, made several attempts to induce the Ming emperor to abdicate in exchange for a princely title under his new regime, but without success. The passing of the Mandate of Heaven to the Chinese rebel would have been disarmingly convincing if it had been acknowledged by the dying dynasty. As it happened, Zhu Youjian's suicide note (above p. 180) dealt his challenger a fatal blow, psychologically no less lethal than the rope that terminated his own life. Thereafter no Ming subject could give service to the rebel leader with an unsullied reputation and a clear conscience.

In practical terms, the Qing dynasty regained the empire's financial solvency without institutional change. It merely enforced the Ming laws with the kind of discipline that had one time been imposed by Zhang Juzheng (p. 176). It is very doubtful that Li Zicheng could have attained the same degree of authority with less violence, being labeled as a bandit as he already was.

Here was a dilemma for Ming veterans. Traditional statecraft, growing out of the teachings of Mencius, taught them to value the satisfaction of the population at large regardless of the origin of the ruler (see above, p. 114). On that count, they had no cause to raise their standard against the Qing. Yet, bound by the practice of those days, to acquiesce was to collaborate, which would always be a source of inner conflict. Most likely Wu Meicun (above p. 181), who blamed the entire confusing situation on a beautiful woman, had composed his lyrics under such stress.

With the complexities, anti-Manchu sentiments did not die easily. For those who refused to give in, national pride was entwined with personal and dynastic loyalties. Some felt that their manhood was being tested. Others, who resisted the alien forces in their hometowns, may have mixed their vested interests with a motivation for martyrdom.

An immediate issue that sparked waves of resistance in the Yangtze Delta had to do with an order that all men had to trim their hairlines. Regulating hairdos was in fact a traditional dynastic practice. The Ming had demanded that all males roll their long hair into buns on the back of the skull and affix them with hairpins. For some reason, it was Manchu practice for men to shave off the front part of the hair up close to the crown. The new dynasty proclaimed in 1645 that this would apply to the entire male population throughout the empire within ten days. Failure to comply was to be regarded as open defiance of the throne. The more the Chinese took the decreed haircut as slavishly degrading the more determined were the Manchu authorities to enforce it, as if the destiny of the empire were hanging in the balance on the badge of obedience made out with the hairline of the citizenry. A court academician who merely criticized the policy in private was condemned to death by beheading. As he was close to the throne, the sentence was actually carried out by strangling. It is difficult to estimate how many thousands chose to die rather than live with this humiliating sign of submission, because the issue was mingled with other causes of the resistance movement.

Another infamous Qing deed was the literary inquisition. Any published item suspected of being seditious was investigated by the official circles at length and as a rule brought to the attention of the emperor. There were only a few cases in which the authors explicitly stated their Ming loyalist sentiments. Most works involved historical references that were considered to make insinuations about the present dynasty—satirical poems, forbidden characters, unorthodox expressions, puns, etc. When an item was judged to be subversive, not only were the author and the sponsor of the publication punished, but so were the readers, plate engravers, printers, and book sellers. In the most serious cases the offenders were tortured to death and their family members executed, exiled, or enslaved. The deceased offenders were dug out of their graves and their bodies desecrated. When the imperial vengeance raged, an inquiry could involve several hundred persons. In a number of cases, however, the accused were found not guilty and dismissed. Scattered cases ran through about half the duration of the Qing period, until the closing years of the eighteenth century.

But all the atrocities and provocations did not lead to "racial tensions" in the modern sense. The absence of a permanent grudge helps us to understand that nationalism in its present form and as we experience it today is a product of modern society, where cultural influence and economic interest make the individual feel so conscious of the corporate uniqueness of which he is a part that a drastic alteration of those values by foreign intervention inevitably incites massive and intense reactions. In the seventeenth and eighteenth centuries neither did the Manchus make a serious effort at alteration nor did the Chinese feel that their cultural tradition was in fact threatened. Only a small segment of the population was incited.

For the majority of the people, this one and a half centuries (from the Qing takeover to about 1800) was a period of prolonged peace and prosperity. Traditionally, the first four Qing emperors received credit for this turn-around.

Shunzhi (his personal name was Fulin, reigned 1644–1661) ascended the throne as a minor. The earlier part of his reign was managed by his uncle Dorgan. A religiously inclined person, Shunzhi was under the influence of the Jesuit missionary Adam Schall von Bell. Yet he also became infatuated with Buddhism. Kangxi (Xianye, reigned 1662–1722) was every inch a model emperor of the Chinese image. Kind, gentle, yet resolute, he made vital decisions in internal affairs and led expeditions beyond the border. His reign, which lasted for sixty-one years, did much to solidify the dynasty. Chinese scholars did not forget that on one of his

Beijing under Kangxi

inspection trips, his boat moored in the countryside, people heard him reciting books beyond midnight. While Kangxi was magnanimous, his son Yongzheng (Yinreng, reigned 1723–1735) was stringent and calculating. His emphasis on discipline might have been necessary for officialdom, but the sovereign's surveillance of the bureaucrats, in part motivated by personal and family intrigues, led to the extensive use of the secret police. Some of the stories circulated by the Chinese about the spy activities during his reign clearly fall into the category of "thrillers." The last of the four, Qianlong (Hongli, reigned 1736–1795), reigned for sixty years. He did not die in 1795, but abdicated in favor of his son. Afterward as retired emperor he continued to wield power behind the throne until his death in 1799. At no other time in Chinese history did so many emperors have consecutively linked reigns of benevolent despotism over such a long period. Although they had distinct personalities, these four were all energetic and distinguishably capable. Their devotion to their office was also unprecedented. At the founding of the dynasty, staffs for interpretation and translation were provided for the throne; before Shunzhi's reign was over, they were no longer needed. The throne was versed in the Chinese language. Yongzheng used Manchu only to curse. Kangxi and Qianlong were scholars of Chinese studies in their own right, even though the degree of their accomplishment has been contested by historians.

Less mentioned, however, is that this period of peace and prosperity was fostered by a combination of favorable circumstances. In these one and a half centuries, international trade worked to the best interest of China. Tea was in demand in Russia. Silk and raw silk had been exported to Japan since the early Tokugawa period. Chinese porcelain, rugs, lacquerware, jewelry, and furniture gratified European capitals during the age of salons and Enlightenment. Unbleached cotton piece goods called "nankeens" were exported to Europe and later to the United States. Before being overtaken by the West and its Industrial Revolution, China's cottage industry and handicrafts enjoyed a twilight of qualitative superiority. The earned foreign exchange boosted the traditional agrarian economy, and the steady inflow of silver bullion, mainly from Japan and the Philippines, expanded the volume of money. The circulation of money was facilitated by the minting of bronze coinage undertaken by Beijing and the provincial mints. The mild inflation was accompanied by a steady population growth and the opening up of new agricultural land.

The elimination of the southern Chinese army commands in the 1680s, noted above, permitted more remittance of tax money to the north. This was the age when the banner system still functioned effectively. In 1696, Kangxi himself led an army of 80,000 men and improved artillery of Western design to meet his challenger, the Mongol leader Galdan. The battle of Urga is generally recognized as having put an end to the nomadic domination of frontier wars in which cavalry charges had been invincible for two millenniums. After the battle Galdan probably committed suicide. The unfinished business with his followers had to be settled by Qianlong, who in 1759 completed the occupation of the area called Xinjiang (now the Xinjiang-Uighur Autonomous Region), which at that time extended beyond Lake Balkhash.

In this period, contacts were made with the forces of tsarist Russia. The Treaty of Nerchinsk in 1689 and the Treaty of Kiakhta in 1727, negotiated at the zenith of Qing power, secured China's northern frontier, with China's border stretching much farther to the north than it does now.

With Korea as a protectorate even before the Manchus entered China, the Qing empire now extended its suzerainty over Siam, Burma, Vietnam, Bhutan, and Nepal. Outer Mongolia and Tibet were treated as peripheral territories administered differently from the interior provinces.

Toward the end of Kangxi's reign, the state of national affairs was already such that the monarch could declare that the empire's poll tax would be permanently frozen at the current level. The census figures taken before 1711 would be maintained as a permanent quota; further increases in the population would never again be taxed. In reality, this probably promised more than it delivered because the unit of taxation, the *ding*, theoretically an able-bodied male, had always been a relative quota. Perhaps at no time had the *ding* figures ever come close to the

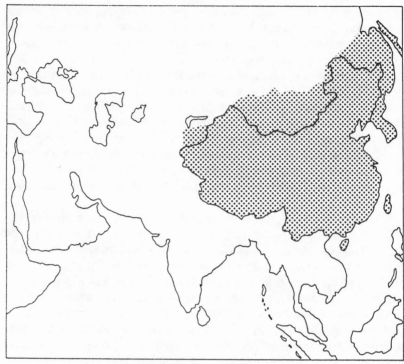

The Qing Empire at Its Zenith

actual head count. The assessment differed from one district to another, and the rates of collection could also be adjusted up and down to suit national and local needs. But Kangxi's decree reflected the boundless confidence of the throne in that era.

Overall, the Qing made few changes of Ming governmental institutions. Office salaries were only nominal, and the supplementary income of the officeholders derived from a variety of irregular sources, such as a surtax on silver payments called "melting charges." Yongzheng demanded that this quasilegal income be regularized. Subsequently, an "honesty-nourishing allowance" was authorized for fiscal officers of all echelons.

But if the Qing copied the organizational chart of the Ming, the new dynasty also made the offices function somewhat differently. For one thing, the Manchu emperors, during the time of fiscal expansion, exercised more authority than the ritualistic figureheads of the late Ming. The Qing monarchs held that imperial succession was a family matter, not for public discussion. They institutionalized a system of allowing princes of the blood to give counsel to the throne. To do away with the Ming fiction of letting child emperors make state decisions, a regent was formally appointed when the emperor was a minor. This effectively put an end to partisan controversies among Chinese bureaucrats, and debates on abstract matters by censorial officials were no longer allowed. Eunuchs were kept under control within the palace.

After the initial wave of resistance, Manchu relations with the Chinese improved. Intermarriage, forbidden by law, actually went on all the time. Indeed, several Qing emperors had Chinese concubines. Both Kangxi and Qianlong were reported to have had Chinese mothers. Opportunities for the Chinese to participate in government were theoretically unlimited, the only condition being that at the highest levels they had to share power with the Manchus. For each ministry, there were two ministers and four vice ministers, with the Chinese and Manchus equally divided. A similar arrangement was made for the grand secretaries. In 1729 the Yongzheng Emperor created the Grand Council; the members, appointed by him, were usually selected from among the grand secretaries, ministers, and vice ministers. Since the council members kept their concurrent portfolios, their bureaucratic influence further overshadowed the Manchu nobility. As time went on, more and more Chinese bureaucrats served as governors and governors-general.

It is not surprising, then, that when modern-minded historians search through the Qing records for the causes of Chinese nationalism, they find none. For imperial subjects who were born after the Manchu conquest were not even collaborating with an alien dynasty; they were serving *their* empire, which to them was a duty.

17
1800:
A Point for Reflection

In 1800, Napoleon attacked the Austrians in Italy, Jefferson and Burr were tied in the presidential election in the United States, and William Pitt seemed to have achieved the union of Ireland with Great Britain. In China, the Qianlong Emperor, who called himself "the old man who completed a perfect record," had been dead for barely a year. His favorite confidant, He Shen, had been arrested and ordered to commit suicide. Goods confiscated from his household were worth billions. The rebellion of the White Lotus Sect was getting out of hand. In Hubei, Shanxi, and Sichuan, the rebels gained large followings. The government forces repeatedly announced that the insurgents had been routed and annihilated; yet subsequently it became evident that the rebel camp had actually gained strength. On the recommendation of the governor-general at Guangzhou, the emperor decreed the prohibition of the importation of opium; the export of unminted silver had been proscribed a year earlier. These developments ushered in the new century, for China to be one of repeated defeats and insurmountable difficulties.

In view of the success and splendor mentioned in the preceding chapter, the reader may wonder: How could China's fortunes change so quickly?

Chinese writers tend to emphasize the working of the dynastic cycle. By the time Qianlong retired, the Qing Empire had already exhausted its growth potential. The martial spirit of the bannermen had evaporated. The banner system itself declined no differently from the way that the Ming hereditary military households had vanished from the rosters. Yongzheng's "honesty-nourishing" allowances, although increasing the salaries of key personnel by several times, were insufficient to cover the administrative costs of their posts, not to mention the personal expenses necessitated by the living habits of the bureaucrats, and not to mention the fact that numerous middle and lower officials were still paid with little more than nothing. As a result, corruption ran rampant. In the wake of misgovernment came neglected public works and unrelieved natural disasters, and, therefore, banditry and peasant rebellions. The chain reaction followed earlier patterns that had unfolded in history over and over again. Before facing the Western powers, China had weakened itself.

Today, almost 200 years later, we may have to expand on this observation. The combined reigns of the four early Qing emperors, splendidly successful as they seemed to be, were in the vision of macrohistory anachronistic. With all the fiscal surpluses passing through their hands, those rulers did little to revamp the superstructure of the empire or to strengthen the middle echelon of the government. A central treasury was still missing. The empire's financial resources were still handled by lateral transactions, thus yielding vital statistics always of doubtful quality. Civil laws that could have linked governmental operation with the rising economic trends were still not in place. China remained a conglomeration of village communities.

Again with the benefit of hindsight—the passing events of the subsequent 200 years in view—we further acknowledge that reform in China is always easier said than done. The peasants could only be maneuvered in blocks. The bureaucrats, who took the close to 1,500 counties in China proper as their interchangeable posts, could not be encouraged to compete among themselves for technical specialization. The experiences of the Tang and Song forewarned of this. To accommodate the mass, the governance of the Third Empire had worked its way toward the common denominator; it anchored itself in ideological cohesion. This is evident when we review the format of the civil service examinations, the procedure for personnel evaluation, and the operation of the local government.

But when inertia took hold, China was to remain like a submarine sandwich. There was a huge piece of bread on the top called the bureaucracy, there was a huge piece of bread on the bottom called the peasantry, both undifferentiated. The makings in between, be they cultural norms or the quintessence of governance or the substance of the civil service examinations, were basically a moral platform that suited the agrarian simplicity within a country of many millions of small self-cultivators. Relying on these moral precepts to supplement the penal code, China did not have the structural strength to qualify as a modern nation. It did not possess the needed functional maneuverability.

A modern nation is one in which the society is managed monetarily. The division of labor and the interchangeability of services and goods, together with the accompanying rights and obligations, are legally defined. A pluralistic society is possible because the mathematics of it, guided by the concept of equitability, enables the citizenry to attempt things that have never before been allowed. New churches are supported by their congregations. Artists and professionals compete for new patrons. It is most unfortunate that the process of moving in this direction has to be, historiographically, labeled as a development from feudalism to capitalism.* The connotation of class struggle comes to obscure all other aspects of the movement. The moral implication also hinders technical analysis of its application in the East and the West.

Given the constitutional differences between the Qing empire and its contemporary national states in western Europe, it would have been impossible for the Chinese to follow the path of the latter. Civil liberty in the West developed from the matrix of municipal franchise; the monied strength of the burghers alone was insufficient to bring about social change. In the age when foreign trade began to weigh heavily on the national economy, the power of mercantile interests grew substantial enough to convert some of the landed interests and compel the government, after a struggle of some duration, to realign its entire operation according to commercial principles. China had no such experience. Let us see what Adam Smith had to say about the situation. He wrote: "China has been long one of the richest, that is, one of the most fertile, best cultivated, most industrious, and most populous countries in the world. It seems, however, to have been long stationary. Marco Polo, who visited it more than five hundred years ago, describes its cultivation, industry, and populousness, almost in the same terms in which they are described by travelers in the present times. It had perhaps, even long before that time, acquired that full complement of riches which the nature of its laws and institutions permits it to acquire."

*Fernand Braudel points out that the word "capitalism" was used only sparsely in the nineteenth century, and never by Marx. He believes that the term was first used in its current sense as a natural opposite of socialism by Werner Sombart in the opening years of the twentieth century. See *Civilization and Capitalism 15th–18th Century*, Vol. II: *The Wheels of Commerce*, trans. from the French by Sian Reynolds (New York: Harper & Row, 1982), p. 237. Sir George Clark believes that "capitalism" as a name for the "modern economic system" was invented in the middle of the nineteenth century by socialists. See Clark, *The Seventeenth Century*, 2nd ed. (New York: Oxford University Press, 1947), p. 11.

Adam Smith, a contemporary of the Qianlong Emperor, had no idea that he would be held up as a spokesman for capitalism. He considered that there are "two systems of political economy"; one is "the system of commerce," the other "that of agriculture," and the system of commerce is "the modern system." *An Inquiry into the Nature and Causes of the Wealth of Nations*, Vol. I, Book IV, "Introduction."

His observation about the limits Chinese laws and institutions put on capital formation is undoubtedly true. As the government of the Ming and Qing was set up, its permanent policy was to foster the multitude of small self-cultivators, whose production techniques, having reached a plateau, could not be further improved. We have already observed that the basic farm implements remained virtually unchanged over a period of 600 years (pp. 144, 175). On the other side, modern commerce depends upon the wide extension of credit, impersonal management, and the pooling of service facilities. The feasibility of those conditions hinges upon trust, which must be legally enforceable. Thus merely refraining from interference in the free exchange of services and goods by the government is not enough; it has to be the patron, judge, and policeman of the movement. In view of the style of fiscal management of the Ming and the Qing, the government of the Third Empire neither intended nor had the capability to facilitate such an operation. With China's own house remaining mathematically unmanageable, its sermons on self-restraint and mutual deference were an ineffective substitute for an equitable administration over its millions.

But Smith's comment on China's being stationary requires clarification. No country could have remained stationary for centuries. In fact, during this period China went through several major policy changes and reversals. As early as the eleventh century, Wang Anshi's reforms intended to partially commercialize the empire's fiscal operations. Ironically, one of the reasons leading to their failure was the lack of mercantile participation and civil support (pp. 118–19). The painful effect was felt for a long time. When the policy of fiscal expansion stalled, the alien Yuan dynasty offered no alternative. The Ming resolved the dilemma with a bold retreat. Budgetary control and limitation stepped forward to substitute for the actual handling of the financial resources by the government itself. Staying away from the advanced sectors of the national economy altogether, the dynasty accentuated its virtues of being earthbound, and in doing so frankly acknowledged that to improve the standard of living was not its purpose. The Manchus, diverted from innovation as they were, at least liberalized the most rigid features of the management of their predecessors, such as letting more money go into circulation, taking fiscal matters realistically up to a point, and permitting the widening of trade at Guangzhou. But as a whole, the pattern was established. The regime's primary function was to hold the village communities together. Ideology came before technology, cultural influences were valued more than economics, and the passiveness of the bureaucrats as a rule took precedence over adaptability. Even frontier wars did nothing to alter this internal setup. Compared with the volatile character of the Second Empire, the Third

Empire was clearly immobile. It is the net result that may have induced the author of the *Wealth of Nations* to make his observation about a "stationary" China.

Whose fault was this? Should we point the finger at the Song reformers for their hastiness? Did their failure discourage further attempts at monetary management for a millennium to come? Or should Khubilai be blamed for his insatiable urge to conquer and thus his failure to organize China proper into a system? Or was Zhu Yuanzhang, as the founder of the Ming, responsible for overreacting to the Song failure by turning the clock backward far beyond a reasonable limit? Or were the Qing emperors, in their effort to live up to the image of Son of Heaven, equally guilty for being inhibited from reviving China's cultural pattern in substance, even though the times had changed, and in the seventeenth and eighteenth centuries they had far more awareness of conditions in the outside world? Suffice it to say that for short-term historical studies either pro or con, any or all of the above arguments could be developed into convincing theses.

But when the pieces are put together, we shall see instead the inescapable effect of geopolitics, more potent than the deeds of all individuals and dynasties combined, that kept China as it was. The many arguments scattered on the foregoing pages can now be summed up as one attributed to the mighty power of the Asian continental land mass. Being fringed with a vulnerable frontier of 2,000 miles, China had to maintain its national unity to survive. Military preparedness had to emphasize not only striking power into the desert lands, but also endurance on the home front, and above all the logistical capabilities to support both. These requirements implied that numerical superiority might count far more than quality. The weather over the continental land mass was such that the emperors and ministers had to constantly think of famine and starvation and along with them mutiny and rebellion before entertaining any thought of abundance. To prevent regional power from challenging the center, manorial estates had to be avoided. Direct taxation on individual peasant households remained the only solution to these simultaneous requirements. Simplicity and uniformity were therefore essential. Litigation, moreover, was not something that such a political system could easily accommodate, given court expenses and the cost of training a professional legal staff. When these factors accumulated, the economically more rational arrangements, such as laid out in the more compact southern kingdoms that existed between the Tang and Song (p. 110), were destined to be transitory. The unified empires of the Han and Tang were built up on crude foundations. Monetarily, the technically more advanced approach of the Song had to regress to make way for the far less enlightened administration of the

Ming. The Qing emperors, with their merits and faults reexamined in the light of the long-term rationality of history, could now be seen as having been invited to break a constitutional deadlock. Their relatively uncultured background actually appeared to be an advantage: Being uncommitted, they could be impartial. They had more aptitude and capacity to learn within a social environment supporting a statecraft that always stressed the fundamentals and basics of human values.

This is an alarming picture. It foretells that when China was forced to modernize, the revolution was expected to undo the works of a millennium. Unlike what happened in western Europe and Japan, where the adaptation of commercial practices could be started at the middle level, with the merchants playing an active role, in China it was to apply to thousands of bureaucrats and millions of peasants amidst a cultural tradition that paid little attention to the civil law, and where property rights had always been rendered ambiguous by the custom that gentlemen never spoke of profit, which was unbecoming in the face of the spirit of self-restraint and mutual deference. Needless to say, the revolution had to be excruciating and protracted.

Now let us take one more look at 1800 and the dynastic cycle.

Qianlong's record was not as perfect as he claimed. To begin with, he did not inherit a sound fiscal foundation, as recent research bears out. Moreover, as exemplified by the case of He Shen, his reign involved a number of unpalatable details that were carefully concealed in his lifetime. In traditional bureaucratic style, truth always came downward from the top; statistics reflected the wishes and demands of high authorities. The "old man" emperor's military campaign, conducted principally by Chinese troops called the "Green Standards," suffered several setbacks that were rarely mentioned. The formation of the White Lotus Sect had been going on for some time; in fact its rebellion broke out in the last years of his reign.

Closely related to the popular uprising, an undesirable consequence of the one and a half centuries' internal peace and prosperity was a phenomenal population growth. The total number of mouths that China had to feed in 1800 seems to have been in the vicinity of 300 million. There is little doubt that the number had doubled during the combined reigns of the four early Qing emperors. In agrarian China, labor was capital. The farm surplus, unable to be transformed into other kinds of materialistic benefit, was utilized to support a large population. With the number of newly opened fields diminishing, the country fell into the category of the "dismal science" of Malthus, whose treatise emerged with the French Revolution, or a whole decade prior to the Qianlong Emperor's demise.

Toward 1800, the draft banks of Shanxi appeared and established branches in the principal cities. Silk looms counted by the tens of thousands were reported in Suzhou and Nanjing. Salt-making, copper-mining, and porcelain manufacture were supposed to have employed prodigious numbers of workers. These reports, often appearing in brief and scattered references without detailed accounts to back them up, have puzzled and confused present-day readers. In reality, they at most suggest that on the eve of Industrial Revolution in Europe, China might still have had a few cases of concentrated wealth unattained by Westerners. But those exceptional cases in no way constituted a social system. Capitalism, if this word must be used, specifies an organization and a movement. When a society transforms itself from the norms of the "system of agriculture" to those of the "system of commerce," not only the legal instruments must be revised to suit, but also, the citizenry has to be prepared for it, so that compliance with the new laws becomes a social compulsion. The monetary trust extended between individuals and corporations signifies that property rights have been settled, so that division of labor and interchangeability of services and goods are self-evident and naturally inviting. The question is not how much wealth is on hand, but how this richness can be transferred and reinvested, and continue to grow and multiply. So far all the nations that have experienced such a breakthrough have found the process irreversible. China by 1800 was nowhere close to such an eventuality. To cite the aforementioned exceptional cases as evidence of an "inceptive capitalism" is therefore meaningless. It is tantamount to saying that a child is not a child, but a pre-adult.

The Qing was a period of scholarly pragmatism. Before 1800, several great novels were produced. But by pragmatism we mean that the philosophers of the age merely stayed away from the metaphysical speculation of the Song and the meditation school of the Ming. Lacking a physical environment that truly encouraged independent thinking, they could never depart from the social values anchored in the literary bureaucratic management, which they took so much for granted. Some pretensions of the past had been corrected by those thinkers. But the pragmatists, working closely with the Confucian classics and historiography, could not develop a penetrating vision to see what eyes could not see. What's the point of having pragmatism? Essentially it is to break away from one system as a step toward building another; as Bacon and Descartes discovered, science develops from prolonged and persistent disbelief. Lacking such thoroughness, the Qing pragmatists could not be said to have arrived at the wisdom of the Greek thinkers, who held that Natural Law must be gradually discovered—a belief that later was to spark the thinking of Renaissance men. Nor did the Qing pragmatism lead to the kind of variety reminiscent of the "Hundred Schools" of China's own Warring States period.

The Qing novels indeed have their unique qualities. They portray contemporary life with leisurely details to a degree unattained by any other form of literary presentation. But from the historian's point of view they remain products of China under bureaucratism. *The Dream of the Red Chamber*, aesthetically composed, is too nostalgic, too sentimental, too feminine. *The Scholars*, sharply satirical, is written like a collection of essays. Both the anger and self-pity of the authors reveal the limitations of their lives, which must have been sensed and shared by many of their admiring readers.

Have we been too negative in evaluating an era? Undoubtedly we would have been had we been writing on the eighteenth century for its own sake. One could, of course, dwell on the vision of the Enlightenment and see China as a model of social harmony, or with the Physiocrats admire the Chinese for always being able to put their emphasis on the fundamentals and basics, or follow a generation of craftsmen to marvel at everything that is *chinoiserie*, from the carefully carved latticework on teakwood chairs to the satin-like surface of lacquer vessels several feet tall. But elegance and polish on one side leads to crisis and danger on the other. After all, 1800 was only forty years away from the Opium War, when Chinese and Manchu soldiers had to carry swords and spears against a foe who came with 540 canons mounted on sixteen ships. And there are the subsequent events of the one and a half centuries yet to come. The pressure and tension that originated from the same fundamental cause eventually led to the occasion of the Great Proletariat Cultural Revolution, so much so that foreign observers begin to wonder where "the roots of madness" lie.

With all the unkind words said about eighteenth-century China, we merely try to explain that there are roots but no madness. An explanation of what seems to be incomprehensible is there, if the reader is willing to go back far enough. The roots may be found in geography as well as in history. In that sense the year of 1800 is not even a breaking point; it might be a good point for stopping for reflection.

18

From the Opium War
to the Self-Strengthening Movement

Today, with the additional span of one and a half centuries behind us, we can review the events leading up to the Opium War in a perspective quite different from that of our predecessors, even though the basic facts remain unchanged. Lin Zexu, the imperial commissioner at Guangzhou, exercised sufficient initiative to compose a letter to Queen Victoria and had more than twenty copies of it made so that every European ship sailing home could be entrusted to convey the message, one that asked for the voluntary suspension of the opium trade by Britain. Yet Lin minimized the importance of the news that in England warships were gathered in preparation for an expedition to China as no more than "an intimidating gesture designed to scare us." On the one hand he inquired about Emeric de Vattel's *Law of Nations*; on the other he enforced Chinese prohibitory laws, which were in the statute books but so far had been ignored by everybody, with a sudden severity and urgency characteristic of traditional Chinese legal practice. Above all, his principal method of enforcing the laws took the form of "group responsibility," that is, rounding up offenders by categories and by association, serving the convenience of the bureaucratic system rather than individual justice. Charles Elliot, of course, had no intention of solving the problem by peaceful means. He urged the British merchants to surrender the opium to him, and, as the superintendent of trade, handed it over to Lin, to make the commissioner responsible to the British Crown for the goods thus confiscated and destroyed. It provided the grounds for the later demand for compensation, set at a value of six million dollars and to be a part of the twenty-one-million-dollar war indemnities that the British were able to extract from the Chinese. The way that the Daoguang Emperor (personal name: Minning, reigned 1821–1850) conducted his office throughout this sequence of events could never be considered fair or even-handed. He demanded from his officials more than they could possibly accomplish; he encouraged them to act boldly, yet when things went wrong he did not hesitate for a moment to mete out the death sentence, although, by custom, the penalty was commuted to exile to the frontier provinces.

The war itself was a simple matter of first puncturing the formidable facade of the Celestial Empire with an expeditionary force of 4,000 men, enormously better organized and better equipped than their Chinese counterparts. War was declared by the Indian Government on behalf of the British Crown in early 1840. Soon the redcoats occupied Dinghai on Zhoushan Island and blockaded the mouth of the Yangtze and then that of the Pearl River before proceeding north to threaten the capital. The Qing empire could have capitulated at this point. A preliminary convention was worked out in the field, but it was repudiated by both governments. Beijing felt that the terms made too many concessions; Westminster regarded them as not having made enough.

When hostilities resumed in the autumn of 1841, the British occupied Ningbo on the Zhejiang coast. The expeditionary force was gradually built up to 10,000 men and fourteen steamers. Chinese resistance at the mouth of the Pearl River and on Zhoushan Island was heroic but futile. A counterattack, led by a general who was the emperor's cousin, only added blunders to the setback. The staff of his command consisted of many literati who had no professional training. Ten days before the engagement, with the recovery of Ningbo in mind, these men of letters competed in drafting victory announcements in advance. To finance the campaign the general had set up four paymasters' offices in separate cities to receive grants and remittances directed by the central government. Large sums of money passed through those agencies, but the figures did not tally. Firearms were manufactured in the field by inexperienced personnel from instructions in handbooks printed some 200 years earlier. During the operation, Chinese fire rafts, which were supposed to set the British warships ablaze, were themselves ignited miles away from the target by the enemy and rendered harmless. The night attack on Ningbo fell into a British trap. In the summer of 1842, when the organized fighting collapsed, the British took Shanghai and Zhejiang, the latter being vital to Beijing's communication to the south. A month later the Treaty of Nanjing was signed.

The settlement provided for a payment of war indemnities, as mentioned above, the cession of Hong Kong, the opening of five ports— Shanghai, Ningbo, Guangzhou, Amoy, and Fuzhou—to trade, a fixed tariff on imports and exports, and equal positions in official correspondence between the two sides. A supplementary treaty signed the next year fixed the tariff at an average of five percent *ad valorem*, the authorization of extraterritoriality to permit the British consuls to try their own subjects, and the "most favored nation" clause, by which in the future any concession that the Chinese government granted to a third power would be simultaneously and automatically extended to Britain as well. This clause was also incorporated in the treaties that China subsequently signed with France and the United States.

For over a century, there have been more than enough charges of arrogance, complacency, irresponsibility, and corruption leveled by Chinese and Western writers alike at the Daoguang Emperor and his functionaries. While no one could ever clear them of those charges, in retrospect, neither could anyone else in their position have done much better in view of the institutional burden and cultural heritage weighing so heavily on them. China being a conglomeration of village communities, its major problem was worse than official corruption. It had a constitution that was mathematically unmanageable. Left by itself, it relied on the power of belief to compensate for its lack of organizational integrity. Aesthetics in governance was indulged in with religious fervor. Thus even during the period of crisis, we find Commissioner Lin composing poetry and enjoying a moonlit night. Custom dictated that moral perception would precede reality in his reports and public announcements. Yet Lin Zexu was never a dishonest person. Suffice it to say that self-deception was a part of Chinese public psychology. Truth was not all that was objectively observed; it represented the will of the emperor. The utmost virtue of the Son of Heaven was not being just, but being impartial. Daoguang could send Lin Zexu into exile; he could also sentence his own cousin to death. It was with just such impartiality that he held the bureaucracy together.

The Qing was not as introverted and noncompetitive as the Ming; but as a succession dynasty it inherited certain characteristics of its predecessor. Its reluctance to realize fiscal innovations and technological progress reflected an unspoken wish not to disturb the delicate balance that had up until then kept millions of peasants in place and thousands of literati-officials placidly employed. We may note here that after the Opium War the court in Beijing never conducted an inquiry to determine what happened, or sent observers overseas, or made institutional readjustments. The blueprints of modern military equipment offered by the American envoy were politely declined. Of all the clauses included in the Treaty of Nanjing and the supplementary treaty, the one that grieved the Manchu and Chinese officials most was that thenceforth diplomatic correspondence with the barbarians had to be handled on an equal basis. In his report to the emperor, Jiying, who negotiated the treaty settlement with Sir Henry Pottinger, continued to belittle the constitutional features of the several Western nations. Their lack of regularity and constancy was seized on as a sign of moral inferiority. China's falling short in many vital areas was not mentioned.

But unfortunately for the Chinese, even before the war was declared, the exchange of gunfire near Chuanbi Island in the Pearl River on November 3, 1839, had shattered their noncompetitive position forever. Their rectitude in fighting a war to stop drug traffic had little bearing on future events; Chinese history in the coming century and a half was to be a prolonged national struggle to survive. Fundamentally, this involved a process through which a large agrarian country loosely constructed on social values with a generous tolerance for administrative anomalies had to transform itself into a nation that was mathematically manageable.* It was more difficult than it is ordinarily recognized because the task had to be accomplished, ultimately, by a mass movement of millions of peasants led by the poet-magistrates— the dominant components of the social constitution (p. 193). Nevertheless, to tighten internal cohesion around modern technology was more than, as Adam Smith has advocated, to "enrich the people." As the events of the past century and a half show, it was a matter of life and death.

The prospect was, however, far from being clear on August 29, 1842, when the Treaty of Nanjing was signed on the deck of the *Cornwallis*. Even as recently as several decades ago, we ourselves still had no idea that to a great extent the turmoil and violence unfolding before our eyes were still a necessary part of the protracted and painful struggle that ran continuously from the days of the Daoguang Emperor and Commissioner Lin to the present. Only with all the events laid bare do we begin to realize the magnitude of this stupendous movement.

---

*Rarely mentioned in this connection, England too had to go through some kind of transformation before becoming a major commercial power. Prior to the Reformation, Italian bankers in England handled the remittance of papal dues. They usually made advances to the Vatican, then used local collections to contract English sheep farmers, thus controlling the export of wool to the continent. London's banking district, called the Lombard Street (in those days all Italians were known as Lombards), might be considered a forerunner of the "concessions," or business and residential districts in China's treaty ports administered by the Westerners. In this case the Italians, too, enjoyed extraterritoriality, which, nominally reciprocal, had little meaning to the Englishmen, since few of them had business interests in Venice or Genoa or Siena. England had to take the inferior position because most of the commercial laws were inoperative in the rural areas. In that sense the country could not be said to have qualified as monetarily or mathematically manageable. This later awkward situation was corrected only after the Civil War and during the late Stuart period.

Today most provisions of the Treaty of Nanjing and the supplementary treaty have been nullified by later events. The recovery of Hong Kong by the People's Republic has yet to be achieved; but a plan for handing it over peacefully has been agreed upon. The Crown Colony includes the island of Hong Kong, ceded in 1842 as described; the Kowloon Peninsula on mainland China, ceded later under the Beijing Convention of 1860; and the New Territories, which, farther inland behind Kowloon and consisting of more than 90 percent of the Crown Colonies area, was leased to the British for ninety-nine years, the provision to run out in 1997, which is also the target date for the return of the entire colony. Pledges allowing local autonomy and not to alter the present economic and legal systems in the next fifty years have been made by Beijing.

How well the present regime's promise of "one nation, two systems" works in the future remains to be seen. What the historian can point out for sure at this point is, once again, the gigantic scale of the problem at hand of converting a nation with a huge population and land mass from the mode of agriculture to the mode of commerce. The preliminary indication is that before all is settled, even the accepted usage of conventional labels such as nationhood and Marxism may have to be modified in order to accommodate the case of China. Clear enough, the compromise solution on Hong Kong made sense only when the issue is reviewed as a part of the larger problem behind it, which is deeply affected by geography and culture no less than by economics and politics.

Now let us return to the mid-nineteenth century.

A decade after the signing of the Treaty of Nanjing, a greater dissatisfaction was registered by the victors than by the defeated. The peace settlement opened China for trade; but trading required voluntary and active participation on both sides. What would happen if the local population, under the direction of the magistrates, remained hostile to the foreigners arriving at the treaty ports? What would happen if the Chinese merchants contracted to do business with foreign firms should default and run inland, beyond the reach of the consular offices? To whom should the foreigners protest if, after the regular tariff was paid, the inland provinces should add exorbitant transit taxes on the goods? There was a great deal of ambiguity hanging over the opium trade, as the 1842 settlement had refrained from clarifying whether it was now legalized or the Chinese laws prohibiting it were still in force. All told, in order to make the treaty system effective, offices of residential ministers should have been established in Beijing, the inland provinces should have been opened up for business and travel, transit taxes should have been regularized, and the legalization of the opium trade should have been made official. A new opportunity for raising these issues occurred in 1856, because the American and French treaties, signed in 1844, included clauses for revising the terms after twelve years. The British, invoking the most favored nation status, could have claimed the same privilege if renegotiations got under way.

Since 1854 the diplomats and naval officers of the three powers had shuttled between north China and the south to seek a hearing for their proposals without success. Among the Chinese officials, Ye Minchen, governor-general at Guangzhou, was the most obstructive. Moreover, the populace in the city had already successfully resisted the British entry for several years. This was exacerbated by the fact that the new emperor, Xianfeng (personal name Yichu, reigned 1850–1861), was a hardline xenophobe. These conditions induced the two European powers to take up arms once more. So there transpired the Anglo-French War against China in 1856–1860, sometimes referred to as the Second Opium War.

A Chinese vessel registered at Hong Kong, flying the British flag, was boarded by Ye's soldiers, and this provided the British a pretext for war. Soon the French joined in, on the grounds that a French missionary had been judicially murdered by Chinese officials in Guangxi. The Crimean War and the Sepoy Rebellion in India delayed the joint operation somewhat, but once the forces were gathered, they had no difficulty in taking Guangzhou in the closing days of 1857. Governor-General Ye Minchen was captured and later died a prisoner in Calcutta. The city of Guangzhou was under British occupation for the duration of the war, which was to drag on for another three years.

In the summer of 1858, warships of Britain, France, the United States, and Russia converged along the shores of Tianjin, with those of the former two taking action and those of the latter two watching a short distance offshore. The Dagu Fortress was taken and the city occupied. The so-called Treaty of Tianjin, concluded in June, actually involved four separate treaties. In general they authorized residential ministers in Beijing, a five percent tariff and 2.5 percent transit tax on imports and exports, and ten additional ports for trade, which opened up the inland provinces, Taiwan, and Hainan Island. Inland navigation by foreign ships was consented to by the Chinese government. Passport bearers from the signatory countries were free to travel in China. Legalization of the opium trade was agreed to with Britain. War indemnities were to be paid to Britain and France.

Those treaties were supposed to take effect upon exchange of ratified copies. The next year when the Western foreign ministers arrived on warships for this purpose, the Dagu Fortress was under repair, and obstacles had been set up in the river leading to the port of Tianjin. The American minister alone took the Chinese advice by detouring to the north to arrive at Beijing. The exchange of copies was in time accomplished, even though his reception by the Chinese was less than cordial. The Russian representative, arriving overland, did the same thing. But the British and French ministers, with a flotilla of eighteen ships, decided to clear the obstacles and force their way through. In so doing they exchanged fire with the newly replaced shore batteries. This time the Chinese, under a Mongol general, scored a victory. The allied forces suffered more than 400 casualties, with four ships sunk and six damaged. Yet in the long run the Chinese had to pay for this act.

In 1860, a reinforced allied expeditionary force included 18,000 British troops and 7,000 French soldiers, with 2,500 Chinese laborer auxiliaries recruited from the south to cover the rear. It seized the Dagu Fortress by overland encirclement before reoccupying Tianjin. Peace negotiations delayed further advance for weeks, but by October the Anglo-French forces were in Beijing. The Xianfeng Emperor had to flee to Rehe, never to return. His summer palace, close to the present site of Beijing University, was at first looted by the allied soldiers and later set afire by orders of Lord Elgin. The Beijing Convention of 1860, initiated by Prince Gong, the emperor's brother, recognized the treaties concluded earlier, provided additional indemnities, ceded Kowloon to the British, and permitted French missionaries to purchase property in the interior provinces.

The greatest beneficiary of this sequence of events was tsarist Russia. Claiming credit for serving as the mediator who had persuaded the Anglo-French forces to withdraw from Beijing, the Russian ambassador demanded and obtained for his homeland the territories north of the Amur River and east of the Ussuri River to the sea, including today's Khabarovsk and Vladivostok, an area of over 300,000 square miles. It happened that during the preceding years when the court in Beijing was preoccupied with other matters, the tsarist forces had made inroads in this remote region and intimidated the local Manchu general into accepting them. The 1860 Treaty of Beijing merely confirmed the Russian position and enlarged its scope.

While all this was happening, the Manchu dynasty was fighting for its life to fend off another challenge. Since 1850 large areas in central and south China had been embroiled in internal rebellions, and the most threatening of them all were the Taiping rebels, led by Hong Xiuquan. This village school teacher, who had received a Christian tract given to him by a foreign missionary in the streets of Guangzhou, fell ill after repeatedly failing the civil service examinations. In his delirium he saw visions. After he recovered and had an opportunity to read the tract he came to believe that he himself was Jehovah's second son and Jesus Christ's younger brother. The distress of the local people in Guangxi Province owing to hard times and misgovernment made his Messianic message attractive to many, and several of his cohorts who had a social background similar to his own directed the converted peasants. Members of his God-worshiping Society pledged themselves to righteous living, god fearing, and universal brotherhood and sisterhood. The purge of the world of demons applied to village idolatry as well as to corrupt officials and government runners. In early 1851 Hong proclaimed his Heavenly Kingdom of Great Peace. He himself became the Heavenly King; five of his close followers were made auxiliary kings. Long hair in front and no queue in back gave the rebels a distinctive physical mark. Contingents of the Qing army were no match for the mass of peasant zealots incited by spiritualism. In 1852 the Taipings besieged, within a span of several months, Guilin and Changsha, respectively provincial capitals of Guangxi and Hunan, yet failed to capture either. Hong then abandoned the sieges to move on, taking Wuchang, capital of Hubei in early 1853. Large quantities of inland shipping were seized, along with supplies and military stocks captured from the Manchu forces. By this time his followers had grown to half a million. In another two months the Taipings had established themselves in all the major cities on the Yangtze River from Wuchang to Nanjing. The latter became the "Heavenly Capital" and remained so for a period of eleven years—until the summer of 1864.

From today's perspective, the positiveness of the Taipings can no longer be exaggerated. They vaguely suggested that the traditional mode of governance that treated the peasants as an undifferentiated and inarticulate body of producers needed to be altered, or else China could never establish a new order to cope with the changing circumstances of the world. Yet the Heavenly Kingdom was not the solution. In the past, many historians, adhering to the immediate context, faulted Hong Xiuquan for not pressing the northern expedition with vigor once Nanjing was taken, for his failure to form effective alliances at first with the Nian rebels in north-central China and later with the Small Swords arising in the Shanghai area, and for his inability to court foreign sympathy at a time when the Westerners, exasperated over their negotiations with the Qing Empire, thought that the Taipings, being Christians, might offer a better alternative. A constitutional analysis of these considerations, however, greatly diminishes their speculative value.

The Taipings, with their combativeness, irrationality, distrust of government, and primitive communism, resembled in certain ways the

Protestant Left during the Reformation era. Yet even in Europe such leftist movements are remembered only as interruptions in certain urban centers. Hong Xiuquan derived less substance from the distorted rudimentary Christian teaching with which he attempted to lead a national movement, since freedom of conscience had so little relevance in rural China. The theological foundation of the Taipings never rose above the level of shamanism because their movement, originating in the lower strata of the population, did not seriously anticipate an organizational phase to bring forth an integrated society in this world. When everybody was emancipated, the social order vanished.

Here once again, the durable structure of the traditional Chinese state and society, obsolete as it was, came into play, especially for its interlink in the civil service examinations, which subtly delivered materialistic incentives for the subscription to orthodox social values handed down all the way from Mencius to keep the rural communities in line. When the gentry members, given the protected privilege of landholdings of modest size, invoked the ancient virtues in unison, it was difficult to say where the cultural influence ended and the political power of the state began. Nor could anyone say for sure whether this was an economic order or a social custom. The fatherly image of the emperor, sanctioned by history, came closer to this unitary constitution of China's than did the God of the Old Testament. He derived his operational capacity from his ceremonial functions. While it is true that by the mid-nineteenth century the Qing empire might have abused this all-embracing arrangement, as later events showed, it was far too early to expect a replacement of the dynasty along with the institutions that it represented.

The Heavenly Kingdom proscribed prostitution, footbinding, concubinage, gambling, and opium-smoking. Yet the patronage of equality for women did not prevent its own hierarchy from maintaining harems. Nor did the "kings" abide by simple living once they became masters of the Heavenly Capital. After 1856, the hierarchy was preoccupied with internal strife. Its land redistribution program, derived from the traditional schematic design, remained a paper scheme. The extant copies of its version of the civil service examinations reveal that the examiners did not grasp the socio-economic leverage of such an institution.

The person most responsible for rallying traditional orthodoxy and the Manchu empire to defeat the Taipings was Zeng Guofan, a former court academician. Like Qi Jiguang 300 years earlier (p. 171), he built up his Hunan Braves by recruiting in the rural areas and officering the force with natives hand-picked by himself, most of them Confucian scholars and many of them small landowners from his own Xiangxiang County. An espirit de corps was established. Supplies were derived from a universal transit tax authorized by Beijing and local contributions, voluntary and forced. A new element was that a marine corps drilled in ship-to-ship fighting and quartered on river junks equipped with firearms kept the operation mobile. At first recruited to protect their home province, the Braves soon outperformed the army regulars and from 1854 on saw action in other provinces. Their strength expanded from the original 20,000 men to several times that number. In the hard fighting with the Taipings, seasaw battles developed along the middle section of the Yangtze River and its two major tributaries, the Xiang and the Gan. The war now entered into a phase in which the walled cities were contested not only for their strategic value but also for their effect in controlling manpower and food supplies. Atrocities were committed by both sides; prisoners of war were indiscriminately slaughtered. Epidemics broke out amidst food shortages, and depopulation in the war-torn areas was a factor contributing to the eventual end of the civil strife.

Yet in the 1860s the Taipings, after losing control over the inland provinces, made one more upsurge by carrying the war into the coastal region. Hangzhou, Ningbo, Suzhou, and Shanghai changed hands. The cutting down of mulberry trees caused irreparable damage to China's sericulture. In this phase of the war Li Hongzhang, one of Zeng Guofan's associates, distinguished himself. He recruited and organized a Huai Army, patterned after the Hunan Braves, from his native Anhui Province. Now that the war with the Anglo-French forces had ended, the "Ever Victorious Army," a regiment of Shanghai volunteers organized by the merchants and officered by Westerners, could see action on the side of the government with the blessing of the foreign powers. Its operations built up the romantic fame of Frederick Townsend Ward and Charles George Gordon (the Chinese Gordon). With their assistance Li cleared the eastern seaboard, enabling Zeng's Hunan Braves to enter the Heavenly Capital on July 19, 1864. The Heavenly King had committed suicide earlier.

The mopping up of the Taiping remnants in Fujian was concluded the following year. Even just this phase of the struggle was contemporaneous with the entire duration of the American Civil War. And yet, with bloodshed incalculably greater,* it solved fewer problems.

The term "Self-Strengthening Movement" comes from a sentence in the *Book of Changes*: "Heaven moves on strongly; the gentlemen therefore incessantly strengthen themselves." This motto, applied to the imitation of the West by the Chinese in the 1860s and 1870s, does reveal

---

*Estimates of total casualties in the Taiping Rebellion run as high as 20 million.

some kind of defense mechanism at work. As the promoters of this movement never felt completely assured that they were beyond criticism, they quoted the classics to stress that there was a change of time and circumstances that justified their following the foreign lead. Another argument that they made defensively was that they borrowed Western learning for its utility; for the fundamentals they never deviated from China's cultural tradition.

In practice, the criticisms that they were exposed to were mild. But the attempted reform, with so narrow a scope, ultimately defeated its own purpose.

For about a decade after the conclusion of the Convention of Beijing, there was a short period of good feelings. The Westerners, having already extracted from China all the concessions they needed, refrained from applying further pressure. When such hawks as Harry Parkes and James Bruce (Earl of Elgin) were gone, a new breed of diplomats, men like Rutherford Alcock, the British minister, Anson Burlingame, the American minister, and Robert Hart, the Irishman who acted as the inspector general for the newly created Chinese Customs Service, advocated a conciliatory policy. They believed that given proper encouragement, China would proceed to open its door further for its own benefit. In the meantime Prince Gong, acting for the minor emperor Tongzhi (personal name Daichun, reigned 1862–1874), realized that the treaty system was here to stay and that China should go ahead and follow the terms faithfully rather than fantasize about their abrogation and a return to the tributary relationship. Within this cordial atmosphere the Self-strengthening Movement came forth apace.

An office called the Zongli Yamen was set up in 1861. Coexisting with the old-fashioned boards and bureaus, the yamen specialized in handling the affairs of the foreign powers under the treaty relationship. An interpreters' college was organized in Beijing the next year, and several language schools soon opened up in the port cities. Henry Wheaton's *Elements of International Law* was translated. During the last few years of fighting the Taipings, the scholar-generals were deeply impressed by the firearms and steamers of Western manufacture. So, under Zeng Guofan, Li Hongzhang, and Zuo Zongtang (another Hunan general), who became governors-general after the suppression of the Taipings, machine shops and shipyards were established in several southern cities, with equipment purchased and technicians hired overseas. In the 1870s when foreign relationships deteriorated, this trend nevertheless continued. A steamship company was organized, a group of teen-age Chinese students arrived in the United States for Western studies, a coal mine opened up in North China, and telegraphic services linked China's major cities.

With all this the combined effort of the Self-Strengthening Movement demonstrated a single-minded purpose: China wished to take advantage of Western technology to boost its military strength, but for nothing else. It was guns and steamships that the reformers wanted, so it was arsenals and dockyards that they built. The changes were compartmentalized so as not to interfere with Chinese laws and institutions. The personnel trained in "foreign affairs" were expected to become technicians auxiliary to the literary bureaucracy, so there was no change in the regular education system and the civil service examinations.

The limited goal was unattainable, for a reason that is not difficult to pin down. So-called "foreign affairs," which in reality meant "things Western," were the end products of the entire range of modern Western civilization, resulting from its maximum efficiency and greater emphasis on precision. It was the antithesis of a bureaucratic management system that, persisting in its noncompetitive characteristics and its sprawling structure, had for hundreds of years been used to maintain a more modest level of performance in order to assure internal cohesion. As the two modes of life were structured, they took root respectively in mercantile and agrarian communities, and the different living habits thereof affected every producer and every user of the weapons and contrivances, not to mention their coordinators and organizers, on every occasion and on any given day.

The arsenals and dockyards were set up as business enterprises but they had no contact with correspondent firms; they were manufacturers but they had no subcontractors and retailing distributors. Many business contacts were loose at best. Office accounts could not be seriously audited. There were no adequate budget for their operations since none existed for the government itself. A general standard for personnel management was lacking since there was no such standard in China's entire economic life.

To call all of this "corruption" risks misrepresenting the situation. Such a moral charge would imply that the arrangement was workable.

As it happened, it was not. An immediate test came in 1884, when China found itself at war with France for suzerainty over Vietnam. In short order the French fleet neutralized the Jilong Fortress in Taiwan and occupied the Pescadores. When they turned their attention to the mainland, within hours the warships destroyed the Fuzhou Dockyard, which had been built with French aid.

Stripping the Chinese Empire of overlordship over Vietnam may have been a blessing in disguise, but at the conclusion of the war in 1885, the loss of influence over the peripheral areas left China more exposed than ever, and it would have to fight for its life thereafter. Japan had already sent an expedition to Taiwan a decade before. Russia had detached a large section of territory from China's northwest frontier. By the Treaty of Petersburg in 1881, which was counted as a Chinese diplomatic victory, China still had to pay the tsar nine million rubles and surrender the Balkhash Lake area. In the same year that the war with France was concluded, Britain reduced Burma to a protectorate.

The late nineteenth century, at the maturity of the Industrial Revolution in the West, was an era of Social Darwinism. Losers in practically any struggle were deemed inferior in character. China's repeated failures in foreign affairs made the Self-Strengthening Movement look very bad, as it had wasted twenty years' of precious time. Yet, in modern Chinese history, the movement constituted only the first of a long series of "failures" that China was to experience. The opportunity to offer a more positive view of this sequence of events has occurred only recently. With more historical depth, we can now see that failures though they seemed to be, they were necessary steps toward a immense revolution. Compared with the inaction after the Opium War, the reform in the 1860s made a serious commitment, so much so that the reformers had to protect the movement with an indigenous and ancient label. Timid as they were, they dared to punch a hole in traditional China's solid structure. The scope of their "self-strengthening" is of course a disappointment to us. But in view of the time and circumstances, it is not surprising. When we remember that to make this effort at industrialization China had to produce from scratch its first mathematics textbooks, and the students selected for foreign language studies had to be fourteen years old or younger, we begin to realize what a long way China had to go. The Self-Strengthening Movement was based on technological application. More than three decades later, however, in 1898, the Hundred Days' Reform (next chapter) attempted to rewrite the constitution and introduce institutional changes. Another twenty-one years later, during the Republican era, China's intellectuals came to the realization that change had to come not only from themselves, but also from within their minds. Even though unplanned and uncoordinated, the progression of these events causes us to marvel at the power of history. It has a logic; its long-term rationality also allocates the Chinese Revolution sufficient time for preparation and applies enough pressure to it to enable it to follow through. The magnitude is always appropriate for the size of the problem at hand.

19
The "Hundred Days,"
the Republic, and May Fourth

China's defeat by Japan on land and sea during the war of 1894–95 brought serious repercussions. The war aim of the Chinese was to maintain Korea as the last tributary state, but in the process it was lost forever. The Liaodong peninsula, Taiwan, and the Pescadores had to be ceded to the victor. The war indemnity of 200 million ounces of silver put an unbearable financial burden on the defeated. Other commercial concessions were similar to those granted earlier to the Western nations. But in addition, the Treaty of Shimonoseki, as this latest settlement was called, also authorized Japan to operate factories in Chinese cities. Through the most-favored-nation clause this privilege was soon extended to all other treaty powers. Thanks to joint intervention by Russia, France, and Germany, after the signing of the treaty the Liaodong peninsula was "saved" from transfer. China paid another thirty million ounces of silver in its place. But the tsarist government waited only three more years before demanding a twenty-five year lease on the territory. Thereafter it changed hands between tsarist Russia and imperial Japan, and then fell again into the hands of Stalin's Soviet Union, for altogether close to sixty years. China did not recover it until 1955.

The defeat by Japan deeply wounded China's pride. The Chinese had fought the Japanese before, but never accepted that the latter could be their superior. Undoubtedly, ethnocentrism resided on both sides, which had helped fan up the hostilities in the first place. Less noticed was the fact that modernization is essentially a process of applying the principles of commercial organization to state affairs, so that an extended system of division of labor in the public domain parallels that in the private sector and the resultant higher level of functioning endows the nation with better maneuverability apart from its character. Japan, moving in that direction ever since the late Tokugawa period, was much more efficacious than China's undifferentiated agrarian mass, and the differences inevitably showed on the battlefield.

World-wide racism had reached a high-water mark around the turn of the century, and it found an ardent spokesman in William II. The Japanese were receptive to the kaiser's message that they, patriotic and sanguine, had appeared as a chosen group over the indolent and spiritless Chinese. Ito Hirobumi in his negotiations with Li Hongzhang must have seized the opportunity as the representative of the victor to seek revenge for the contempt that Chinese writers had in the past habitually and insensitively heaped on Japan; or else his rough treatment of Li, China's senior statesman, served no practical purpose.

The humiliation was so shocking that the public reaction in China swung to extremes. One school of thought urged the acceptance of Japanese superiority: Ito could be invited to become China's premier. Another school agitated to repudiate the peace treaty altogether. The concessions demanded by Japan could then be parceled out and handed over to the tsarist and Western powers as an incentive to induce them to fight the Japanese. Not exactly endorsing this, Li Hongzhang was, however, sufficiently moved by the suggestion to sign the Li-Lobanov Treaty of 1896, which, among other things, granted Russia the right to construct a railroad in Manchuria. A rumor continued to circulate that Li received a handsome sum from Petersburg for putting his signature on the document.

Still, for China the greatest difficulty arose from the war indemnity. The funds could only be raised from foreign loans. At this time there was no lack of lenders. But each of these, representing a foreign power, was anxious to capitalize on the opportunity to control Chinese customs revenues and to secure mining rights. Before the Sino-Japanese War, China had negligible external debts. Thereafter, its public finance was thoroughly under the control of foreign banking consortiums. The proceeds from import and export duties, the salt gabelle, and inland transit taxes became collateral for the loans. It was the issue of financing the railroads that sparked the Revolution of 1911. The situation hardly changed during the early Republican era. It was the dispute over the disposition of customs revenues that led Dr. Sun Yat-sen to break off his alignment with the Western powers to befriend the Soviets.

Back in the nineteenth century, 1898 was an events-crowded year. So-called "spheres of influence" were established in China by Britain, France, Germany, Russia, and Japan. If a particular province fell under the sphere of influence of a foreign power, China was compelled to announce that that province would never be ceded to another nation. When a major port was leased, the leaseholder had the claim for ninety-nine years and was free to fortify it, and the Chinese were not allowed to send troops to within a specified distance, usually fifteen miles. The power controlling the sphere of influence had exclusive rights to railroad construction, telegraphic service, and the mineral resources. If China should initiate a project of its own, no capital could be contributed by a third power; nor could technicians of other nationalities be hired. Some of those concessions were wrested from China by forty-eight hour ultimatums. Those conditions caused Dr. Sun to call China a subcolony—a status below a normal colony which served only one master. At the turn of the century China was subject to the domination of a host of foreign powers. The "Open Door" policy announced by Secretary of State John Hay in 1899 and 1900 did not substantially change the situation.

In the summer of 1898, official circles in Beijing experienced something that they had never experienced before. From June 11 to September 21, for a period of 103 days, more than 200 rescripts, decrees, and edicts came down from the throne proclaiming that governmental offices would be reorganized, a budget prepared, the army and navy modernized, the entire educational system and civil service realigned, and agriculture, industry, and commerce promoted and brought up to the world's standards. If those measures could have been carried out by proclamation of the throne, China would have been instantly transformed into a modern nation. But the move toward Westernization was proclaimed in a characteristically un-Western manner. The "Hundred Days' Reform," in line with traditional make-believe, invoked an age-old doctrine that truth always emanates from the top downward. A pronouncement from the throne was a deed accomplished, according to the practice.

Although reformers were not entirely unaware of the fallacy of their approach, they went ahead regardless. At the abrupt suspension of the movement after 103 days, the emperor was put under house arrest for life, never to regain his freedom. A half dozen of the reformers were executed. Two prominent leaders had to escape overseas. More than forty important officials were dismissed from governmental service.

The Guangxu Emperor (personal name Daitian, reigned 1875–1908) was the son of Empress Dowager Cixi's sister and Prince Chun, a son of the Daoguang Emperor. When his cousin the Tongzhi Emperor died in 1874 without an heir, Guangxu, at three, was named successor by the strong-willed and power-conscious Cixi. He did not gain control of the government until 1889, yet until her death in 1908, Cixi never relinquished her position as *de facto* ruler. Whenever she was not regent she was pulling strings behind the scenes. A trusted eunuch and a member of the Grand Council served as her liaison with the courtiers. Governors-general and senior army and navy commanders had to rely on this back-door connection to remain secure in the power base of the waning dynasty.

Guangxu was an intelligent and sensitive person; he could shed tears at reading a touching report. The cloistered life within the palace and the lack of an opportunity to exercise his own will since childhood were serious handicaps for a monarch whose ambition was to reshape the destiny of a large nation. His advisers in the reform were Kang Youwei and Liang Qichao, both from Guangdong. Kang was the classic scholar, able to muster the debunking elements in traditional Chinese literature to serve present-day purposes. Liang, more a pragmatist, was a writer of popular appeal and eloquence whose erudition went beyond the classical sources. Before 1898 they had been agitating for the reform for at least three years. They organized meetings, gave lectures, published journals, and solicited funds to popularize their cause as a form of public education. A number of foreign missionaries participated in their activities and added considerable input to the movement. If the Self-Strengthening Movement could be called a program of constructing arsenals and dockyards, the Hundred Days' Reform could similarly be labeled as aiming at budgetary control and constitutional monarchy, even though the reformers, men of a wide range of temperament and interests, had visions of more radical things beyond this immediate scope.

Cixi had been watching her nephew's reform with guarded interest but for some time had refrained from interfering. The immediate issue that caused her to act seemed to involve personnel management. As the emperor began to discharge important courtiers who were opposed to his reforming platform and to promote the reformers, a clash between the old and new became inevitable. It also touched on the jealousy and rivalry between the Manchus and the Chinese. A great alarm was raised when word spread that Guangxu would grant an audience to Ito Hirobumi and might be persuaded to tour Japan. The last straw came when the emperor held a private audience with General Yuan Shikai, bypassing Commander-in-Chief Ronglu, a Manchu and the empress dowager's confidant.

Should we accept Yuan's justification for his turning informer, which he gave to *The London Times* in an interview many years later, that the reformers urged him to murder the empress dowager, the emperor's adopted mother, or should we believe the account of *The North China Daily News* and the *Shen Pao*, which said that Yuan received a secret order from Guangxu, asking him to protect the throne? Whatever the case, Yuan turned informer and went over to the side of Ronglu and the empress dowager. When Cixi suddenly returned to Beijing from the suburbs, the scheme of the reformers was foiled. The purge was set in motion; everything was to return *status quo ante*. The emperor and his close advisers had to pay the price.

In the present case the historian is obliged to cover the pertinent events in line with his predecessors. But repeatedly he has to caution his readers not to follow those early writers too closely for interpretation, since they, reviewing the occurrence with less historical depth than we have, tended to stress the personal influences of the key figures on the scene, therefore understating the institutional causes. The Hundred Days' Reform antagonized the entire corps of army officers who had risen through the ranks of the banner system and Green Standard, no less than the whole body of the literary-bureaucrats who had distinguished themselves through the old-fashioned education and examinations. Although this was amply explained by historians in the past, we must now further emphasize that those groups were more than vested interests; they represented the logic of the Chinese state and society. For several hundred years, China had relied on the professional military caste who had a minimum of technological exposure, and a civil service hierarchy, whose ideological cohesion stood as a cornerstone of a permanent constitution. The arrangement, foregoing progress for stability, had made homogeneity and uniformity prevail over an immobile empire. To do away with those supports would have immediately dissolved the imperial order. Yet the other side of the dilemma was that unless some indication was given that those institutions would eventually be replaced, it made no sense even to talk about reform.

After the failure of the Hundred Days, Guangxu was blamed for his timidness and indecision. Yet there was no evidence that he could have acted otherwise, since as the emperor, he was supposed to personify the traditional virtues that permeated the whole Chinese society, from the village communities all the way up, and culminating in filial piety. To be slightly more resolute he would have had to compromise his image as well as his office. Perhaps he could have, as Kang Youwei had suggested in early September, resettled himself in Shanghai, but that would have been taken as a revolt against social custom in addition to a desertion of his own dynasty. If the reformers were ready to go that far, one might ask, why must they stick with Guangxu and the Qing, nothing but liabilities in time and circumstances? Would not it have been simpler if they had gone straight for republicanism? Eventually history's answer affirmed this latter course.

But the enormity of the problem would not make the process any simpler. Bitter struggle and a great span of violence still lay ahead. The long revolution was foreseen by Tan Sitong, one of the six who forfeited their lives to Empress Dowager Cixi's vengeance. Determined to be a martyr, Tan refused to flee. "Unless," he wrote, "blood spills over all parts of China, the country will not see salvation. That being the case, let me shed mine first."

That he did on September 28, 1898. The official whom the empress dowager dispatched to oversee the execution was Gongyi, later one of the patrons of the Boxers.

After the coup of September 21, Cixi had intended to replace Guangxu with another child emperor of her selection. However, she met expressed opposition from several southern governors and a large number of civil leaders in Shanghai, who were under Western protection. Kang Youwei had escaped to Hong Kong with British assistance. Liang Qichao was given safe conduct by the Japanese legation. Foreign envoys continued to show concern about the safety of the emperor and pressed the palace with questions. Her wish unfulfilled, the empress dowager's antiforeign feelings intensified, and this eventually affected her judgment in dealing with the Boxers.

The *Yihetuan*, or "Righteous and Harmonious League," was one of the secret societies gathering followers in north China. The members practiced martial arts and mystic rituals, from which the name Boxers was derived. Some of them claimed that by controlling their breath and muscles they could withstand bullets. In the closing years of the century they took advantage of the spontaneous clashes between the local population in Shandong on the one hand and the Germans and native Christians on the other. Soon they attacked all foreigners on sight and attempted to destroy all things of Western origin. In 1899 the governor of Shandong, a xenophobe himself, called the Boxers "righteous subjects" and incorporated them into the provincial militia. The next year they move into the metropolitan Beijing area. Among Cixi's favorites, only Ronglu disputed them.

The psychology of the empress dowager at this point is a subject of speculation. Apparently, at times she exposed herself as in a state of fear and hesitation rather than being firm and resolute. Imperial edicts throughout the period fluctuated, calling the Boxers in turn "bandits," "children of China," "bad elements," and "righteous subjects." General Nie Shicheng, who later died in the outskirts of Tianjin resisting the allied invasion force, found his position untenable as he had simultaneously to fight the Boxers and the foreigners. It seemed that the harder the foreign powers pressed Cixi to suppress the lawless Boxers, the more determined she was to accept the external challenge. Those details thoroughly exposed the inherent hazards of the Chinese monarchy. In an age when the complexities of world affairs demanded the governmental machinery to remain alert on a large number of technical issues, the court of Beijing still handled its business in a thoroughly amateurish and personal manner. In that sense Cixi the dowager provided a useful service by exposing this institutional awkwardness, thus hastening the liquidation of China's imperial order, which had been in existence for 2,000 years.

Her war was declared on June 21, 1900. It was not against one nation, nor against a specific list of nations, but against all foreign powers in contact with China. Inside Beijing, the attack on the foreign legations and the burning of churches by the Boxers had been taking place for ten days. On June 11 a secretary of the Japanese Legation was murdered. On June 16 the allied forces demanded that the local commander at Tianjin surrender the Dagu Fortress the next day by 2 a.m. When he did not, they opened fire at 6 a.m. and took it. With that, on June 19 the Chinese government notified the personnel of the foreign legations that they had to leave Beijing within twenty-four hours. Still trying to negotiate, the German minister Baron Klemens von Ketteler was shot to death in the streets of Bejing on June 20 while on his way to the Zongli yamen.

Before the meeting deciding on the declaration of war the antiforeign faction presented the empress dowager with a message alleged to have been delivered by the foreign legations, demanding her retirement. Even then she still asked the more than 100 courtiers kneeling before her to speak up. Yet two of them who did dare to speak up against the hostilities were executed by her order.

The siege of the foreign legations in Beijing lasted for fifty-six days. Three times a truce was arranged. In late July the Chinese government delivered flour, vegetables, and watermelons to the beleaguered foreigners. (Dr. L. Carrington Goodrich, then close to six years old, was with the foreign missionaries. He told me that so far as he knew the delivery did not occur at the Beitang Cathedral as was generally believed.) General Ronglu's refusal to use artillery against the legations must have saved countless lives. During the siege some 250 foreigners lost their lives. Deaths among the Chinese Christians were not counted. After the siege was lifted, the allied troops, comprising contingents from eight nations and numbering 18,000 men, committed killing and raping against the civilian population in reprisal. In central and south China, the governors assured foreign consuls that imperial orders after June 20 would be ignored, thus maintaining a neutral stance. The event was labeled "Boxer Rebellion," as if the capital had been overpowered by insurgents.

The empress dowager and the emperor escaped from the palace one day after the allies entered Beijing. Their journey to Xi'an and extended stay there enabled Li Hongzhang to negotiate with the foreign powers at a leisurely pace. The Boxer Protocol was signed in September 1901, barely two months before Li's death. The allies demanded the death penalty for eleven high officials who had been responsible for the hostilities; four of them had already committed suicide, three were ordered to commit suicide later, and two had their sentences commuted to life imprisonment in a frontier province.

In forty-five cities where the Boxers had caused disturbances to foreigners, civil service examinations were suspended for five years, and special envoys were dispatched by China to Germany and Japan to apologize for the slain diplomats. Chinese fortifications along the coast to Beijing, including the Dagu Fortress, were razed, and foreign legations in the capital were permitted to station troops for their self-defense. An embargo on military equipment from abroad was in effect for two years. The indemnities that China was to pay were set at 450 million ounces of silver, approximately five years' state income of the Qing; with interest coming close to the amount of the principle, the last payment would not be cleared until 1940. (Later the United States had a change of heart and undertook to return the outstanding indemnity funds to China for educational purposes. Several other nations followed suit.) After the settlement, tsarist Russia refused to pull out of Manchuria, which was to be one of the causes leading to the Russo-Japanese War of 1904–05.

Still in Xi'an, Cixi was already issuing proclamations to reverse herself. After returning to the capital, she virtually reactivated Guangxu's reforms, which she had stamped out earlier. Moreover, she even broadened their scope. Eleven ministries were created to replace the old offices, the civil service examination was terminated for good in 1905, and a mission headed by a prince of blood was to make constitutional studies overseas. A call for national and provincial assemblies was planned.

Of course she could not know that responsible government would be difficult to implement in China in the late twentieth century, much less in her time eighty years earlier. The fundamental obstacle rose from the fact that the traditional Chinese state and society had a different anatomy, as if being fish, it could not be transformed to fowl. The lack of adaptability went even beyond the character of the Manchu dynasty, which in a sense was a victim of its time. Its large and undifferentiated bureaucracy worked well under the arbitration of the throne so long as

China remained introverted and noncompetitive, in which case there was a consensus on public issues, and the role of the Son of Heaven could be carried out with ritualistic serenity. The large and undifferentiated peasantry would remain as a "good element" as the agrarian population was held docile within the boundaries of the administrative districts. In all this there was culture and discipline. In the summer of 1900, under the full force of foreign pressure, the top turned into a despotic demon, both uninformed and unsure of itself. The bottom appeared to be an uncontrollable mob. Clearly enough, such an organizational structure needed more than liberation and paper reform to go through the new century.

On November 14, 1908, the Guangxu Emperor died. The death of the empress dowager followed in less than twenty-four hours. This amazing coincidence gave rise to suspicion of foul play. Although he is known to have been sick for some time, she was robustly active and, in fact, had on November 13 presided over a meeting to name a successor to the throne. Actually, what really happened makes little difference in the long sweep of history because the successor that Empress Dowager Cixi picked, Xuantong (personal name: Henry Puyi, reigned 1908–1911), then three years old, was destined to be the last emperor of China. In less than three years, at the proclamation of the Republic, not only was the Manchu dynasty swept away, but also the Chinese monarchy that started at Xi'an under Shi-huang-di of the Qin 2,132 years earlier.

Dr. Sun Yat-sen, the revolutionary, had at one time hoped to advance his ideas of reform without overthrowing the Qing; otherwise he would not have sought an interview with Li Hongzhang (which was never granted). After 1895, the year China was defeated by Japan, he turned against the Manchus. Being a Cantonese and proficient in English, he had an advantage in approaching Chinese communities overseas. Yet, as his memoirs show, the early effort to win support was never easy.

Before October 10, 1911, Sun had attempted to overthrow the Qing dynasty ten times; each failure brought the loss of life, some of the dead comrades being his close friends. His party was essentially made up of the educated elite and thus lacked means to address the masses in those days. The martyrs-to-be involved themselves in the classical approaches of disseminating incendiary literature, assassination, and seizure of governmental offices; but gradually they learned to make use of the secret societies and infiltrate the modern army and navy being organized by the Qing.

Sun indicated that the reaction to the Boxer Rebellion gave his revolutionary effort a new impetus; party membership increased rapidly and solicitations of overseas support became easier. Yet the tenth attempt at armed uprising, which took place in April 1911 at Guangzhou, again failed, and seventy-two members of the party laid down their lives. The success six months later did not come about in any planned manner. The underground in Hankow exploded a bomb by accident. The subsequent police investigation led to the disclosure of partisan membership rolls, most of those involved being soldiers and junior officers of the new army. They were compelled to act prematurely, with neither an overall leader nor an immediate sense of direction. A brigadier general of the imperial army was pressed into command. At this crucial moment the Manchu governor-general ran away, giving the revolutionaries the breathing space that they badly needed. One after another, other provinces responded to the revolution. The new empress dowager, Guangxu's widow, had to accept abdication on behalf of the child emperor.

The first two decades of the Republican era were an ignominious beginning. Sun Yat-sen yielded the presidency of the new republic to Yuan Shikai, the betrayer of 1898, in consideration of the Qing forces at his command, which were still capable of putting down the revolution. A peaceful settlement was quickly achieved, but not for long. As soon as Yuan consolidated his position he proceeded to proclaim himself emperor. When World War I broke out in Europe in 1914, Japan seized the opportunity to put before Yuan the Twenty-one Demands, which, if complied to in full, would have reduced China to a protectorate. Yuan died in 1916, after having been emperor for eighty-one days. In the confusion, a pig-tailed general who professed to be a Qing loyalist brought back the dethroned Xuantong for a restoration. This time the revived monarchy lasted even less time—twelve days. From this point to the establishment of the Nationalist government in Nanjing under Chiang Kai-shek in 1928, China sank into a period of warlordism.

There were two national governments, one in Beijing and the other in Guangzhou under Sun Yat-sen's Constitution Protection Movement. Neither controlled much territory, however. Civil wars, never ending, turned the railroad trunklines into a revolving stage. Army commanders assumed a variety of titles; they were distinguished from one another by the cliques to which they belonged. Tibet and Outer Mongolia slipped out of China's control, the latter permanently. Foreign gunboats cruised China's inland waterways. Foreign concessions in Chinese cities organized international trade for the short-term interests of the merchants rather than the long-term development of the nation as a whole. Exports chiefly comprised agricultural products, imports consumer goods that suited the taste and purchasing power of a new urban bourgeoisie that was too small in number and too much oriented toward the West to change the destiny of China, a country of great land mass and population.

These deeds and affairs, in their kaleidoscopic confusion, only begin to show their historical consistency more than half a century later. China's major problem can be pinned down as the incompatibility between the modern concept that everything has to be mathematically managed and the traditional sense of organization that made the center, instead of representing the sum total of the parts, an alleged moral force which held them together, their mutual effectiveness neutralized and canceled out, in a delicate balance and in a serene manner. At the establishment of the Republic this conflict was recognized. The monarchy had to go, not only because the potential occupant of the throne was a habitual betrayer or a child who could be manipulated for the rest of his life, but also because the absoluteness of the throne supported the uncompromising character of China's social order. If this had not been the case, the revolution of 1911 would not have won so easily or the two attempts to restore the monarchy defeated so overwhelmingly.

But opposition to a negative influence cannot be instantly translated into a positive force. Recognizing that China's problem was constitutional, we must emphasize, however, that by constitution we do not mean a document that is signed, sealed, and solemnly kept, but its basic definition, denoting the bodily structure of a nation that affects its disposition, character, and range of performance. The Chinese, overly proficient in the style of management by the literary bureaucracy, placed too much faith in the constitution as a piece of paper, ignoring the fact that whether it provided for a unicameral or a bicameral legislature, presidential power or a cabinet form of government, the written constitution had little relevance to China's conglomeration of village communities, where the literacy rate was generally said to be 5 percent, the millions of peasants could only be manipulated in blocks, and vital statistics were unavailable. The traditional governing principle that held men to be superior to women, the aged over the young, and the educated above the illiterate bore no relation either to universal suffrage or economic opportunities for all. Nor could the thousands of stone arches in the countryside praising chaste women, engraved tablets eulogizing selfless civic leaders, and clan temples and village idols—elements of the great tradition and the little tradition (p. 72) that in the past had been utilized as auxiliary instruments of government—be converted into tools to advance the cause of democracy and create a pluralistic society. Besides, with the termination of the civil service examinations in 1905 the links between the superstructure, the governmental apparatus, and the infrastructure, the local communities, had already been severed. Under these conditions parliamentarianism was a sham. Whatever political platforms the newly organized parties might advance, none of them could field candidates that had genuine ties with constituencies. Of course the urban social classes had never been potent enough to determine the direction of national politics; if they had been they would surely have tried, as their counterparts in other areas of the world had done whenever the opportunity arose. In other words, modernization would have been simpler if historically Chinese civilization had developed in parallel with the West, with civil liberties growing out of municipal franchise, or in a similar pattern to Japan's, where the wealth of private business firms outpaced the power of the *daimyos*.

We read numerous accounts of manipulated elections, the abrupt dissolution of parliament, and abuses of the constitution during those chaotic early years of the century. But the real tragedy was that none of the generals who occupied the offices of the presidency or premiership, villains or not, could even emerge as a strongman. A major reason for their ineffectiveness was governmental finance; the Republic had inherited an empty treasury. The traditional source of revenue, the land tax, had been assessed for the maintenance of the old-fashioned *yamen* only. The proceeds were too small and too scattered to be of any value to the central government. Other items of income had been put up as collateral to pay foreign loans and war indemnities. Floating domestic bonds would have been impracticable as there were few potential subscribers. The only door left open was foreign borrowing. Who would lend money to China at this moment? Banking consortiums backed by foreign governments. This arrangement inevitably made Chinese leaders appear to be tools of alien masters who would remain overbearing toward the domestic population. During World War I the so-called Nishihara loans, named after their Japanese negotiator, were handed out to the Beijing government with the alleged purpose of preparing China for entering the war on the allied side. Actually, however, the funds boosted the strength of the recipients who were recognized as serving Japanese interests in the internal strife.

Warlordism in those years became endemic. When the old system was dismantled, and the new one had not been built up, personal military power remained as the only means of maintaining some measure of interim cohesion. But the fraternal bond among the senior commanders could no longer be counted on when their power stretched beyond territories of provincial size. *Realpolitik* set in; plots and coups took their toll. The situation was extremely fluid.

The warlords, tragic heroes of a sort, were not necessarily evil by nature. A British observer commented that many of them would have made good generals in the British Army. Identifying their personal ambitions with whatever schemes of national salvation they had in mind, they encountered great difficulties when they had to explain their positions before their subordinates and the general public. Zhang Zuolin was a protégé of the Japanese who turned into an ardent nationalist. Feng Yuxiang was called the "Christian general" before he became a follower of the Soviets. Yan Xishan organized a "heart-washing society" and applied all sorts of religious touches to it. Tang Shengzhi was almost converted to Buddhism; he rationalized his slaughters with a message of redemption. Not all the warlords were rough-hewn. Wu Peifu was a poet. But the roguish Zhang Zhongchang, having risen from the ranks of coolies, was said to have lost count of the troops he commanded, his bankroll, and the women in his harem.

We have to admit, however, that the overall damage done by warlordism was serious. Its adverse effect on the Chinese economy was immeasurable. In an age when social reconstruction was badly needed, the acts of the warlords, with a few extremely rare exceptions, were destructive. Moreover, their actions dampened the national spirit. Warlordism deprived the new republic of its last shred of respectability and ushered in decades of forlorn hope and despair. If the warlords served any historical purpose at all, it was that they had intensified the internal pressure, which, combined with eighty years of foreign aggression, compelled the educated youth of China to work out a formula for national salvation by themselves.

With the "May Fourth Incident" the young people found a line of action; and the "May Fourth Movement" furnished the ideological support to their acts.

May 4, 1919, was a Sunday. At 1:30 P.M. some 3,000 students from thirteen universities and colleges in Beijing gathered in front of the Gate of Heavenly Peace for a demonstration against the decision of the Versailles Peace Conference to award to Japan the treaty rights previously held by the Germans in Shandong Province. Those rights consisted of everything that made the "sphere of influence" (p. 214) the most onerous feature of an unequal treaty. China, by declaring war against Germany in 1917 and sending laborer battalions to the western front, was supposed to have been on the winning side of the war. Moreover, the declaration of war alone was sufficient to wipe out all treaty obligations. Yet at Versailles China found that instead of sharing the fruits of victory, its representatives had to sign away rights affecting its territorial integrity to satisfy another victor. This was unprecedented and outrageous. Yet with the disclosure of the secret treaties of several years before, China's position was compromised. Previously, to induce Japan to enter the war, the great powers had agreed to, on separate occasions, the transfer of those rights. More damaging to the Chinese cause was that the previous exchange of notes between Tokyo and Beijing, now made public by the Japanese delegation at the conference, confirmed that the Chinese warlord government had also consented to the terms.

The May 4 demonstrators distributed handbills declaring that the Chinese people would never accept the selling out of China's sovereign rights by traitors. They marched to the legation quarters and left letters to the ministers of the foreign powers. Late in the afternoon they decided to have a confrontation with the three Chinese officials of cabinet rank who had been responsible for the secret communication with the Japanese. One of them was beaten and another's house was set on fire. At this point the police intervened, and thirty-two students were arrested.

The news soon spread throughout the nation. The press echoed the demand of the students, and protests, strikes, and shop closings spread like wildfire. The Beijing government yielded. The arrested demonstrators were released, the three accused officials were dismissed, the cabinet was compelled to resign, and the Chinese delegation at Versailles refused to sign the peace treaty. The Shandong problem was finally settled at the Washington Conference, called by President Harding and planned by Secretary of State Hughes. Japan withdrew its claim to rights allowed by the secret treaties. The Twenty-one Demands were effectively buried with the signing of the Nine-Power Pact of the Washington Conference in 1922.

Today when student riots are commonplace and scenes of "confrontation" appear daily on the television screen, it is difficult for us to imagine how unusual the May Fourth Incident was, occurring at a time when modern communications were in their infancy. The reader would do well to remember that traditional China was like a submarine sandwich (p. 193). Even though the civil service examination had been terminated in 1905 and the monarchy abolished in 1912, no social reconstruction of substance had followed. By 1919, it was estimated that there were from one million to two and a half million factory workers in China—still a drop in the bucket when measured against the enormous population. On the whole, agrarian China remained unchanged. The undiversified economy offered few jobs and little of the variety found in a modern society. Professional jobs, moreover, were likely to be concentrated in the treaty ports under the municipal administration of foreign powers. Those we refer to as the "intelligentsia" found themselves by circumstances a class of misfits. Few of them could identify comfortably with any existing socio-economic group. Without alternatives, there was a tendency for them to fall back on the old social customs. Even as students enrolled in modern colleges and universities, many of them maintained the outlook of the literati-bureaucrats of the past. Being the educated elite, they counted themselves successors to the old-fashioned officialdom and thus entitled to the lifetime security and all the privileges that went with it. The May Fourth Incident was more than a demonstration and a protest. It demanded commitment. If the educated young people felt that lettuce and mayonnaise in a submarine sandwich were not substantial enough to provide structural firmness for a modern nation to sustain its functional maneuverability, they themselves had to step in to solve the problem. When this message began to spread, for the first time the large and undifferentiated piece of bread on the top, an institution of 2,000 years' standing, showed signs of being converted to an instrument to carry on China's long revolution over the next half century.

This was possible owing to an environment of intellectual agitation and ferment. To trace its origin further, we should cite the work of foreign missionaries and the contact with foreign concessions in the Chinese cities, the preparation of new textbooks and sending students overseas after the Self-Strengthening Movement, and the contributions by great translators such as Yan Fu and Lin Shu, who made the works of Montesquieu, Smith, Dumas, Balzac, Dickens, and others available to Chinese readers. But since the May Fourth Incident came to be seen as a student action, historians maintain that the "May Fourth Movement" was an action-oriented preparation, mainly organized by professors within educational institutions, with Beijing University as its citadel and 1917 as its clear starting point. After May 4, 1919, the movement spread far and wide. But as the momentum continued to build, this period of preparation could be said to have run its course by about two years later, or mid-1921.

The major credit for creating the appropriate intellectual atmosphere should go to Cai Yuanpei, chancellor of Beijing University since 1917. He was the rare individual who combined training as a young court academician under the Qing with subsequent study in Germany and France. After the founding of the Republic he served as minister of education. At the university he appointed as dean of letters Chen Duxiu, another degree-holder from the civil service examination of the imperial era who had studied in Japan and France. A veteran revolutionary, in 1915 Chen had founded a monthly magazine call *New Youth* ("La Jeunesse" on its masthead). As dean, he continued his editorship, and several prominent members of the Beijing University faculty frequently wrote for the magazine. Its circulation climbed to 16,000 copies, an impressive figure for those days. Chiang Kai-shek was a regular reader. Mao Zedong admitted that he was influenced by *New Youth* and even contributed an article to it.

In an oft-cited editorial in the January 1919 issue, Chen argued that if the magazine had any constant guiding principles at all, they were no more than science and democracy. The editorial created far more of a sensation than this brief summary might suggest. In the context of the editorial, by science Chen stressed social sciences rather than natural sciences. And, as several faculty members of the university interpreted it, they were to be held as methodical and persistent ways of disbelieving, not fundamentally different from the standpoint of Bacon or even of Descartes. When cast against the Chinese background, which asserted that the moral code was immutable, truth always came down from the authorities at the top, and when that was not enough, make-believe was brought in to fill in the gaps, Chen Duxiu's platform did not lack revolutionary implications. Even democracy, before being elaborated to mean representative government, was seized on by this editorial writer as an iconoclastic tool to do away with tradition and Confucianism. Chen used the word democracy almost interchangeably with the word individualism, until then in Chinese usage a label that carried a negative overtone, it implied a wanting of public spirit.

Several writers joined in the attack on China's "quintessence." Among them was Lu Xun (the pen name of Zhou Shuren), a former medical student in Japan and now a minor official with the Ministry of Education. While Chen Duxiu discoursed in general terms, Lu made the argument in short stories and followed them up with pungent short essays. One short story, published elsewhere several years later, is typical of this writer's attitude toward the traditional code of ethics. "The Brothers" is in fact partially autobiographical. An office worker who had the reputation of being selflessly devoted to his younger brother found the latter seriously ill. While waiting for the doctor to come late that night he had many anxious moments. Scarlet fever was suspected to be the cause of the illness. He was afraid that his younger brother might die and then he would be unable to send his own three children to school in addition to his two nephews. Relief came when the physician announced that the brother had only contracted measles. But that night in his dream this man saw his brother dead and himself sending his own children to school, but not the nephews. As one of the nephew cried and begged to go, he slapped the child on his ear. He saw blood come out of the boy's face until he woke up, sweating and panting. The next morning in the office he was complimented by his colleagues for his brotherly love.

Serving on the editorial board of New Youth and working closely with Chen Duxiu was Li Dazhao, the Beijing University librarian. Li had studied at Waseda University in Japan and been exposed to Marxism through Japanese writers. He contributed a series of articles on Marxism and the Soviet revolution to *New Youth*. Reflecting the dilemma of China's intelligentsia in this age who were facing numerous theoretical options but had few practical means to handle the problems at hand, Li showed an endless tendency to eclecticism in building up a universal system through which the values of the East and West could eventually be synthesized. But the result was by no means a colorless compromise. Unlike Chen Duxiu, he had never fully abandoned nationalism; Li anticipated a strong peasant movement in the revolution. He justified violence as means to overthrow a regime that itself was founded violently. And he went on to interpret freedom and democracy with a bend toward moral coercion reminiscent of Rousseau. In all these he exercised a significant influence on Mao Zedong, whom he hired as a temporary office assistant.

The American import of the group was Hu Shih, who had graduated from Cornell and received a Ph.D. from Columbia. At this time a professor of philosophy at Beijing University, Hu's major contribution to the May Fourth Movement was his advocacy of the use of the vernacular to replace the archaic writing style. Of a different temperament and intellectual stamp from his peers, Hu Shih was averse to "isms," and for that he was less appreciated in an age when most of the young people, being revolutionary romantics, were seeking an ideological formula for quick salvation. His pragmatic approach, a heritage of his American mentor John Dewey, could be crystallized into six words: "Bit by bit, drop by drop." That, however, was hardly in step with the tempo of the times. In the long run Hu was not entirely wrong. The Chinese revolution was destined to take a course unexpected even by the revolutionaries. The problem was larger than the existing vocabulary. In the face of it all "isms" seem to have been twisted and over-stretched.

In view of what had happened in the previous decades, China by 1919 had indeed taken a long stride forward. At the conclusion of the Opium War the nation made no readjustment whatsoever. With the Self-Strengthening Movement, it still limited its borrowing from the West to technology, which had to be related to armaments. The Hundred Days' Reform, even though it failed, at least put forth a proposal to restructure the entire panoply of governmental offices. Now during the May Fourth period the intellectuals went another step further. Their readiness to bring out the entire stock of China's cultural elements for reexamination and for possible liquidation was the furthest any Chinese had entertained going. It took seventy-nine years to reach this stage. When we speak of the "Western impact," only the perspective of macrohistory empowers us to say that the all-or-nothing response on the part of the Chinese does give an indication of the technical difficulties of solving the problem before the time was ripe.

After May 4, 1919, events moved faster. The Chinese Communist party (CCP) was founded in July 1921. Sun Yat-sen's party, having taken four different names in the previous three decades, was finally settled on as the Chinese Nationalist Party (Kuomintang, or KMT). At the convening of its first national congress in January 1924, the KMT was reorganized to follow the Soviet line, and Russians and the Comintern began to play an important role in Chinese politics. Sun's policy of allying with the Soviet Union and the admission of CCP members to his party as individuals was put into effect. Many students who had been active in the May Fourth Incident by this time had left school to participate in the movement in the south.

The first KMT-CCP alliance worked for a little over three years. Sun Yat-sen died in 1925, and his role as the most prominent Chinese leader, after some manuever and finesse, was taken by Chiang Kai-shek, whose Northern Expedition started the next year. This campaign to eliminate warlordism was militarily successful. But in April 1927 at Shanghai, Chiang launched a "party purification." Soon the hunting down of CCP members took place in all KMT controlled cities. The Generalissimo and the Nationalists pleaded self-defense. They maintained that the Communists had conspired to take over from within; that at the encouragement of the Comintern they might even do bodily harm to Chiang, the commander-in-chief. The CCP and a number of foreign observers charged Chiang with betrayal, since now that he had financial support from banking interests in Shanghai he could act without Russian help.

The "tragedy of the Chinese revolution," as Harold Isaacs aptly termed it, is best illustrated by the destiny of the May Fourth leaders. Li Dazhao, a founder of the CCP, was arrested by the warlord Zhang Zuolin and strangled to death in 1927. Chen Duxiu, another founder, was elected the CCP's first secretary general. For the setback of 1927 he was at first removed from his office and them expelled from the party. Then he was arrested by the KMT government and given a prison sentence. He died of cancer in 1942. Cai Yuanbei used his influence as KMT elder to promote civil liberties and curb political control of the student movement until he died in 1940. He was never regarded with favor by the Nanjing government. Lu Xun wrote a column for a newspaper and remained an exile in the International Settlement in Shanghai. He was active in both the League of Leftist Writers and the Union for Human Rights, in the latter organization of which Cai Yuanbei was also a leading figure. Lu died in 1936 at the age of fifty-five. Hu Shih became Chinese ambassador to the United States and later served as chancellor of Beijing University under the KMT government. His work was severely criticized by Marxist scholars. After 1958 he was president of Academia Sinica in Taiwan until his death in 1962. Several other student leaders from the May Fourth period, Lo Jialun and Fu Sinian, for example, remained prominent as educators in Taiwan. But twentieth century China's preeminent philosopher, Feng Yulan, stayed in Beijing and was brought to public criticism more than once.

The cross-sectional view suggests that the problem behind all this was so large that neither the KMT nor the CCP could exercise full control. In the 1920s, it brought sufficient pressure to bear to cause China's educated elite, who would have been literati-bureaucrats in the past, to break away from tradition; but the work was still less than half done. To make China mathematically manageable, the transformation had to affect the bottom layer, the peasant masses. Although Li Dazhao and Mao Zedong had some vague ideas about how to do this, no one at this time could have drawn up a precise plan for carrying it out. Still beyond anyone's imagination was the future task of applying "the system of commerce" (see p. 194, note) to this large and undifferentiated piece of bread on the bottom. In 1927, Li was dead, Mao had decided to take to the field, and Zhou Enlai had escaped capture in Shanghai. While they were unaware of it, both the men in power and the opposition had ventured into a no man's land where history offered no guidance. The most ardent Marxists could only keep faith with the inevitability that feudalism was bound to give birth to capitalism and then socialism and then communism. Juggling the "isms," they hoped that somehow China might be able to follow the Soviet example to telescope history and shorten the path by one stage or two. But the idea of working with the peasants had already made Secretary General Chen Duxiu furious. He could not see how one arrived at the highest level of human accomplishment by means of the least enlightened species. It would be judged lunatic if anyone had at this point dared to predict that only to put monetary management into effect, China was yet to see Chiang's five suppression campaigns against the Communists, the CCP's Long March, the Xi'an Incident, the war against Japan for eight years, another civil war that lasted more than four years, and then a decade of turmoil called the Great Proletarian Cultural Revolution. Nor can we believe that all this was necessary if we do not keep in mind the evolution of the three Chinese empires that preceded our time. It was a Herculean project to implement a different organizational principle in a country whose population in the meantime grew from 500 million to one billion.

20

Contemporary China and Its Place in the World

Strictly speaking, the time for writing a definitive history of contemporary China has not yet arrived. The Chinese revolution is like a long tunnel that has taken more than a century to grope through. As it gradually unfolds, it is most difficult for anyone inside or outside of it to describe its course. Even the revolutionaries themselves may be confused by its tortuous passage and momentarily lose their sense of direction. Today most primary sources are full of words of anger and frustration, giving negative emphasis to how things have not turned out as they should have done. When dealing with macrohistory, however, we are naturally inclined to be positive. What do we mean by the long-term rationality of history? It implies that even though the events may not suit us and may seem unreasonable and absurd in the short term, when taken together the entire sequence makes sense. It delivers us to a certain destination.

An undeniable fact about contemporary China is that although until the 1920s the country was mathematically unmanageable, now it is on its way to becoming mathematically manageable. Signs are that Chinese history, distinguished in the foregoing chapters for its incompatibility with the history of Western civilization, has finally found a link and can now be docked with the latter. Before we explain how this happened, we may broaden our vision to take note of a number of external factors. The most convincing evidence can be found beyond the immediate subject itself.

A current question of interest is how far China might go in its capitalist experiment before causing serious ruptures. Since this indeed is related to our background analysis, let us start with this topic.

Capitalism is a confusing word. Based on the British experience after World War II, it could be instantly labeled socialism and then bounce back to capitalism without any constitutional amendment. Until the Cold War, few would have felt that being labeled as capitalistic was desirable. The present higher regard for the word in the West has sprung from political considerations. Cold war and international contention have induced the Western democracies to see in capitalism a common economic cause. All this means that the term is not only vague but also at present broadened in scope to suit purposes beyond its original connotations.

In reality, what makes capitalism work is a system of monetary management distinguished by the following three conditions:

wide extension of credit,

impersonal management, and

mutual sharing of service facilities.

We can further qualify capitalism to mean that the monetary management must extend to embrace the entire national economy including the agrarian sector no less than industry and commerce. A competent judiciary system is necessary to back it up, so that the interchangeability of value can be clarified and enforced and the accumulated wealth can be piled steadily higher. Implementing those conditions, a capitalist country permits private enterprise to play a dominant role; private capital therefore exercises a disproportionately wider influence over public life. With this price paid, the public frees itself from unnecessary governmental regulation and gives free rein to economic forces so that competition can achieve the greatest efficiency. Socialism modifies the system with stronger public participation and control. Such differences, as suggested earlier, can only be relative. Today the economic life of the United States is far from entirely free of socialist influence.

But if we examine capitalism as a historical product, we will see fewer such complications. Before the word capitalism was coined, Adam Smith referred to its prototype as "the system of commerce" (p. 194 note). In the history of the development of capitalism, Renaissance Italy is its birthplace and Venice its pacesetter.

For the capitalist system to develop, however, it had to remove obstacles in several areas to make a start. Politically, in Italy this was accomplished during the contest for power between the Empire and the papacy, which left the cities on the peninsula pretty much to themselves. Religiously, the anti-usury doctrine of the Catholic Church was simply disregarded. Among the autonomous cities, Venice enjoyed the unusual situation of being economically monolithic. The agricultural sector on the mainland was quantitatively insignificant. The unemployed nobles had been pensioned off. The labor problem was solved by the utilization of slaves and immigrants. The city's salt water was moreover unsuitable for manufacture. Venice therefore did not need to struggle with the ecclesiastic courts, divine monarchy, monastery interests, seignorial rights, trade guilds, labor unions, or the complexities of the common law. The entire state functioned like a large trading company; all commercial laws became civil laws. The merchant republic simply followed its natural instinct to build up its sea power and pile up its wealth. In the fourteenth century and the early fifteenth century the city state saw its prestige and influence reach their high point; it became a major maker of European history. But precisely because its capitalism had only a negligible production base, its potential for growth and expansion was limited. When the Turks rose in the east and the Portuguese in the west, it rapidly fell into decline.

When the Italian Renaissance was overtaken by the Northern Renaissance, the Dutch Republic became the next banner bearer of capitalism. Previously, the peoples of the Low Countries had no experience at organizing themselves into national states. But municipal autonomy took a stronger hold in this part of the world than in areas where the territorial princes were in firm control. The towns claimed ancient privileges of a great variety. In many cases a person in residence for forty days could free himself from villeinage and gain burgher status. As rural weavers and itinerant traders flocked into the urban areas, the legal proceedings of those business colonies were readjusted to competently handle the new situation. In the meantime the commuted feudal dues, unreadjustable upward, dwindled to become matters of no consequence. And Amsterdam had been encouraged to develop its carrying trade to counterbalance the influence of the other Hanseatic cities.

The immediate cause leading to the independent movement was provided by the Spanish Inquisition. The 1550 edict declared that anyone who printed, copied, kept, or circulated certain heretic literature along with those who read, preached, or discussed the scripture in private or in public without authorization was to be put to death. For those who recanted the execution was to be carried out by the sword for men and burying alive for women. Those who refused to recant were to be burned at the stake. Any spiritual judge could mete out the penalty; informers were rewarded with 10 percent of the possessions of the accused. New bishoprics were to be organized to subject the natives to stringent control. When Philip II was ready to apply the inquisition in its full force, a sales tax was collected from the local businessmen to finance the military campaign. Thus for the population, a new economic grievance was tied to the issues of religious freedom and self-government.

The revolt of the Low Countries was a long-drawn-out affair. It started with the arrival of Alva's army in 1567. His "Court of Blood," with some 18,000 executions, was part of the story, so was the defeat of the Spanish Armada in 1588. Dutch independence was declared in 1581. But not until the truce of 1609 did the new republic feel reasonably secure of it success; and not until the end of the Thirty Years' War at the Peace of Westphalia in 1648, or eighty-one years after the initial conflict, was the hard-won independence confirmed and guaranteed by international recognition.

There were a few surprises as one event gradually triggered off another sequentially.. The southern portion of the Netherlands, the original hotbed of unrest, was to remain a Hapsburg possession. Independence took effect in the north. Calvinism, having made inroads in Flanders, was to become the religion of the Dutch, while today's Belgium and Luxembourg would remain Catholic. Another unexpected development was that during the protracted struggle the United Provinces, as the new republic was called, received a powerful influx of skilled labor and capital. The cloth industry in particular grew phenomenally at the expense of the south.

Now the Hapsburg yoke was off; the influence of Rome was also erased. Even though the Reformed Church did not immediately bring peace to all the Calvinists and the interpretation of predestination sparked a dispute between the Remonstrants and the Counter-Remonstrants, the controversy failed to pick up the needed social forces to ignite an armed conflict. It was allowed to fade into the background. One more key factor was that during the struggle for independence the regional princes had stood behind the population. After the war they, with their titles of nobility, appeared on the payroll of the rising bourgeoisie. Under those circumstances there was no other logic of constructing the new republic except to turn it capitalistic. Maritime power and trade occupied the future thoughts of the nation rising on the shores of the North Sea. They became a national purpose. Civil laws encompassing property rights, maritime usage, and international application were promoted, with the universities of Leyden and Utrecht supplying the brain power. For the next century and more, Amsterdam remained the foremost center in the Western world for the carrying trade, maritime insurance, commodity exchange, and money markets. Adam Smith devoted a whole section of his treatise to a discussion of the operation of the Bank of Amsterdam, indeed a capitalist instrument par excellence.

The rural part of the republic, however, was basically a country of butter and cheese. Furthermore, derived from the ancient charters of the towns, customary laws showed great unevenness from one place to another, Federation provided an answer to this unusual situation. The flexibility of a two-tier government allowed some of the outdated practices, without being formally abolished, to fall into disuse; in the meantime a new mode of organization could arise from experiment. The contemporaries were amazed that not only was the United Provinces a confederacy of seven sovereign states, but also, it even let many towns and cities within the provinces retain certain marks of sovereignty. The Dutch East India Company, formed from the merger of existing firms, retained their regional "chambers," each of which had its own directors, ships, and sales schedule. The Netherland navy was divided among five admiralty colleges. Until 1752, Amsterdam still operated its own postal service to foreign countries. With two thirds of the population and contributing three quarters of federal revenue, in the early years, Holland even insisted that it had the power to enter into diplomatic agreements with other nations independent of federal authority.

But for all this, apparently the system of monetary management worked. The greatest appeal of capitalism is its *laissez faire* spirit, which derives economic benefit from a geographically unbalanced situation. Undoubtedly it worked better in the early modern era than it does now. For the Dutch Republic, internal tensions existed but never reached a point of rupture. A measurement of the success was that the accumulated wealth could be fed back into agriculture. Dikes, windmill pumps, cattle breeding, intensive cultivation, artificial meadows, and drainage canals soon transformed the country's landscape.

In the seventeenth century the Dutch Republic was both a major rival of and an inspiration to England. The two nations were at war more than once. Yet in the end the Englishmen took a Dutchman as their king. If that is not confusing enough, the records also show that England itself went through a civil war that was fought twice. Interregnum followed regicide. There were experiments with commonwealth and protectorate. There was a restoration that was upset by another revolution. To this day rarely can two historians completely agree on what was going on, or why a nation had to go through a complete circle more than once in order to discover itself.

From our viewpoint of macrohistory, however, the picture is clear enough. In the early part of the seventeenth century England had not been mathematically manageable. Toward the end of the century the

Amsterdam Stock Exchange in the seventeenth century—this could not have happened in China.

situation improved enormously. During the middle decades the unsettledness had invited a great variety of potential solutions to the problem, ranging from absolute monarchy to parliamentarianism, from Laudism to religious independency, from military dictatorship to communism. While the advocates of these various doctrines were unaware of it, they had ventured beyond a new frontier of historical experience. Never before had a nation with a sizeable agrarian base like England managed to institute a system of monetary management until it could be governed as if it were a city state.

The outdated conditions of the country's hinterland revealed the enormity of the problem. The feudal system had been gone for several centuries, so had the manorial system as a system. But components of land tenure derived from medieval usage, unreadjustible to modern conditions, had been hanging on. In theory feudal land was inalienable. But in practice buying and selling had been going on for centuries. A landholder could dispose of the estate he held but did not own by enfeoffing the buyer nominally in exchange for service, to the extreme for no more than "a rose in summer." Villeins, having been emancipated since the depopulation caused by the Black Death in the fourteenth century, held the acreages under cultivation as "copyholders." Protected by the common law against eviction, they passed on their holdings to their children along with the lingering service obligations to the manor lords, which appeared in a bewildering variety. Commuted rents, in an age of inflation, usually came close to the vanishing point. During the reign of James I, some remaining royal land was alienated at prices which were criticized as being a give-away. Yet, in fact, the suggested prices amounted to the cash equivalents of 100 years' rental income. Rent increases in this age, if possible at all, had to take the form of "entry fines." Some aggressive landlords managed to quadruple the rents in a span of a dozen years, others not at all. The resourceful ones bought out the copyholders and leaseholders; the poorly situated ones were unable even to locate their tenants-in-chief.

This confusing situation enriched some speculators but impoverished many others, while tenants, or those who held the right to use the land as a group, were suffering the perennial anxiety of not knowing from day to day what their legal and financial status was. Apparently, there was no way to maintain stability, much less initiate an ambitious program of mobilizing the nation's financial resources to meet a fiercely competitive world.

Had England concentrated on food production for domestic and local consumption, the problem could have been minimized. Trade could then have been compartmented in the coastal cities, leaving the inland sector unaffected. But British exports came almost exclusively from the backs of lambs. Wool and woolen goods accounted for 75 to 90 percent of the commodities sent overseas. Agriculture, connected with commerce by sheep farming, became increasingly sensitive to foreign affairs and to overseas price fluctuations. In parallel with it, domestic trade also gathered momentum. On the eve of the civil war, itinerant merchants became unusually active in the provincial towns. Peddlers crowded the back roads.

The lack of jurisprudential integration contributed to the degree of uncertainty. The common law, basically social practices accumulated by an agrarian society in which local self-sufficiency was the rule, held that what had not been done in the past could not be attempted at the present. This was grossly inadequate for the conditions of the seventeenth century. The principle of equity, *in recognition of justice as to what was equitable* and sometimes under the influences of Roman law and canon law, was sanctioned by the prerogative courts only.

Under these conditions, when the king was compelled to seek new tax revenues to maintain an army and navy in order to cope with circumstances and to enlarge governmental functions out of necessity, the entire nation was embroiled in disputes and became divided. Numerous threads of beliefs and convictions were stirred up in reaction to an issue, undoubtedly with mixed emotions. Religious controversies, originating from the unsettled affairs within and outside of the Church of England since the Tudor Reformation, added intensity to the multifaceted disputes. Indeed, everything was being tossed into the melting pot.

And this was not a case where a change at the top could bring about a settlement. So long as the lower strata remained ungovernable and a set of interlinks between the top and bottom were not in place, a change of command at Westminster could not achieve a breakthrough. The problem, one must recall, was the structure of the nation, not merely its distribution of power or the personalities of its leaders.

By 1689, when William and Mary, the Dutchman and his English wife, were installed as co-sovereigns, the restructuring of the nation had been on the whole accomplished. The decades of turmoil leading up to this were an opportunity to rationalize land tenure in the field; as Professor Tawney put it, foreclosure takes effect cheaper by war than by court proceedings. A measurement of the success was the centrally managed land tax of 1692. By then, landed properties had been so integrated and identifiable for tax purposes that the tax farmers could be done away with. The exchequer controlled the receipts, which, at £2 million a year, far exceeded the annual income from all the revenues combined during the previous years.

The common law courts had been experimenting with the admission of equity ever since the prerogative courts had been abolished by the Long Paliament. At first a kind of stopgap device, the practice in time also accumulated sufficient precedents to lose its ad hoc outlook. The merger of the two legal traditions was at hand. In 1689, John Holt became chief justice of the King's Bench. Among the many things that he did was to direct the common law courts to treat litigations involving merchants in accordance with mercantile practice. This decision had a profound influence on the life of the citizenry, especially in the areas of inheritance, mortgages, legal disposition of chattels, and damage settlements for nonfulfillment of contracts.

The fact that William of Orange, a foreigner who had little intrinsic interest in the domestic affairs of Britain, and Mary, an obedient wife who carried the Stuart name, could be elected king and queen was evidence that the new bottom structure had been reasonably settled; now the new chief of state could be someone whose lack of interest in internal politics appeared to be an advantage. With the reorganization, parliamentary supremacy became the rule; property rights were confirmed as the logic of a new mode of governance. The cabinet form of government and a two-party system were possibilities of a not too remote future.

The Mines Royal Act of 1693, terminating the crown's claim to precious metals found in ores, which in the past had inhibited the growth of the mining industry, instantly stimulated investment. The next year witnessed the birth of the Bank of England, which lent money to the state to cover the national debt as a permanent institution, therefore relieving the king of personal responsibility for it. In fact, William and Mary themselves became the first two stockholders of the new enterprise, clearly separating them as private individuals from the public offices that they occupied. With this innovation England's modern era had come of age. There was no longer any doubt that state affairs could now be handled according to commercial principles.

The revolution of 1689 was "glorious" not only because it was bloodless, but also because it succeeded in cashing in on the efforts of the preceding decades. A milestone had been reached. Judiciary review did most of the work in tightening the knots and trimming the unevenness of the new system.

If we review the three conditions characterizing the monetary management of capitalism, i.e., extension of credit, impersonal management, and pooling of service facilities (p. 233), we will see that England in the opening years of the eighteenth century had all of them in place, ready to be adopted and expanded by the public as general practices. Ever since the organization of the Bank of England in 1694, the country was experiencing the first credit inflation of modern proportions. From 1702 to 1714, the annual governmental expenditure of Britain increased from £5 million to £7 million, while the national debt was piling up from £13 million to £36 million. Marlborough's war was won with the credit advanced by a dozen or so business communities in continental Europe. Knowing that the merchants of London were behind the Bank of England, the lenders needed no great amount of persuasion to join the winning side. The financing could be considered the first "international monetary fund"; it also established the modern trend of war as a business. The reader may at this point appreciate what Professor Braudel has said: "Capitalism only triumphs when it becomes identified with the state, when it is the state."

Having reached this stage, Britain began to overtake the Dutch Republic as the center of international finance. An immediate benefit was the instant rise of the insurance business in London, to replace that in the hand of Hollanders, who had, among other things, monopolized the coverage of British shipping during the previous century. It seemed that what the Dutch could do, the English could do better. The secret was that once the new infrastructure of the national economy was set up and its interlinks with the superstructure were realized through the merger of the common law with equity, the agrarian wealth and mercantile interests found a channel of interflow. The operation of agriculture therefore became consonant with that of commerce. The landed squires of Britain blended well with the rising bourgeoisie. Religious controversies, which had rocked the nation ever since James I arrived from Scotland, seemed to become irrelevant to the modern mind. Of course, additional work still had to be done. More enclosure acts had to be enacted to further rationalize the use of agricultural land, so that turnpikes could be constructed and an urban proletariat could be created out of the displaced labor force. But a point of no return had been passed. Looking back, the British could always see 1689 as a major milestone in their history. Other acts were modified and reversed, but the effect of the Glorious Revolution was permanent.

What does all this have to do with Chinese history?

These are not legends of other lands. Nor are they passing incidents whose effects are binding only within the boundaries of the countries where they took place. Arising from the universal urge of self-preservation, the desire to accumulate worldly goods has found fulfillment through commercial operation; the pattern has in turn become the guiding principle of governmental organization. While the practices may involve good and evil, and they may be abused, vulgarized, and perverted, the organizational principle based on the extensive interchangeability of services and goods enforceable by law is here to stay. It has broadened the basis of scientific inquiry and technological application. It has enriched human life, and it has helped to rank the nations. The materialistic life, given ideological justification by Machiavelli, Hobbes, and Locke, has supplied a major component of Western thought. In the closing decades of the twentieth century, when a one-world history is needed, we cannot see how the story of capitalism, synchronizing the establishment of banks in Venice, Amsterdam, and London with the rise of the Italian Renaissance, the Northern Renaissance, and the English Renaissance, can be divorced from the study of Chinese history. In a rather crude but quite straightforward manner, we can say that Chinese history since the Opium War is a series of continual efforts at readjustment to meet this challenge. The settlement that we have in mind is essentially a merger of China's cultural tradition, developed on a huge continent, with this oceanic influence.

In the past, with historical development reaching an insufficient depth, reformers in China and Chinese historians alike had a general tendency to underestimate the effort required for the readjustment. An often cited comparison put the Chinese revolution on the same footing with the Meiji Restoration in Japan. But the fact is that the

Japanese during the late Tokugawa period, within a country of competitive fiefdoms, had already structured their economic and social life along commercial lines. The feudal lords appointed their business agents, or *kuramoto*. Wholesale dealers, called *tonya*, were organized into groups. The associations of merchants, *kabu-nakama*, paid taxes through a government license system. Banking was conducted in the major cities by the large family concerns. Inns ranged along the main highways. Shipping services, *kaisen*, carried the insurance business as a sideline. All three conditions that are features of capitalistic monetary management were in place. The restoration merely provided a political cloak to accommodate components that were already operational. Furthermore, the rapid adaptation with little consideration for egalitarianism is sometimes cited as a factor leading to Japan's crisis situation prior to World War II.

Nor is the Chinese revolution comparable with the Russian revolution. China lacked the groundwork of Westernization which had been laid in Russia by Peter the Great; yet, on the other hand, there was no such an institution as serfdom, which had lingered on in tsarist Russia until a little over a century ago. Indeed, orthodox Marxism had no technical advice to offer the Chinese. Often cited as a piece of revolutionary literature, *The Communist Manifesto* should be read for its practical approaches to problems. "Revolutionary mode of production" is reserved for the economically most advanced nations. As several breathless paragraphs in the document suggest, the formation of the bourgeois society takes centuries to reach maturity. Communists are not supposed to organize separate parties aside from those of the working class.

Although rarely lacking good will toward the Chinese throughout their protracted struggle, America could not provide historical guidance for China either. The United States was formed when the merger of equity with the common law, while incomplete, had been in progress for over a century. Few Americans remembered what it was like when neither the management of farm operations nor the administration of rural communities could be done monetarily, or understood that modern laws would simply become inoperative when the enactment was not backed up by social compulsion. Business efficiency of the American type, made possible on the one hand by the good fortune of extending a proven workable system gradually over a continental span and on the other by all kinds of toil and trouble involving Shays' rebellion, the Whiskey Rebellion, nullification, state rights, civil war, emancipation, specie, banking, antitrust acts, labor legislation, interstate commerce—issues particular to the landscape of the Northern American continent—could not easily be copied by an Asian nation. This makes the experience of Western Europe, involving the prototypical rise of capitalism, more than ever an essential clue to our understanding of contemporary China.

In the language of macrohistory, we take the position that nothing in the world happens twice in exactly the same fashion. Every event or deed has its own matrix. Historical lessons, therefore, should be drawn from cause-and-effect relationships at length rather than in incidental parallels.

In the foregoing pages we have seen that there is a persistent trend that all nations in the world have to break away from the management of agrarian experience to adapt to mercantile practices—whether the result is called capitalism or socialism. It spreads from small nations to larger ones, from oceanic nations to those of continental background, and from nations of less cultural rigidity to those with profound and immobile heritages. Not only the French Revolution and Russian Revolution should be considered as major readjustments within this general trend of reaching a modern transformation, but also, most of today's struggles around the world, including those between the have's and have-not's, and between the mathematically manageable and the mathematically unmanageable, are still inseparable from this organizational problem.

When reviewed within the wider frame of world history, the sequence of events involving China since the Opium War no longer appears as an endless assembly of blunders which leads nowhere. The Chinese response to the Western challenge has been vigorous and persistent. Compared with the pattern established elsewhere, the initial effort to resist change, to limit change to the particular areas, and to rally behind traditional values as a countermove can only be expected. And in view of the long-drawn-out struggles in the Netherlands and England to reach settlements, nor has China wasted a great deal of time. The reader is invited, once more, to appreciate the metaphor that China is a submarine sandwich (pp. 193, 226). The May Fourth Movement commissioned the large piece of bread on the top, potentially literati-bureaucrats of the past and awakened young intellectuals of the present day, to be the driving force of the forthcoming revolution. Logically the bottom layer of society, the large and undifferentiated peasantry, will supply power of locomotion. Neither the enlightenment of the former nor the emancipation of the latter will mark the end of the struggle, however. The ultimate goal is to render the nation and society mathematically manageable by modern standards, to boost their functional maneuverability and to reinforce their structural strength.

In that perspective the history of contemporary China can be outlined with clarity. Chiang Kai-shek and the Kuomintang (KMT) provided a new superstructure for such a reorganization. Mao Zedong and the Chinese Communist Party (CCP) worked out a new infrastructure to overtake Chiang's superstructure. And the historical mission of the present leadership and its successors is to provide interlinks between the top and bottom, thus making the system work.

Chiang has often been criticized for his improvisation, for his inability to clean house, for his reliance on personal loyalty and emotional appeals to command his subordinates, and for his straddling the old and the new, the ancient and the modern. There is plenty of truth in these charges; but the critics have never explained how these shortcomings could have been avoided and what the alternatives were.

The fact is that the approaches could not have been avoided. If there had been an alternative, the Chinese would have elected a different leader. One must remember that Zhou Enlai, whose own life was threatened by Chiang's arrest in Shanghai in 1927, had to negotiate his release during the Xi'an Incident in 1936.

We realize that it is much easier to condemn Chiang Kai-shek than to call attention to his accomplishments. Nor can we defend all of the Generalissimo's words and deeds. But Chiang is a historical figure whose life and times sum up a mass movement, one of the greatest of its kind, which in turn has built up the foundation of the People's Republic. Without giving recognition to the positive side of his role, no one can technically explain why China in the 1980s differs so much from China in the 1920s.

From the continuity of history, we must further admit, warlordism was a natural consequence of the dissolution of the imperial order (pp. 221–22). Chiang, picking up the pieces, could not afford to be selective. With the graduates of the Whampoa Military Academy forming the core of his followers, he managed to hold an assembly of provincial strongmen and politicians together. Most of those men, self-made, claimed no mandate from their home constituencies. The lack of financial sinews marked another weakness of Chiang Kai-shek and the KMT. Imperial China had no such capability to mobilize the entire nation as one body to wage a war or enter into economic competition with rival states so organized and mobilized. (In that sense, China in the early twentieth century was similar to England in the early seventeenth century.) During the decade prior to the war with Japan, the KMT's Nanjing government achieved tariff autonomy, established a central bank, and derived its revenue from maritime customs, the salt gabelle, and excise taxes. The deficit gap was closed by floating domestic bonds. Yet, for all this, on the eve of the war the annual budget of the national government amounted to only 1.25 billion *yuan*, or at a 3:1 exchange rate, something close to $US 400 million. Even though it had greater purchasing power then, this was an extremely small amount.

It was with this organizational capacity and these assets that Chiang Kai-shek won worldwide recognition as the hope of China and provoked Japanese militarists to armed conflict, a war which he frankly acknowledged that China had no chance of winning on its own. International assistance was needed. In taking such a position he was not less honorable than other world leaders of his class. But at the end of the war he brought no joy to those who had lent him a hand. Instead, alliance with him was a liability and an embarrassment. For that Chiang Kai-shek was never forgiven; to make matters worse, there was the Stilwell affair atop the charges against his government of atrocities and corruption and incompetence. To this day few Americans would stop to think that dollar for dollar, the U.S. aid to the Nationalist cause might still have been a bargain. When the long-term consequences of the KMT's struggle are assessed, the historian may draw a different conclusion from the negative view of the years of Marshall and Truman, and Chiang Kai-shek may be remembered as the man who provided China with the first prototype of a national government which, however imperfect it was, managed to win the country's first foreign war in more than 100 years, and that was a war for self-defense and for survival.

Modern warfare has a characteristic that is usually neglected by the belligerents themselves. The mass mobilization and the relentless drive for efficiency set in motion behind the lines a process of social reconstruction that deviates from the original war aims of the contestants. Neither the kaiser nor the tsar had the remotest idea that World War I would serve to terminate autocracy as an institution, regardless of where it was situated and for what cause it had been compelled to take up arms. When Hitler launched his campaign for *lebensraum*, he could not have imagined that when his scheme backfired, racial equalization as a countermove would soon spread to all continents as a global trend, unexpected even for Churchill and Chamberlain. Although civil war in China progressed quite differently from those cases, it yielded a fair share of surprises, nonetheless.

Some thirty or forty years ago, no one expected that the ultimate effect of land reform in China would be the creation of an infrastructure for the new China that would one day render the country mathematically manageable. The most ardent Communists were talking vaguely about the "release of the productive forces" in the agrarian areas; others accepted the implied egalitarianism as a goal in itself. Apparently, the latter meant a great deal to Mao Zedong, or else he would not have launched the ill-conceived Great Proletarian Cultural Revolution. Yet, as the aftermath of the Cultural Revolution as well as the outcome of the civil war testifies, history's rationality in the long run may overrule the intentions of the originators of those events.

This is not to say, however, that Mao's achievement should be minimized. Some forty or fifty years ago few would even have had the vision to rebuild China up from its structure of a submarine sandwich. Economic betterment of course starts from the most advanced sectors. Its humanitarian appeal notwithstanding, the suggestion of working with the Chinese peasants in order to alter China's destiny sounded hopelessly quixotic in those days (see Chen Duxiu, p. 231). It was owing to Chairman Mao's singlemindedness that this resolution carried. With a combination of courage and endurance, ingenious maneuvers and luck, his program obviously accounted for the astounding success of the People's Liberation Army. An irony during the process was that once again, the traditional method of relying on the homogeneity and uniformity in total mobilization to maintain organizational simplicity managed to overcome the technological superiority of the opponent, which, unevenly distributed, became cumbersome in the field. (With some modifications, this was essentially the same technique with which later the Vietnamese rendered the U.S. military ineffective.) During the Chinese civil war Mao's army, moreover, fought without a formal superstructure. Large cities under CCP control were the rare exception. Urban culture and contact were deliberately avoided. Battle formations were coordinated with radios. In the field, personnel for civil and military administration were on the whole interchangeable. The rustic character of this peasant army enabled it to recuperate faster than the KMT forces after every round of engagement during which they inflicted heavy losses on each other.

But of more enduring historical value is Mao's rural reconstruction. Before the war, China's agrarian problem had been sketchily presented by John Lossing Buck, Richard H. Tawney, and Fei Xiaotong. The roots of the problem, traced back for centuries, could be assessed from the local gazetteers. They were summed up as land scarcity, overpopulation, and peasant indebtedness. Yet, as detailed data began to surface, the extent of the problem still took the field workers by surprise. Tenancy of agricultural land was by no means the entire nexus of the grievances. Parcelization of land sometimes cut the plots down to the sizes of a room. Partial mortgages were not unusual. In many cases the landlords were not much better off than the poor peasants, being only a few steps removed from starvation. Usury was universally practiced, frequently against the lender's own neighbors or relatives. Exploitation furthermore took the form of hiring help by paying wages below the subsistence level. It became most difficult to draw a line separating those who should be relieved and who should give relief. This fact was not easy to absorb. Yet when the historical background was unveiled one had to accept the truth that all these were the natural consequences of an outmoded village economy that had been allowed to progressively worsen by itself. It had been further weakened by war and pestilence and harassed by internal strife and foreign aggression over decades if not centuries.

Mao Zedong, one the greatest propagandists of all time, made "Chiang Kai-shek and American imperialists" responsible, portraying them as trying to perpetuate the distress. Traditional Chinese elements were labeled "feudal." During the civil war years, young men and young women, educated or partially educated, were induced to work behind the front lines. A generation thoroughly dissatisfied with the current state of affairs assured the CCP of plenty of recruits.

A detailed account of the land reform as it was conducted in a village in Shanxi Province has been presented by an American writer, William Hinton. His *Fanshen* is a classic on the subject. The proceedings he describes started with a reign of terror. Rural riffraff were encouraged to take possession of the village. By inducement and by coercion, the party cadres organized the villagers. Men and women who had been inhibited by cultural norms of the past were stimulated to air their grievances. Inflamed with anger, they started to seize the property of the well-to-do and beat some of them to death. Yet, the initial violence served only as a prelude. Once the village was under CCP control and the district was secured, a second echelon of cadres moved in. Excessiveness was curbed and revenge for its own sake discontinued. A village election took place. The entire roster of the local CCP branch was exposed to public scrutiny; one by one the members were readmitted to the party upon ratification by the village assembly. (Those were ordinary people, not CCP members.) The Marxist labor theory of value was taught to the villagers. Redistribution of agricultural land gave consideration to the needs of each household and the manpower available. Nothing was too trivial to escape the attention of the partisans. The data-processing went beyond any conventional limit. The moral persuasion penetrated individual souls. Methodical thoroughness marked this most unusual program conducted by Mao and the CCP. Reading *Fanshen*, one gets the impression of a society literally dissolving itself and turning every individual into a "noble savage" in order to introduce a new social contract. It involved endless discussions and conferences. Every major move was coordinated, deliberated, given a trial run, revised, put into effect again, reviewed, and modified a second time until it was considered fit and proper. Outside the village, regional conferences often engaged hundreds of delegates who deliberated for weeks. A gigantic marathon conference in 1947 is said to have been attended by 1,700 delegates from four different provinces, all of the rank of regimental commander or county magistrate, that lasted for eighty-five days.

In the end Mao and the CCP created an infrastructure for the new China. The land redistribution not only made the subsequent organization of cooperatives and communes a relatively simple matter, but also, with the work done, the Greatest Peasant Leader and his followers succeeded in building a channel of command from the clusters of village congresses up, who were supported by the local branches of the peasants' association and the poor peasants' league. Those units functioned as constituencies of a sort. With the overwhelming majority lined up, the CCP no longer had any difficulty in closing in on the KMT forces as the latter's territory dwindled, and their defense lines were pushed in on themselves against the city walls.

Successes in the early 1950s, including the fact that Chinese divisions fought American forces in Korea at least to a standstill, greatly boosted Mao's prestige and influence. The economic side of the story is not difficult to explain. Before 1949 China had three separate economies. Situated in Manchuria was a component of Japan's economic system, which used to be linked with Korea and the Japanese islands. In the coastal cities a modern economy was oriented toward the West and relied on foreign influence for operation. The agrarian sector, the great hinterland, was more or less a neglected child. Under the People's Republic for the first time the three systems were put under a unified management. Soviet aid, small by today's standard but put to work in key areas, made its contribution. The integrated land utilization, which eliminated the wastefulness of small plots and the duplication of labor, also showed impressive results. Above all, China had a low industrial profile which was also wartorn; rehabilitation and rebuilding could quickly make a difference. But by 1958 these favorable but nonrecurring factors had either vanished or been used up.

At this point the 1958 Great Leap Forward reflected Mao's idea that will power alone can solve all problems. The "backyard steel mill" made the point. When no additional funds were available for reinvestment, Mao decided that an intensive application of muscle power could create the needed capital. When the service sector of the economy had been used to the limit, he decided that on-the-spot production could do away with transportation and the needed technology. In this way he recreated a primitive economy in which all the components within his power became excessive but those beyond his reach remained absent. A great imbalance appeared among all these primitive cells, contrary to the growth strategy of a modern economy in which all the imbalances among the different regions and various sectors can be coordinated and induced to compensate one another to achieve a new balance on a higher plateau. The disastrous consequences of the Great Leap Forward movement were well publicized. Yet, behind the blunder lay a different philosophy of life. As Liu Shaoqi rebuked him in late 1958, Mao fancied that the classless society he had created already qualified as communism, a society whose members picked up the necessities of life "each according to his need." The attempt to skip the socialist stage of development and go directly to the communist stage, according to Liu, was "a Utopian dream."*

When the economic program failed, and the Soviet withdrawal was followed by several years' bad harvest, Mao Zedong's fortune reached a low ebb. The Great Helmsman was not to be elbowed aside from his command position for good, however. The Cultural Revolution of 1966 enabled him to stage a comeback. When that took place, policy reversal was accompanied by the settling of accounts of personal grudges; one begins to wonder at this point: How could this happen? What made one individual so immune to the public opinion of a whole nation, a people who, with sober thought, would eventually admit that a decade of ideological campaigns which got nowhere was, after all, madness? That being the case, how could we justify it with the long-term rationality of history?

At all events, the Cultural Revolution cannot be explained from the words and deeds of its participants or even by its immediate observers. Its historical meaning may have evaded Mao Zedong himself. Having worked with the Chinese peasants incessantly for forty years, and in doing so having solved one of the most difficult problems faced by any generation in the entire length of Chinese history, as one of his poems claims, and in the process having suffered the violent deaths of two brothers, one sister, and at least one wife and one son, Mao Zedong felt that he had the right to protect his own work from being subverted. Getting things done without a superstructure, moreover, suited his

*The criticism was published as the resolution of the CCP's Central Committee of December 10, 1958, in which neither Liu's nor Mao's name was mentioned. The Chinese text appeared in the *People's Daily*. For English translation see Conrad Brandt, Benjamin Schwartz, and John K. Fairbank, *A Documentary History of Chinese Communism* (Atheneum paperback, 1966 [Harvard University Press, 1952]), pp.111–132.

I take the responsibility for interpreting the resolution as a rebuke of Mao Zedong by Liu Shaoqi.

style and habit. Being human, he probably derived certain malicious satisfaction in ripping and crippling the new bureaucracy, and along the way, cutting down those artists and men of letters who did not share his sense of rustic simplicity. Rarely mentioned, the infrastructure that the CCP and Mao had created, in the form of communes and production brigades, had not been tied to the top structure of the state by institutional links, such as defendable rights and ownership claims, but by the uncertain cords of ideology. When *realpolitik* set in, Mao had no reason to believe that he himself should abdicate as the principal spokesman of the Chinese revolution. Alliance with Lin Biao and mobilizing the Red Guards completed all the preparations for him to regain leadership supremacy.

Assiduous student of history that he was, Mao Zedong could not conceive of himself as an instrument of destiny whose lifetime work constituted no more than a segment of the Chinese revolution. He had cleared the cancerous complexities of inter-household exploitation within the villages, which in the past had been one of the most fundamental obstacles to China's modernization. But the egalitarianism would be meaningless if the new system should remain as it was. Ultimately, it constituted no more than a modern form of *juntian* (p. 81), the erosion of which, as past records show, could not be prevented by government orders. It seems that Mao was not unaware of this dead-end. He might or might not have cautioned his wife against teaming with others to form a "gang of four"; but undeniably, in the last years of his life he broke off from Lin Biao and authorized Zhou Enlai to contact Kissinger and Nixon, signalling that he was ready to look for an alternative.

But if his work and that of the CCP should break away from the traditional dynastic pattern at all, the new infrastructure must be established as an unencumbered economic base, which could be utilized for future growth and expansion. Diversification and a higher level of interchangeability and division of labor would be in order. Only then could the crude structure of the Chinese society—the anatomy of a submarine sandwich—be put behind forever. In that sense the Cultural Revolution was not a total waste. Despite a decade of turmoil, it also provided an opportunity for regrouping. Above all, its trial-and-error nature had a profound educational value. It demonstrated that Mao's China, tenacious but unstable, still needed the stabilizing force in the middle to qualify as a final settlement.

The historical experience of several developed nations indicates that modernization is always accompanied by economic growth and expansion. Not all the steps can be planned beforehand. On the whole it comes as a result of the convergence of internal and external pressure. Once a breakthrough is reached, furthermore, the established pattern will work out its own future path. Government guidance and assistance, while still needed, will take a secondary position. The features of a pluralistic society will emerge as a byproduct of economic diversification. This is to say that a great deal of spontaneity will accentuate the process. The prerequisite of such a breakthrough is the removal of all existing obstacles, not the introduction of ideal solutions for hypothetical problems. For all we can see, China has already passed this crucial point.

The lack of a strong Western-style legal tradition works both to China's advantage and its disadvantage. The reader must realize that the picture of a law-abiding citizenry being abused by a lawless ruling class that the foreign observers habitually employed to categorize China is no more than another view of the submarine sandwich repeatedly referred to in this volume. It is an outmoded constitution; for its awkwardness both China's citizenry and the ruling class have paid dearly over the past 100 years, and certainly few would shed tears at its obliteration. This background suggests that the decades ahead may promise to be a most challenging and creative era for persons engaged in China's legal profession. New laws have to be enacted to keep pace with the new dimensions of materialistic life. These things could not be adequately done in the past, just as it would have made little sense to impose modern traffic regulations and street signs before the automobile was invented. The history of England in the seventeenth century further encourages us to think that conflicting ideas, when pressed by necessity, can be simultaneously accommodated by law. Whereas when legislation fails to carry, it can be accomplished by judiciary process.

As for the question that we brought up earlier as to where China is heading with the present experiment with capitalism, our answer is that the question itself may have to be reconsidered. When a nation of one billion persons completes a revolution that lasts more than a century, the magnitude of the movement may justify the reconsideration of the terminology and phraseology settled on before such an earth-shaking event. Undoubtedly, China's problem in modern times, tracing its origin hundreds or even thousands of years back, is not something that can be easily characterized by labels developed from the Western experience. The nation's early unification was dictated by geographical requirements (pp. 20–24). As a result, local institutions and regional interests were not sufficiently free to grow toward a plural society (p. 98). To facilitate bureaucratic management, schematic designs, ignoring internal diversities (p. 16), run through almost the entire length of Chinese history. The fostering of individual self-cultivators (p. 42) more-over remained, with few exceptions, an obsession of emperors and statesmen. The governance was noted for its lack of depth and preci-sion. All the while, Chinese civil laws remained undeveloped; citizens' rights to private properties remained uncertain (p. 119). Millenniums later, economic exploitation was not distinguished by organizations such as baronial estates and industrial combines, but on a minute scale within the villages and, for the most part, among the villagers them-selves (p. 247). The reason for this is not difficult to pin down. The development of capitalism requires governmental participation (p. 233), since the extension of credit, impersonal management, and sharing of services cannot do away with trust, which has to be secured by law. In China's case, the withholding of support by the government in these matters was sufficient to prevent capitalism of the modern Western and Japanese type to take root in this country of such great land mass. Consequently, when the surplus in the rural areas was denied an invest-ment outlet yet the small self-cultivators were short of capital, "agrar-ian exploitation" to the extent described by Hinton became the natural order of things. The contracts, usually unwritten, could be enforced by the village leaders and local strongmen in the name of law and order with or without the blessing of the civil government.

The Chinese Communist Party has cleared away the mess. Yet, as subsequent events have shown, the true meaning of the campaign is to wipe out the encumbering anomalies, not to abolish private accumula-tion of capital altogether. In the time table of development, the Chinese so far still remain at the stage of "primary accumulation of capital"; the dominant majority of the population have yet to experience the life-style of the machine age. The banishment of private wealth at this point, as attempted by the Maoist zealots, can only worsen the general poverty. Once this is recognized, the fundamental cure for the situation, that measures be taken to affirm property rights of the individual within the socialist state, cannot be avoided, even though this is a belated move and rhetorically, the CCP is confronting great difficulties in clarifying its own position on the issue.

The purpose of the current policy of the People's Republic, summed up in the slogan "to get rich is glorious," is double-barrelled. On the one hand, the national economic expansion, so enormous in scope, cannot go very far without private participation. In an assumed situation if Gen-eral Motors should ever become state-owned, its operation would still require so many subcontractors, and even more numerous service and service-support agencies, to include not only dealerships and filling stations but also fast food services, drive-ins, and schools which train secretaries and motel managers. It would be ludicrous to claim that state planning could have provided them all. The failure of the Self-Strengthening Movement in the late nineteenth century, one might recall, was due to the lack of such an in-depth commitment (p. 211).

Not so well understood by the public at this point is the crucial importance of the readmission of private entrepreneurship as a necessary step in recognizing property rights. As the present policy is being put into effect, we have no reason to suspect that the enfranchisement will not be legally binding. When claims of losses owing to untimely revocation by the government are allowed and the immunity of the accumulated wealth from political harassment is universally assured, the solidified rights of the citizenry will provide substance to a sound government.

From the story of Wang Anshi's failure (pp. 119–20) we have learned the lesson that unless the bottom strata of the society are endowed with the power of legal defense, the unlimited taxation power on the top will not be a blessing for those who hold the reins of the government, because the nation, being fiscally unstructured, cannot conduct its business in any good order. It may well lead to a situation in which the tax burden of the populace becomes unbearable yet the proceeds delivered to the treasury fall short of the quota. The paradox can best be explained from a recent case, which may serve as lateral illustration.

The Anshan Steel Works is an industrial complex in Manchuria embracing dozens of mills and shops spread over a wide area. Until several years ago the Chinese Steel Ministry pressed it for tonnage increases for their own sake. The Finance Ministry saw it as a revenue source. Yet the provincial authorities and municipal government demanded that it contribute to local construction. Disputes among the conflicting interests were endless. Technical controversies could easily flare into ideological polemics. To settle the issue, it was finally recommended that the industrial enterprise be reorganized as a publicly owned corporation, paying double income taxes—to the state and to Liaoning Province. Strengthening the property rights of private individuals has a similar effect. It gives the populace something to defend; it endows different constituencies with special interests so that each can develop its character and accountability. Failing that, as the aforementioned case of Wang Anshi and many other cases testify, China can only be governed as a conglomeration of village communities and the peasants can only be maneuvered in blocks. This means that political liberalization and economic expansion must come forth hand in hand. In order to make the country mathematically manageable, it is necessary to supply the numbers. There is no such thing as a "beggars' democracy." In that sense and in that sense alone to get rich is glorious.

It would be out of place for the historian to praise or condemn a contemporary regime from his personal likes and dislikes. He must, however, judge whether such a regime, especially one that involves a mass movement, is consistent over the long term with its predecessors. In the present case we have no reason not to answer in the affirmative. Personal foes as they seem to be to one another, Chiang Kai-shek, Mao Zedong, and Deng Xiaoping in the course of macrohistory represent three segmented phases of a continual movement. The freedom to act that the People's Republic enjoys today could never have been possible without its forerunners. If credit does not go to the leaders themselves, at least it should go to the mass movements that they represent.

In the entire length of Chinese history, the protracted revolution also falls into place in our periodization scheme. The Third Empire, running a course of 543 years (p. 147), is noted for its introverted and noncompetitive disposition. Its constitution was so diametrical to modern usage that excruciating readjustments could not be avoided. China's prolonged struggle can keep company in history books with the English revolution in the seventeenth century.

To return to the question asked twice earlier, whether China is heading toward capitalism, we have to reiterate our position that no thoughtful answer can be given without qualification. Offhand, the answer could be an impetuous yes. If fashion billboards appear on Beijing's boulevards at a short distance from the Great Hall of the People, Cadillacs equipped with refrigerators and air-conditioners are imported and sold for private use, and new enterprises are selling stock to raise capital, it is most difficult to defend those acts as incidental deviations from China's socialist regimen. But in the interest of history, recognition must be given to the fact that "capitalism," a word of Western coinage, carries a connotation of European origin. Within that context capitalism can only be developed from the matrix of municipal franchise. Either intensively or extensively, it has grown up with the imprint of the city state. The bourgeoisie therefore has an unchallenged interest in it. Also, private capital always plays a dominant role in shaping public life under such a system. The Chinese revolution, however, is basically an affair of peasants led by educated youths, made absolutely clear by Mao's campaign. Only in the ensuing nation-building have the Chinese discovered that certain techniques of monetary management, developed by the Western nations and Japan, cannot be avoided. The imitation has since given Deng's China a capitalist image. But the differences between this image and reality are not only numerous but also profound.

Despite the recent decentralization, the Chinese government is never inclined to relinquish its monopolistic control of metallugical, petroleum, and chemical industries, machine-tool production, shipbuilding, public transportation, banking and insurance, foreign trade, broadcasting, and even the tourist industry. Those enterprises contribute the lion's share of the nation's productivity. So far liberalization has only permitted management to exercise discretion in decision-making. Private enterprises are limited to small shops, food services, retail trade, and certain businesses not profitable under public ownership. Moreover, most of those enterprises are not transformed to private ownership outright, but leased for private operation under contract. Otherwise, joint ownership to include private capital has been widened. The agricultural communes can be said to have ceased to function, as food production is being taken over by individual peasants. But it is inaccurate to say that the communes themselves have been dismantled, since they still own the land that is leased to the users. The state still purchases the foodstuff and plans and carries out pricing and distribution. Those are prominent socialist features. The readmission of private capital and borrowing of managerial techniques from the economically advanced nations have in no way threatened China's socialist character.

Nevertheless, in the eyes of the Westerner, China's self-contradictory features are too obvious to be missed. The confusion is compounded by the over-enthusiasm of the promoters of economic rationalization on one hand, who go out of their way to demonstrate how far the program can be stretched, in doing so creating brinkmanship of a kind, and by the inflexibility of the partisan doctrinaires on the other, some of them still clinging to Marxism* as a security blanket rather than a revolutionary tool.

In view of the egalitarianism and collective character of the Chinese

---

*Marxism itself is an amorphous body of intellectual interests. The political pamphlets of Karl Marx do not match his economic studies in thoroughness. Many concrete steps enumerated in the *Communist Manifesto*, revolutionary by the standard of the mid-nineteenth century, have since been adopted by many Western nations, including the United States. On the other hand, as pointed out by Joseph Schumpeter and Joan Robinson, the analysis in *Das Kapital* contains a number of impractical notions, such as that machinery transmits surplus value but does not create it, that professors, being unproductive, are comparable to prostitutes, and that the risk-taking function of the capitalists does not count. These notions contradict Marx's own historical positivism. For one thing, their combined effect would have "talked" the computer industry, and for that matter all high technology, out of existence. On the whole it would be impossible for an individual, much less an entire nation, in the late twentieth to declare that he is in every aspect bound to Marxism.

A reviewer in the People's Republic of China had this to say about me: "This author is not a Marxist; his viewpoint may have debatable features" (*Dushu*, Beijing, No.5, May 10, 1983, p. 11). This comment I gladly accept.

Yet, writing with an emphasis that economic organization has a determining effect on law and culture, I, like many other non-Marxist historians, cannot escape the criticism of being influenced by Marx, especially in the present case when history is examined in long, continuing, and progressively staged segments.

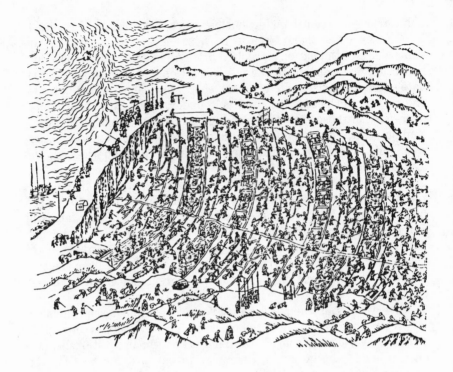

Public works executed with a multitude of manpower were common in the old days.

that is deeply rooted in their history (see above, especially Chapter 2), prototypical European capitalism can be said to contradict China's cultural tradition. The creation of an urban proletariat, the seizing of colonies, and the waging of commercial wars—characteristics which have underlined this prototype—are out of step with the twentieth century and have already been rectified by the nations that started with them. It would be inconceivable for China to pick up what they had dropped.

These is no question that Marxism also has reached the limit of its influence in China. It is no longer premature to say that the Chinese revolution has contained Marxism similarly to the way that the Tang dynasty absorbed Buddhism (pp. 91–92). Fundamentally, class struggle as an instrument of revolution had only limited usefulness during the early phase of China's land reform. Even then the violent excessiveness was already causing some of the participants to shudder. The abuse of class struggle during the Cultural Revolution did not advance its cause. Although no one, not even authorities in the People's Repub-

They are still so nowadays.

lic, can guarantee that the Chinese will never again stage another violent eruption in the name of Karl Marx, in our judgment, historical forces will not rally behind the burned-out case. There is neither the internal desperation nor the external pressure to generate the needed frenzy for such a mass movement. Recent liberation on religious matters further signals that the ideological monopoly of Marxism has been broken.

This means that China may continue to be characteristically self-contradictory without going to the polarized extremes—a situation necessitated by circumstances. The dual policy of fostering private capital while preventing its uncontrolled growth at the very extreme was in fact spelled out early on by Sun Yat-sen in his treatise, which has been in circulation for more than a half century. Not inconceivably, this may well be the solution for all large land-based countries lately restructured in this modern era. For China, however, in the early stage of settlement the divergent aims create a seemingly double image, which leads to the speculation that the country is simultaneously subscribing to two kinds of "isms" that are bound to destroy each other.

Ultimately, all nations may experience this in common after the revolutionary breakthrough: The settlement comes forth in a form of synthesis. We have seen the Netherlands engaging its destiny with the techniques of federation, and England, with the creation of a modern form of jurisprudence by blending the principles of equity with customary law. In a variety of ways they made themselves mathematically manageable, suitable for monetary control. China is no exception. At this breakthrough we can say that Chinese history is being linked with the history of the modern West. Following the established pattern, the officially sanctioned orthodoxy, be it *The Book of Common Prayer* or the doctrine of predestination, Marxism-Leninism or the Chairman's Thought, can now recede into the background as a cultural influence rather than being retained as a feared whip. For both the Chinese and their friends abroad, this is a great moment. It is on such an occasion that millions of tourists throng Tiananmen Square and the First Emperor's mausoleum to see for themselves how this is being done, how the protracted struggle called the Chinese revolution is reaching a settlement.

But no thoughtful observer can be completely unaware of the problems still lying ahead. Land scarcity, overpopulation, and the fundamental conflict between industrialization and ecology have by no means been swept away by the successful conclusion of the revolution. Natural disasters will still occur, despite greater means of public control. Once the Chinese economy is fully under monetary management, vicious cycles of ups and downs are likely to follow. Even though in the coming decades China may command a unique position in mediating between the have's and have-not's, there is also the possibility of a double rebuttal—the developed nations may find excuses to turn back the Chinese challenge with cheaper skilled labor while the developing nations, still shielding their mathematically unmanageable situation behind all sorts of dogmas, will charge Beijing for its aggressive potential, which, regardless of the Chinese cultural tradition, is inherent in a commerce-oriented economy.

No one can enumerate all such future prospects. When we say that for China there is a breakthrough, we mean that certain disabilities have been removed and certain incapacities have been overcome. The freedom to act of a renewed nation will open a fresh vista of possibilities. Normally, the function of the historian is to chronicle the deeds of the past. Convention also demands that he maintain some distance from the immediate present as a safety margin for possible reversals. On this particular occasion and in the interests of macrohistory, however, we no longer see such exercise of caution as necessary. The logic of a continuous drive of many decades behind us plus the orientation of the guideposts from other lands presses us to set up a benchmark on the spot. We would be ineffective even as narrators if we were to evade this responsibility.

The justification for bringing this historical news immediately to the attention of the American public is that it stands as a major turning point in American history as well. Although not formally recognized, our China policy is being made on the basis of just such a premise. For the broadminded reader, the Chinese success is at once an American accomplishment. Again and again we have said that we should never interfere in the internal affairs of the Chinese. But we know that this is only diplomatically, technically, or legally true. It cannot be historically true. For a half century at least, the United States has been a major and busy maker of Chinese history. Americans have fought three major wars in which, for one reason or another, China was a distinct contributing cause. Now the inconsistency can be reconciled, as a sense of common destiny of mankind has emerged from the rounds of conflict, and our understanding of the past is widened by current events. We cannot hold back this knowledge. What is more, when the entire record is reviewed in a worldwide perspective, the conclusions drawn should facilitate our understanding of other nations and civilizations still in various stages of the same struggle, in which the United States may again be involved. Maybe the agony can be avoided or at least lessened, with the Chinese experience as a hindsight. In this connection the major usefulness of a macrohistory of China rests in its magnitude and comprehensiveness. It has the power, vividness, and intellectually intriguing value to deserve universal recognition.

21
Taiwan, Hong Kong, and Macao

This small book of mine would not be complete without a few words about the Taiwan situation. Theoretically, future developments in that island province can upset much of what I have so far put down on paper here. Although they have never acknowledged it publicly, Chinese leaders on both sides of the Formosa Straight are concerned about the future of Taiwan mainly, if not exclusively, owing to such an apprehension.

This is a Chinese province. There have never been enough aboriginees to be reckoned with politically or economically. The territory features a subculture brought over by the immigrants from the mainland who speak the Fujian and Hakka dialects. Lineage influence among them is strong. Under the Japanese rule, Taiwan's agriculture was geared to export its surpluses to Japan, with camphor, sugar, tea, and rice being the staple crops. But cultivation has never been developed to a plantation scale; it is done by intensive farming on homestead plots not basically different from the prevailing conditions in south China. Owing to a more favorable geographical setting, nowhere has the general poverty on the island measured up to the extremes evident in many parts of the continent, the northwest for example.

Taiwan's tenancy rate has been much reduced since the Kuomintang (KMT) takeover after V-J Day. The "Land to the Tiller" Act of 1953, modeled after MacArthur's land reform in Japan, limited the holding of each household to approximately 7.5 acres of medium-grade land. The amount in excess of this limitation was surrendered to the government for redistribution. The compensation, calculated at two-and-a-half

Taipei as seen from the author's hotel room

year's crop yield, was nominal. Of that amount, 30 percent was paid with stocks of enterprises taken over from the Japanese; the balance was paid with commodity bonds, payable in rice and sweet potatoes over a twenty year period, which carried a four percent annual interest. This legislation could be implemented because at that point the island was still under a state of military exigency and the threat of a Communist invasion seemed to loom.

After the land reform came industrial expansion. With substantial U.S. aid, Taiwan's development strategy avoided capital-intensity and prestige industries and concentrated instead on labor-intensive projects for export. In this way the KMT-controlled territory reaped the benefit in a situation when the post-WWII economy of the developed nations left the markets for such manufacture wide open. The program was so successful that American aid was discontinued after 1965. Only in recent years has Taiwan embarked on steel production, the development of high technology, and automobile manufacture, the last in the form of joint enterprises with the Japanese.

The independence movement of the islanders, while attracting considerable attention, cannot be at this point regarded as a serious contender for Taiwan's future. The weakness of the promoters of the self-determination of the Taiwanese in some respects resembles that of the liberal movement on the mainland in the past, which never found the means to translate its idealism into reality. Unable either to make an appeal to the mass or to convert the majority of the educated elite to their platform, the proponents of the movement are campaigning for an unstructured if not a parochial cause. But it embodies a potentially volatile issue, both emotional and real, and there is no guarantee that the situation will not change rapidly.

Despite the displeasure of the People's Republic, the United States cannot be regarded as an obstructing influence in a peaceful reunion of the island with mainland China. Americans cannot possibly block a *rapprochement* if that is the expressed wish of both sides, although legally speaking and from the angle of self-interest, neither is the U.S. government obligated to act as a broker to expedite the process.

As for ideology, the doctrinal differences between the two sides may not be as great as they seem. The KMT, professing to be the party of Sun Yat-sen, is to this day employing large numbers of cultural workers busily compiling the records of its own revolutionary past. The word "socialism" explicity appears in its officially sanctioned literature. Banners proclaiming *Tianxia weigong* ("All that is under Heaven belongs to the public") are on exhibit in many public places in Taipei. The government on the island exercises a firm control over banking and foreign trade. It operates railroads and bus lines. It maintains a strong hold on public education and the mass media. In these aspects its management structure is not drastically different from that of the People's Republic under the Chinese Communist Party's (CCP) direction.

In the areas of culture and education, the KMT's policies, carried on for four decades, leave no room for a separatist movement. Not only are youngsters taught that they are descendants of China, but also, museums and archives give every emphasis to their continental origin. Even engineers and technicians, not to mention teachers and public servants, have never been trained with the thought that they should confine their career and future to an island province. In recent years a kind of "Taiwan literature" has been arising; the dominant portion of published materials, however, shows a wider horizon, not infrequently broader in scope than the works by mainland writers.

Even the ill feelings developed during the 1945–49 civil war should not remain ineradicable grudges. After all, both the KMT and the CCP fought the Japanese during WWII. Not only have they made peace with their former enemy, but also, each in its own way has demonstrated that friendly cooperation can be developed once animosity is put aside. Magnanimity as a desirable character has never been questioned by the KMT or the CCP. Chiang Kai-shek forgave at least a dozen warlords who had taken arms against him. Mao, who lost a son in the Korean War, graciously received Nixon. It is unimaginable that the younger generations who were not involved in the war directly would perpetuate the rift.

But over decades of armed rivalry, both sides have been taking the denial of the *de jure* position of the opponent as a part of their organization logic. For the nationalists in Taiwan, the policy virtually stands for its own *raison d'état*. A sudden abandonment risks dissension and may actually aid the separationists. To a lesser degree, this also applies to mainland China. At the time of this writing, there are many indications that the leaders of the People's Republic are ready to give Chiang Kai-shek a historical rehabilitation. His home in Zhejiang is said to have been refurbished. A huge war museum is planned for a site next to the Marco Polo Bridge. Some streets in Beijing and Hankow have been renamed after KMT generals who died in action during the war against Japan. An alumni association of the Whampoa Military Academy, of which Chiang was the only commandant, has been organized, with Marshal Xu Xiangqian assuming the presidency. But this flurry of activity has yet to be carried to the logical conclusion: the reaffirmation of the positions of Chiang Kai-shek and the KMT by historiography.

The *de facto* independence of Taiwan over the years has also enabled the island province to reach a working order of diplomacy with the foreign powers, the continuation of which may be vital to its economy. Inasmuch as mainland China is striving to become mathematically manageable, reversing the old practice of structuring a nation from the top downward, the preservation of the present order of things, with the potentiality that Taiwan renders to itself a service similar to what Hong Kong is providing, should work to its advantage. Under any circumstances, there is such a wide disparity between the standard of living and patterns of social and public behavior of the two sides of the Formosa Straight that it would be most difficult to govern the two parts, as they are now, from a unitary center.

Hong Kong is an island linked with a peninsula and an adjacent area on the mainland. In terms of real estate, the total area of some 400 square miles is not too small (as compared with Macao's six square miles). Furthermore, with its fine skyscrapers overlooking many natural harbors, Hong Kong's vertical value, enhanced by the picturesque quarried range in the background, may even exceed its horizontal value. As a free port and a shopping emporium, for decades Hong Kong has been a tourist attraction on its own and earned foreign exchange for China, even under the British flag. Recently, it has been noted for its bustling economy, one of the fastest growing in Asia.

In addition to its position as a banking and shipping center of world importance, Hong Kong is a major manufacturer of textile and plastic materials, electric and electronic equipment, and machinery and chemicals. Its printing, food-processing, and motion-picture industries serve the interests of a wide region, not the least Chinese communities overseas.

As this book was going to press, a copy of the Draft Basic Law of the

Hong Kong Special Administrative Region came into my hands, confirming our notion that when a nation reaches a major breakthrough in the modern era, as the Dutch Republic experienced 400 years ago, it may have to pause to recast the concept of nationhood. The Basic Law provides a glimpse of what is possibly in store for Hong Kong after its reunion with mainland China, scheduled to take effect in 1997. There will be separate taxation and monetary systems, a regional flag and regional emblem, and an elected chief executive who, like the elected legislators, must have been in residence for over twenty years; the current judicial apparatus will remain virtually intact. While the laws enacted by Hong Kong will be reported to the National People's Congress in Beijing for the record, the special administrative region will by no means be subordinate to any departments of the central government. Moreover, it may participate in or manage external affairs of special concern to itself. The Basic Law Drafting Committee, having prepared the first draft, is working closely with the Basic Law Consultative Committee. Both are still canvassing public opinion for the widest input. The effort manifests the spirit of home rule, preservation of what is of value, and adherence to the Sino-British Accord of 1984. This is by no means an easy task, yet its success should set a good example for Macao, and the momentum thus built up should be encouraging to both sides of the Formosa Straight.

In conclusion, I would like to sum up my philosophy as a historian in preparing this volume. At a glance, macrohistory seems amoral. The unfolding of human events on a large scale follows certain cause-and-effect relationships independent of any individual's wish, let alone his moral aspiration. In drafting each chapter, I have further underlined the overbearing effects of past deeds, differing from the dynastic historians of the traditional school who habitually present the dawn of each era as a creative period, during which the population and society are malleable enough for men of destiny to proceed from their inventive schemes. While closer to reality, the outline of Chinese history presented here may create an overall impression that what will happen is bound to happen and morals do not count. This brutal positivism could be disturbing if not offending to some sensitive readers. That, however, is not the message that the author wishes to convey.

In the diagram below, the solid portion of the curve is my idea of the configuration of world history. It is made of an infinite number of short thrusts of human effort. For clarity, only three large segments are presented. (Basically this is also the concept of macrohistory.) Called *karma* or predestination, the compulsion of the past is such that our

path runs in a continuous circuit. What freedom of choice we are entitled to starts from where we stand, in the footsteps left by our forefathers. The arrows pointing skyward suggest our idealistic tendencies. Moral power has to be a vital force, since the mass movement represented by the drive of each arrowhead, involving self-sacrifice of an enormous magnitude, cannot be launched without some sense of universal justice, genuine or assumed. But to counter it, there is always a centrifugal pull. Should we call it original sin, or, as Chinese philosophers refer to it, "human desire"? World history evolves out of the inter-reaction of the *yin* and the *yang*.

The ultimate meaning of history, seen in this configuration, resides in its wholesome aesthetic quality. The reader is reminded that the entire written history of mankind extends over something less than 10,000 years, indeed a very short segment within the life of the universe, which may well be a small portion of something else. Following Kant, we can only say that "things in themselves" are unknowable. The dotted portions of the spiral—the prehistory period as well as the unknown future—enable us to sustain our faith in the long-term rationality of history beyond the realm of our mundane experience.

When large chunks of history are reviewed at a distance, the setting is automatically theological. Having no ambition to venture into that awesome sphere, I am more than content to parrot the voice of a giant to relieve myself of the impossible task of relating my limited observations to the unknown. That done, let me say again that the wisdom of the historian is essentially retrospective. To plot some dots in empty space is by no means prophetic.

At this juncture the backlog of Chinese history suggests a number of possibilities. But their combination and timing are so unpredictable that I, after making several strong statements up to this point, feel reluctant to further assert what is bound to happen in days yet to come. Suffice it to say that Pandora's Box has not been totally emptied and that in the future the earth still belongs to the living.

Instead of building any universal system, this small book reverses the practice of some textbook writers who, while narrating the events of the Western world, intermittently add episodes about China and things Chinese, some of them carrying no more weight than footnotes, and count the whole package as "world history." As I see it, the life story of one quarter of mankind deserves to be treated with more care, especially at this juncture when a crucial point has been reached. My scheme of presentation calls out the entire length of Chinese history, together with its inner rhythm and characteristics, for a reconsideration of its confrontation with the modern West. When the baseline of history is rolled back, the protracted struggle before a merger in force makes more sense with the added dimension. The new arrangement does give us an opportunity to see world events in a different light. For one thing, much of the clamor about Chinese absurdity can now be put aside. For another, the effect of geography begins to stand out, and along with it the power of human endurance. Individual reactions to these elements are expected to differ. I, as author, nevertheless hope that together they bring to my readers, tourists and fellow students of history alike, a more pleasant feeling of the reinvigorated longevity of a nation which is, in this jet age, only slightly more than a half day's distance from us.

Epilogue:
Reflections on Tiananmen

Since the last printing of this book, a few things have happened in the world. Perhaps the foremost in the mind of the present reader is the Tiananmen Incident on the night of June 3/4, 1989—a Bloody Sunday in contemporary Chinese history. The author needs to address this tragedy if only to bring the present volume up to date.

That the incident happened at all is of course disturbing and most regrettable, the more so because the true cause of the bloodshed was a profound structural problem of a nation, one that could never be resolved by this kind of confrontation—by a religious war, so to speak. The tragedy, however, does not shake the author's faith in the validity of dividing contemporary Chinese history into three parts: With the war of resistance against Japan, Chiang Kai-shek and the KMT created a superstructure for the new China. With land reform, Mao Zedong and the CCP created a new infrastructure. To maintain history's long-term rationality, whoever succeeds them has the role and duty to establish institutional links between the top and the bottom. The current economic reforms provide an opportunity for the fulfillment of this requirement.

At this point, when so little has been settled, it seems unrealistic to demand immediately from the People's Republic the kind of nuance and strength characteristic of a modern, mature democratic state. Which is not to gainsay, however, that the major responsibility for the Tiananmen Incident falls on the present regime and its partisan caucus.

The greatest weakness of the Chinese Communist Party lies in its inability to maintain a dialogue with those it governs. As a rule, the outspoken among its ranks are purged, yet differences of opinion within the hierarchy have never been successfully camouflaged by Democratic Centralism. We have reasons to suspect that even some of the very highest cadres are unaware of their own roles in history because of the practice of substituting ideology for historiography, and this has been going on for decades. Consequently, technical problems by and large have had to be treated as moral issues.

It is not in the interest of macrohistory to debate whether China is on the road to capitalism, or whether she still retains some of her communist stamina. The urgent task confronting the People's Republic is to bring its public finance and taxation system in line with modern monetary management, so that most problems can be handled numerically. We cannot see how this can be accomplished without organizing private sectors of the economy in depth, providing second- and third-line support. The process requires the establishment of a credit system, starting with the affirmation of property rights. The present reader will know that even with his visionary ambition, Wang Anshi of the Northern Song (pp. 115–21) was unable to provide such a breakthrough, and in the wake of his failure came partisan polemics. More than 900 years later, the present generation should have found a way out.

The origins of the recent controversy are to be found in the two-track price system. A ton of steel, for instance, can be sold for 700 yuan or 200 yuan, depending on which sector of the economy one is dealing with. The products of publicly owned factories, when routinely surrendered to official channels, fetch only standard prices. But when declared as irregulars and sold on the free market, the same articles may earn four times that much (see *The Chinese Intellectual*, New York, Winter 1986, p. 59). This confusing situation makes some officials' "devotion to duty indistinguishable from abusing power," which in turn ushers in a combination of "30 percent bureaucratic economy, 30 percent private connections, and 40 percent money economy" (*Economic Review*, Beijing, 1988, No. 11, p. 19, and No. 12, p. 18). This can be traced back to the "scissors-type taxation" (see this volume, p. xv). For the first thirty years of the PRC, the pricing policy of the government imposed excessive taxation on the workers and peasants alike in order to channel the surplus to heavy industries. The accumulation of capital was thus achieved through self-reliance. A private economy began to appear in 1982. Now, because of the divergence, complaints are heard that "those who play the piano are inferior to those who move the piano" and "the one who cuts the skull open [brain surgeon] is worse off than the one who shaves the head [barber]" (*River Elegy*, Commentaries, the 4th Section).

This double-jointed economy has also exhausted the means of transportation and the supply of energy. Where to turn now thus becomes a crucial issue. Whether to dispose of some of the government's assets, or to invite foreign investment with substantial concessions, or whole-scale retrenchment—whatever future policy is, it cannot avoid disturbing the fundamental philosophy of the government. Not surprisingly, the issue split the Politburo, but the shadow boxing was held *in camera*. Simultaneously, but not uncoincidentally, the marathon mass demonstrations in Tiananmen began to develop in April and May. The protesters brought with them dissatisfaction of various kinds and shades; they never developed a clear common aim. Some of the students were apparently aware of the deadlock within the hierarchy and had been acting in response to it, but it was unlikely true for the majority of the demonstrators, who participated merely to pursue such noble yet vague goals as freedom and democracy. The prolonged stand-off amazed a large number of onlookers, who did little to help.

As the protesters continued to assert their position in abstract yet morally uncompromising terms, the movement gained religious intensity. The final results turned out to be as cruel and shocking as they were unexpected. By the time the rattle of the guns of the army units reached Tiananmen Square, the initial issue about economic structure had long been put aside. A great many of those who died on June 3/4 never really had perceived the sequence of events that culminated with their deaths.

It would be out of place for the historian to predict what may happen next. He can only say that it would be safer to have the aforementioned crucial issues debated in public rather than behind closed doors. In retrospect, a few statements in this volume may seem overly optimistic. But, as I have said, the author's purpose is to establish the long-term rationality of history. He cannot lose faith because of an event, however heartbreaking, that to his mind should never have happened. Instead of hastily making revisions, therefore, he wishes to emphasize that this is a time for reason and understanding. We must not allow outdated doctrinal commitments to confuse the basic facts.

RH

December 18, 1989

Index

Academia Sinica, 230
Aden, 156
Afghanistan, 139
Agrarian problem, 246
Agriculture, 7, 14, 23, 25, 51, 78, 79, 107, 113, 131, 147, 204, 260
Alcock, Rutherford, 210
Altaic languages, 39, 63
Altan Khan, 172
Amazon River, 20
American Council of Learned Societies, xix
Amoy, 175, 201
Amur River, 206
Analects of Confucius, 12
Ancestor worship, 14
Animism, 13
Annam, 105. *See also* Vietnam
Anshan Steel Works, 253
Anyang, 7
Arabs, 90, 92, 105
Architecture, 50, 54, 55, 75, 90, 150, 155, 164
Arik-buga, 139
Aristocracy, 28, 30, 31, 36, 45, 46, 47, 99, 146
Army, 19, 27, 33, 39, 40, 43, 68, 87, 101, 105, 110, 112, 115, 130, 143, 152, 189, 246
Arsenals, 210, 211
Artillery, modern, 189
Asbestos, 137
Assam, 90
Assyrian, 23
Astronomical clock, 133
Audience, emperor's, 166
Avars, 80, 86, 89

Bacon, Francis, 228
Badaling, 38
Baghdad, 138

Bai Juyi, 4, 122
Balazs, Etienne, 25
Ban Chao, 52
Ban Gu, 41, 42, 52
Banner system, 180, 183–84
Banpo village, 3
Banzhang qian, 132
Baotou, 79
Barbarians, 15, 63, 68, 102
Batu Mengke, 166
Beijing, ix, xiii, 99, 125, 137, 144, 155, 162, 183, 206, 210, 219, 224, 225, 254, 262; during Boxer Rebellion, 219–20; as Cambaluc, 137; construction under Ming, 155; present city, 155; site lost to Qidans, 111; as Jin capital, 125
Beijing, Convention of, 206
Beijing Hotel, xiv
Beijing-Tianjin Railway, xiv
Beijing University, 206, 227, 228
Beitang Cathedral, 219
Benaketi, Ahmed, 145
Bhutan, 189
Blast furnace, 107
Block printing, 89
Bonded servant. *See* Slave
Book of Changes (Yijing), 38, 60, 209
Boxer Protocol, 220
Boxers, 218
Bronze, 5, 13, 18
Bronze coins, 47, 62, 108, 129, 158, 162, 185
Bruce, James, 206, 210
Buck, John Lossing, 246
Buddhism, 72, 74–76, 91–92, 134, 145, 173, 187, 225, 256
Bureaucracy, xiii, xvii, 15, 28, 29, 45, 47, 59, 74, 80, 89, 91–92, 98, 102, 111, 125, 143, 144, 160, 168, 200

Burlingame, Anson, 210
Burma, 141, 189

Cai Yuanpei, 227, 230
Calendar-making, 7
Cambulac, 137
Camphor, 158, 260
Canal construction, 90, 144, 155
Canton. See Guangzhou
Cantonese, 8, 221
Cao Cao, 61, 63, 64, 67, 70
Cao Cen, 36
Capitalism, xvi, 194n, 198, 231, 233;
  as developed in Europe, 233–41,
  251
Caspian Sea, 53
Catapults, 133
Cathay, 137
Cavalry, 23, 33, 39, 40, 64, 69, 143,
  179
Censors, 30, 151, 176, 183
Census-taking, 14
Central Military Academy, x, xi
Centralized management, 41–42, 89,
  112, 127, 130, 150
Ceylon, 156
Chairman Mao's Thought, 258
Chamberlain, Neville, 245
Changsha, x, 207
Chariots, 7, 33
Chen, State of, 85, 86–87
Chen Duxiu, 227–28, 230, 231, 246
Chen Ping, 36
Chen Tuan, 134
Chen Yuanyuan, 181
Cheng Hao, 134
Cheng Yi, 134
Cheng Zihua, ix
Chengdu, xi
Chenqiaoyi, 111
Chiang Kai-shek, ix, x, 4, 150, 222,
  227, 230, 244, 247, 254, 262
China Fund, xix
Chinese Army in India, xi
Chinese Communist Party, xii, 230,
  246, 247, 250, 252, 260, 263
Chinese history, xvii, 3, 10, 12,
  13, 20, 26, 49, 56, 127, 167, 208,
  232
Chinese Intellectual, xv
Chinese opera, 3, 71, 123

Chinese writing system, 5, 6, 7, 14,
  30
Christianity, 91, 145, 206, 208; Nes-
  torian, 91
Christians, 105, 138, 207, 218, 219
Chronology of Major Events Con-
  cerning the Chinese Communist
  Party, xii
Chu, 18
Chuanbi Island, 203
Churchill, Winston, 245
Civil law, xvii, 29, 119, 234, 252
Civil Service Examinations, 12, 89,
  96, 118, 125, 143, 148, 162, 168,
  172, 185, 193, 206, 208, 211, 220
Civil war, ix, 66, 231, 246, 247
Cixi, Empress Dowager, 215–16,
  218–21
Cloth manufacture, 174
Coal, 138
Comintern, 230
Commerce, 51, 102, 108, 129, 133,
  154, 170, 188–89, 204
Commercial farming, 174
Communism, xvi, 207, 231, 249
Communist Manifesto, 242, 255n
Communists, 4, 230
Compass navigation, 107
Concubinage, 208
Confucianism, 12, 16, 26, 30, 37, 74,
  97, 145, 228. See also Self-re-
  straint and mutual deference
Confucius, 10, 24, 38, 118, 125
Connoisseurship, 124, 173
Conscription, 24, 28, 43, 84, 88, 120,
  131, 143
Constitution Protection Movement,
  222
Constitutional monarchy, 216
Copper cash. See Bronze coins
Costume, 51, 83, 96, 173
Cottage industry, 170
Cotton, 144, 174
Craftsmen, 174
Credit and banking, 174, 252
Cross bows, 33
Cultural Revolution, xii, 163, 231,
  256

Dagu Fortress, 205, 219, 220
Dai (Tabas), 79

Daily life: Han, 51, Ming, 172; Qing, 188; Song, 129; Tang, 100
Daoguang Emperor (Minning), 201
Datong, 79, 83, 245
Deng Xiaoping, 254
Deng Yu, 49
Depopulation, 80, 209
Descartes, 228
Dewey, John, 229
Di Renjie, 96
Ding, 189
Dinghai, 201
Discourses of Mencius, 10, 12, 22, 24
Disunity, Period of, 66
Dolonor, 155
Donglin Academy, 178
Donglin Movement, 178
Dorgon, 187
Draft banks, 198
Drama, 148
Dream of the Red Chamber, 199
Drought, 22, 30, 45, 96, 149
Duke of Zhou, 14–15, 16
Dunhuang, 75–76

Education, 4, 49, 50, 227, 250, 262
Egypt, 5
Elements of International Law, 210
Elgin, Lord. See Bruce, James
Elliot, Charles, 200
Emigration to Southeast Asia, 175
Epidemics, 105
Erotism, 172
Esen, 165
Eunuchs, 58, 59, 92, 155, 165, 176, 178, 216
Eurasian continent, 138
Ever-Victorious Army, 209
Explosive, 133
Extraterritoriality, 202

Factory workers, 226
Famine, 22, 30, 80, 110, 149
Fan Wenhu, 140
Fancheng, 135
Fanshen, 247
Farm implements, 175
Farm wage, xv
Fei Xiaotong, 246
Feng Yulan, 231
Feng Yuxiang, 225

Fengjian, 14, 15, 24
Fifteen-inch isohyet line, 23
Financial Commission, 108, 114
Firearms, 133, 144, 179, 201
First Empire, 36–41
Five Barbarians and Sixteen Kingdoms, 63
Five Dynasties and Ten Kingdoms, 89, 109–11
Five material agents, 38
Flood, 21, 22
Food plants, 5. See also Rice; Sorghum; Sugar; Peanuts; Sweet potato
Footbinding, 208
Forbidden City (Beijing), 155
Ford Foundation, xv
Foreign trade, 90, 108, 188–89, 222
Former Han. See Han, Former
Formosa Strait, 260
France, 202, 205, 211, 213
Fu Sinian, 231
Fujian, 110, 112, 184, 260
Furniture, 173, 189
Fuzhou, 201
Fuzhou Dockyard, 201

Galdan, 189
Gambling, 208
Gan River, 209
"Gang of Four," 250
Gao Family, 84–86
Gardening, 85, 173
Gate of Heavenly Peace, 225
Genealogy, 74, 134
Genghis Khan, 126, 137, 139
Genghis Law, 139
Gentry class, 53, 54, 58, 68, 161, 173, 183, 184, 208
Geopolitics, 63, 67, 142, 196, 251, 265
Germany, 213, 214, 218–20
Go (game), 91
Golden Horde, 139
Gong, Prince, 210
Gongyi, 218
Goodrich, Dr. L. Carrington, 219
Gordon, Charles George, 209
Governmental monopoly. See State monopoly
Grand Canal, 122, 144, 155, 176
Grand Council, 191

Grand Preceptor, 166
Grand Secretary, 168
Great Hall of the People, 254
Great Leap Forward, 248–49
Great Proletarian Cultural Revolution, xii, 163, 231, 156
Great Wall, 23, 38, 42, 63, 78, 151, 166, 180
Green Crop Money, 116, 120
Green Standard, 197, 217
Guan Yü, 70, 124
Guandu, Battle of, 60
Guangdong, 184
Guangxi, 165, 182, 184, 207
Guangxu Emperor (Daitian), 215–17
Guangzhou, 90, 105, 112, 176, 201, 206
Guilin, 207
Guiqiu Convention, 21
Gunpowder, 39, 107
Guo Shoujing, 144
Guo Ziyi, 104

Hainan Island, 205
Hair styles, 91, 186
Hakata Bay, 139
Hakka, 260
Han dynasty: Former, 36–44; Later, 63–61; map sketch, 44; restoration, 48
Han River, 12
Han Tuozhou, 126, 134
Han Wudi. See Liu Che
Han Xin, 36
Hangzhou, 122, 125, 135, 209
Hankow, 222
Harbin, ix, xiv
Harding, Warren G., 226
Hart, Robert, 210
Hay, John, 215
He Jin, 59–60
He Jintao, 104
He Shen, 192, 197
Hebei, 98
Heilongjiang University, ix
Hemp, 81
Henan, 6
Herbal medicine, 76, 158
Hereditary military system, 143, 152, 169, 176, 184
Hinton, William, 247, 252

History of the Former Han, 41
Hitler, Adolf, 245
Holingeer, 78
Honesty-nourishing allowance, 190, 192
Hong Kong, 201–204, 205, 218, 260, 263
Hong Xiuquan, 206, 209
Hormuz, 156
Horses, 7, 23, 33, 40, 65, 69, 79, 101, 131
Housing, xiii
Hu Shih, 75, 228
Huai Army, 209
Huai River, 125
Huang Chao, 105–106
Huang Zhenbai, x
Huaqing Hot Springs, 3, 100
Hughes, Charles Evans, 226
Huguang, 182
Hunan, 110, 207
Hunan Braves, 208
Hundred Days Reform, 213, 215–17, 229
Hundred schools, 34
Huns, 52
Huo Guang, 44–46
Huo Qubing, 44
Hydraulic engineering, 174

Ice age, 20
Imperial City (Beijing), 155
Imperial unification, 4, 13, 28, 30–31, 36, 56
Imperial University, 49–50, 181
India, 75, 90, 91
Indian Ocean, 156
Industrial Revolution, 212
Industrial wage, xv
Insurance business, 174
Intermarriage, 83, 90, 185, 191
International Settlement (Shanghai), 230
Iran, 89, 90, 105, 139
Iraq, 139
Iron, 5, 41, 25
Isaacs, Harold, 230
Ito Hirobumi, 214, 216

Japan, 8, 52, 90, 93, 110, 139–41, 151, 191, 213, 216, 224, 226, 248, 260

Japanese, 8, 52, 90, 134, 139, 140, 171, 214, 262
Java, 141
Jesuits, 187
Jews, 105
Ji Xu, 96
Jia Sidao, 135
Jianbing, 46, 67, 93
Jiang Qing, xi
Jiankang, 73, 87
Jilong Fortress, 211
Jin (Chinese dynasty), 64–68
Jin (Jürched State), 123, 125, 132, 138
Jing Baiwen, *ix*
Jinling. *See* Nanjing
Jinshan Temple, 123
Jinzhi qian, 132
Jiying, 203
Juntian, 68, 81, 88, 250
Jürched, 123, 127, 134
Jurisprudence, 25

Kaidu, 139
Kaifeng, 107, 111, 115, 116, 124, 127
Kalgan, xi, 79
Kamikaze, 139–40
Kang Youwei, 216, 218
Kangxi Emperor (Xianye), 188–89
Kant, Immanuel, 265
Karma, 75, 145, 264
Kerulen River, 154
Ketteler, Baron Klemens von, 219
Khabarosk, 206
Khubilai Khan, 135, 137
Kiev, 139
King Wen of the Zhou, 12
King Wu of the Zhou, 13, 18
Kinship relationship, 15, 20, 25, 37, 144
Kipchaks, 145
Kissinger, Henry, 250
Kokonor (Qinghai), 23, 39, 52, 172
Korea, 90, 141, 151, 177, 189, 213, 248
Korean War, 248
Koreans, 8, 52, 79, 101, 113, 139, 141
Kowloon, 204, 206
Kuomintang, ix, x, 230, 244, 260, 262
Kyoto, 90
Kyushu, 8, 52, 139

Lacquer, 52, 189
Lai Junchen, 96
Lake Balkhash, 91, 189, 212
Lamaism, 145, 165
Land allotment plan, 102, 103, 153
Land reform, 247
Land survey, 117, 177
Land to the Tiller Act, 260
Landholding pattern, 42, 56, 67, 68, 81, 85, 102, 109, 135, 146, 153, 159, 246
Lattimore, Owen, 23, 101
Law, 18, 26, 29, 56, 93, 119, 186, 251, 292
Law of Nations, 200
League of Leftist Writers, 236
Legalism, 10, 18, 24, 29, 34
Legality and legal practices, 25, 29, 56
Lei Haizong, 75
Leifeng pagoda, 123
Leopard House, 165
Li Chong, 83
Li Dazhao, 228, 230
Li Guang, 43
Li Hongzhang, 209, 214, 221
Li Jiancheng, 94
Li Kui, 41
Li Longji, 100
Li Shimin, 91–94
Li Yuan, 92
Li Zhi, 95
Li Zicheng, 180
Liang Qichao, 216, 218
Liao, 113, 115, 124, 138
Liao Mosha, x, xiii
Liaodong peninsula, 213
Liaoning, 253
Lin Biao, ix, 250
Lin Shu, 227
Lin Zexu, 200
Linan. *See* Hangzhou
Linfen, 87
Lintong county, 5, 27
Lishan, 4, 20
Literary inquisition, 187
Liu Bang, 36
Liu Binzhen, 142
Liu Che (Han Wudi), 37, 39, 40, 42
Liu Daxia, 156, 165
Liu Ling, 75

Liu Shaoqi, 249
Liu Xiu, 49, 53, 54
Liu Yan, 121
Liu Yuan, 68
Liu Yuxi, 77
Liu Zhuang, 50, 55
Liu Ziye, 72
Lo Jialun, 231
Locusts, 30, 45
Loess land, 5, 14, 20, 27
London Times, 216
Long March, ix, 231
Longjiang Dockyard, 158
Longmen, 75
Loyang, 48, 50, 58, 65, 73, 83–84, 106
Lü Buwei, 28
Lü Meng, 70
Lu Xiangshan, 134
Lu Xun (Zhou Shuren), 228

Macao, 156, 175
MacArthur, Douglas, 260
Macrohistory, xvii, 42, 49, 127, 146, 193, 232, 236, 243, 254, 258, 259, 263, 264
Magicians, 51, 165
Maize, 175
Malacca Strait, 156
Manchuria, 5, 23, 39, 78, 96, 106, 124, 141, 172, 181, 214, 248
Manchus, 178, 180, 183–87, 190–91, 216, 220–21
Mao Zedong, x, xiii, 227, 229, 246, 247, 248, 250, 254, 256
Marco Polo, 132, 137–38, 144
Marco Polo Bridge, 262
Marshall, George C., 245
Marxism, 228, 255n, 256
Marxism-Leninism, 258
Matriarchal community, 3
May Fourth Incident, 225, 230
May Fourth Movement, 225, 227, 243
Mecca, 156
Melting charges, 190
Mencius, 10–12, 18, 24, 25, 37, 73, 114, 118, 208
Mengan, 131
Merwin, Douglas, xix
Mesopotamia, 5
Metallurgy, 5

Meteorographical studies, 22, 23
Military colony, 169
Militia, 81, 88, 117, 120, 218
Millet, 51
Ming dynasty, 147, 149–79; map sketch, 155; palace intrigues, 167; tombs, 164
Mingdi of the Han. *See* Liu Zhuang
Mining, 108
Minority groups, 165
Mo Di, 25, 26
Mobilization, 19, 39, 60–61, 90, 131
Mohammedans, 105
Monetary management, 47, 109, 118
Möngke Khan, 135
Mongolia, 52, 154, 189, 222
Mongols, 127, 131, 138–41, 153–55, 166, 189
Moscow, 139
Mouke, 131
Movable type, 133
Mukden, 183
Mulberry trees, 81, 209
Murongs, 79

Nanjing, 64, 65, 150, 154, 164, 207
Nankeens, 189
Nara, 90
Nationalism, 29, 114, 148, 187, 191, 229
Nationalist Army, ix, 246, 248
Natural disasters, 52, 196. *See also* Drought; Flood; Famine; Locusts
Natural Law, 15, 26, 29, 38, 51, 73, 75, 154, 198
Navy, 107, 135, 156, 158
Neolithic Age, 3
Nepal, 189
Nestorianism, 91
New Territories, 204
New Youth, 227
Ni Yuanlu, 181
Nian, 207
Nie Shicheng, 218
Nine-Power Pact, 226
Ningbo, 121, 201, 209
Nishihara Loans, 224
Nixon, Richard M., 250
Nomads, invasions of, 23, 29, 39, 68, 106
North China Daily News, 217

North China plain, 90
Northeast Union Democratic Army, ix
Northern Expedition, 230
Northern Qi, 84-86
Northern Zhou, 84-86
Novels, 172, 198
Nurhaci, 179

Oirat Mongols, 165
"One nation, two systems," xix, 204
Open-door, 215
Opium, 192, 199, 205, 208
Opium War, 199, 200-204, 229
Oracle bones, 7-8
Ordos, 166

Painting, 75, 131, 158
Pamirs, 53
Pan, Lady, 72
Paper, 25, 50, 122
Paper currency, 132, 137, 157, 160
Parkes, Harry, 210
Patriarchal society, 7
Pawn shops, 174
Peanuts, 175
Pearl River, 5, 201
Peasant rebellion, 48, 55, 59, 105, 149, 153, 179-80, 192, 206
Penal code, xvii, 25, 98
Peng Yue, 36
People's Daily, 263
People's Liberation Army, ix, xi, xv, 246
People's Republic, 139, 204
Pepper, 158
Persians, 90, 105, 139
Pescadores, 211, 213
Phags-pa, 145
Pharmacology, 175
Pirates, 142, 151, 156, 171
Poetry, 4, 40, 75, 77, 202
Pohai Gulf, 141
Political philosophy, 17, 19, 55, 63, 134, 163
Political purges, 95, 150-51
Polo, Marco, 132, 137-38, 144
Polo, Niccolo and Maffeo, 144
Population, 36, 45, 50, 78, 89, 175, 180, 197
Porcelain, 158, 174

Portugal, 156
Pottery, 5
Pottinger, Sir Henry, 203
"Pragmatism" of Qing thinkers, 198-99
Primogeniture, 13, 169
Printing, 133
Privy Council, 108, 114, 126, 142
Prostitution, 208
Purple Mountain, 150
Pyongyang, 89

Qi, Duke of, 21
Qi Jiguang, 151, 171
Qian Mu, 70
Qianlong Emperor (Hongli), 187
Qiantang River, 122
Qidan, 96, 98, 101, 113, 124, 138
Qin Dynasty, 27-32, 39
Qin Gui, 123
Qin Shi-huang-di, 27-35
Qing Bu, 36
Qing dynasty, 180-221
Qinghai. *See* Kokonor
Quanzhou, 90
Quinsay, 137

Rainfall, 22, 23
Recommendation system, 57, 89
Recruited soldiery, 130, 132
Red Guards, 250
Regency, 190
Reho, 100, 206
Reischauer, Edwin, 104
Renminbi, xiii
Republican Era, 221-59
Research Center for Rural Development, xv
Revolution of 1911, 214
Ricci, Matteo, 173, 176
Rice, 51, 101, 131, 260
Ritsuryo seiji, 93
Rituals of the Zhou, 85, 96-97
Robinson, Joan, 255n
Rock gardens, 173
Ronglu, 216, 219
Rugs, 189
Rural industry, xvi
Russia, 139, 189, 205-206, 213, 214, 220. *See also* Soviet Union
Russo-Japanese War, 220

Sale of rank, 183
Salt, 41, 105, 173
Sang Hongyang, 41–42, 44
Sangha, 145
Sapanwood, 158
Saracens, 138
Schall, Johannes Adam von Bell, 187
Schematic design of state institutions, 14, 82, 85, 97, 120
Scholars, The, 199
Schumpeter, Joseph, 255n
Sculpture, 33–34, 51, 75–76, 100
Second Empire, 88–136
Second Opium War, 205–206
Secret police, 48, 87, 95, 178, 188
Secret societies, 48, 97, 95, 178, 188, 221
Seismography, 57
Self-restraint and mutual deference, 37, 69, 70, 98, 143, 168, 195, 197
Self-Strengthening Movement, 209, 216, 229
Semu, 145, 151
Serfs, 79
Seven Sages of the Bamboo Grove, 75
Shandong, 105, 218, 225
Shang, 6–7, 13
Shangdu, 147
Shanghai, xiii, 201, 209, 230
Shanxi, 39, 69, 87, 247
Shanyin, Princess, 72
Shen Pao, 217
Shi Le, 68
Shi Tianze, 142
Ship construction, 64, 107, 122, 133, 141, 144, 155, 210
Shu Han, 64
Shun, 114
Shunzhi Emperor (Fulin), 187
Siam, 189
Sichuan, 63, 112, 132, 135, 184
Siege, xvii, 19, 87, 135, 138, 207
Silk, 6, 50, 51, 80, 100, 107, 115, 125, 129, 158, 174, 188, 209
Silk Route, 76
Silver, 115, 125, 162, 178, 183, 184
Sima Guang, 117
Sima Qian, 27, 33, 40, 42, 56
Sima Zhao, 64
Sima Zhong, 72

Single-whip method, 170
Sinicization, 83, 113, 185
Sino-Japanese War, xi, xii, 245
Slaves, 47, 52, 67, 68, 151
Small Swords, 207
Smelting, 108
Smith, Adam, 194
Social Darwinism, 212
Song dynasty, 71, 107, 111–36; leading thinkers, 134; Northern Song, 111–21, 124–25; Southern Song, 122–36; state income, 129; theory of commercial revolution during, 127
Song of Eternal Grief, 4
Sorghum, 144
South China Sea, 135
Soviet Union, ix, 139, 213, 214, 230, 248
Sphere of influence, 214–15
Spring and Autumn Annals, 17, 21
Spring and Autumn Period, 13, 17, 19
Spring Festival on the Bian River, 128
State Council, xv
State monopoly, 41, 45, 47, 51, 55, 109, 128, 254–55
Stilwell, Joseph, 245
Strategy of Warring States, 17
Su Chao, 85
Su Dongpo, 122
Sugar, 260
Sui Dynasty, 61, 85–87, 89, 90
Suiyuan, 78
Sun Yat-sen, x, 150, 214, 221, 222, 230, 257
Sungari River, 123
Suzhou, 159, 209
Sweet potato, 175
Syrians, 90

Taba, 78–84
Taba Gui, 79
Taba Hong (Yuan Hong), 84
Taba Wei, 78–85
Taiping Rebellion, 150, 206
Taishan, 55
Taiwan, 90, 184, 205, 211, 212, 213, 230, 260–63
Tamerlane, 157

Tan Sitong, 218
Tang dynasty, 88–106
Tang Minghuang. *See* Li Longji
Tang Shengzhi, 225
Tanmachi, 143
Taoism, 10, 18, 74–75, 91, 134
Tariffs, 202, 204
Tartars, 138
Tawney, Richard H., 246
Taxation, 28, 40, 41, 47, 55, 67, 80, 99, 104, 110, 146, 152, 159, 169, 182, 189
Tea, 110, 116, 130, 131, 188, 260
Telegraphic service, 210
Tenancy. *See* Landholding pattern
Terracotta army, 4, 27, 33–35
Thai, 92
Third Empire, 149–222
Three feudatories, 184
Three Kingdoms, 64
Tian Hainan, xi
Tian Han, x
Tiananmen, xii, xiii
Tianjin, 205, 218
Tibet, 145, 189, 222
Tibetans, 40, 52, 55, 65, 67, 79, 89, 96, 101, 104, 106, 113, 125
Timur, 147
Tobacco, 175
Tongzhi Emperor (Daichun), 210
Tonkin, Gulf of, 52
Tonkinese, 90
Tourist interest, 3, 4, 20, 33–35, 63, 75, 122, 131, 150, 155, 164, 180, 258, 263
Toyotomi Hideyoshi, 177
Trademark, 128
Tradition, great and little, 72
Treaties: Kikhata, 189; Li-Lobanov, 214; Nerchinsk, 189; Nanjing, 201–204; St. Petersburg, 212; Shimonoseki, 213; Tianjin, 205
Treitschke, Henrich von, 29
Tributary relationship, 151
Truman, Harry S, 245
Tungusic people, 124, 131
Turks, 63, 89, 101, 106
Twenty-one Demands, 222
Typhoon, 140

Uighurs, 89, 104, 189

Ulan Bator, 52
Union of Human Rights, 230
United States, 202, 206, 210, 259
Urga, Battle of, 189
Ussuri River, 206
Usury, 170

Vattel, Emeric de, 200
Versailles Peace Conference, 225
Vietnam, 40, 52, 91, 135, 151, 154, 159, 189, 211
Vladivostok, 206

Waley, Arthur, 10, 34
Wang Anshi, 115–21, 124
Wang Chong, 57
Wang Jingwei, 124
Wang Mang, 46, 47, 55, 57, 82
Wang Qishan, xvi
Wang Seng, 64, 77
Wang Yangming, 173
Wangfujing Dajie, xiv
Wanli Emperor. *See* Zhu Yijun
War indemnities, 200, 205, 213–14, 220
Ward, Frederick Townsend, 209
Warfare, 19, 30, 40, 43, 60, 67, 68, 69, 78, 87, 117, 123, 135, 138, 139, 141, 189, 201, 209
Warlordism, 55, 109, 110, 222, 224, 225
Warring States Period, 13, 17, 19, 31, 34, 36; map of, 11
Waseda University, 228
Washington Conference, 226
Water power, 107
Wei, 64, 68; Northern, 79
Wei Qing, 43
Wei River, 12
Wei Zheng, 93
Weibo District, 104
Well-field system, 15, 16, 28
Wencheng, Princess, 89
Wenming, Empress Dowager, 83
West Lake, 122
Whampoa Military Academy, 244, 263
Wheat, 51
Wheaton, Henry, 210
White Lotus Sect, 192, 197
White Snake, 123

Wine, 41, 45, 128, 130
Wokou (Japanese pirates), 171
World War I, 224
Wu, 65
Wu, Empress, 94–99
Wu Meicun, 181
Wu Peifu, 225
Wu Sangui, 181
Wuchang, 207
Wudi of the Han. See Liu Che
Wuhan, x
Wuxi, 178

Xi (Tätäbi), 101
Xia, 6
Xia Yuanji, 157
Xi'an, 3, 9, 10, 12, 20, 45, 47, 48, 50, 56, 65, 73, 100, 104, 105, 182, 220, 221
Xi'an Incident, 4, 231, 244
Xianbei, 78–85
Xianfeng Emperor (Yichu), 205–206
Xiang River, 209
Xiangxiang county, 208
Xiangyang, 135
Xiao Baojian, 73
Xiao He, 36
Xiaolian, 57, 61
Xibai, 12, 71, 114
Xingzai, 125, 128, 137
Xinjiang-Uighur Autonomous Region, 189
Xiong Tingbi, 183
Xiongnu, 39, 43, 45, 52, 68, 79, 89
Xixia, 113, 116–17, 125, 126
Xu Da, 151
Xu Heng, 142
Xu Lanxu, ix
Xu Xianqian, 263
Xuantong Emperor (Henry Puyi), 221–222
Xuanzhuang, 91

Yalu River, 52
Yan, 10
Yan Fu, 227
Yan Xishan, 225
Yang Guang, 90
Yang Guifei, 3, 103
Yang Guozhong, 100–103
Yang Jian, 85–87

Yang Tai, 133
Yang Zhu, 25, 26
Yangtze Delta, 135, 159, 184
Yangtze River, 90, 110, 149, 183, 201, 207
Yangtze Valley, 12, 62, 125, 141
Yao Shu, 142
Ye Minchen, 205
Yellow Emperor, 114
Yellow River, 20, 21, 69, 90, 165, 182
Yellow Turbans, 59, 61, 65
Yelüchucai, 142
Yin and yang, 54, 264
Yinxian, 121
Yongzheng Emperor (Yinreng), 188
Yuan An, 60
Yuan dynasty, 135, 137–48
Yuan Liang, 60
Yuan Shao, 59
Yuan Shikai, 216, 222
Yue Fei, 123
Yuegang, 175
Yungkang, 75
Yunnan, 142, 184
Yuwen Family, 84–87

Zanzibar, 156
Zayton. See Quanzhou
Zeng Guofan, 208
Zhang Heng, 57
Zhang Juzheng, 176
Zhang Rang, 59
Zhang Xianglin, ix
Zhang Xueliang, 4
Zhang Zeduan, 128
Zhang Zhongchang, 225
Zhang Zuolin, 225, 230
Zhao Guangyi, 115
Zhao Heng, 115
Zhao Ji, 118, 124
Zhao Kuangyin, 107–12, 127
Zhao Xi, 117
Zhao Xu, 115, 116–17
Zhao Yi, 97
Zhejiang, 102, 110, 112, 113, 140, 201
Zheng He, 155, 156, 165
Zhong Chong, 50
Zhou Dunyi, 134
Zhou dynasty, 10–26, 28, 62; Eastern, 13, 17, 19
Zhou Enlai, 231, 244

Zhou Gou, 123
Zhou Sheng, 160
Zhoushan Island, 140, 201
Zhu Changluo, 167
Zhu Changxun, 167
Zhu Di, 154-60
Zhu Gaozhi, 158
Zhu Houcong, 166
Zhu Houzhao, 165
Zhu Qiyu, 164
Zhu Qizhen, 164
Zhu Quanchong, 106, 109

Zhu Xi, 134
Zhu Yijun, 164, 176-79
Zhu Youjian, 164, 180
Zhu Youjiao, 178
Zhu Youtang, 165
Zhu Yuanzhang, 148, 149-54, 176
Zhu Yunwen, 154
Zhu Zhangji, 155
Zongli Yamen, 210, 219
Zoroastrianism, 91
Zuo Zongtang, 165